Women in the
Texas Populist Movement

NUMBER SIXTY-SEVEN:
*The Centennial Series of the Association
of Former Students, Texas A&M University*

Women in the Texas Populist Movement

Letters to the *Southern Mercury*

EDITED WITH AN INTRODUCTION
BY MARION K. BARTHELME

FOREWORD BY JOHN BOLES

Texas A&M University Press
College Station

Title page photo: Populist party convention, Austin, Tex., 1896. Courtesy The Center for American
History, The University of Texas at Austin

The paper used in this book meets the minimum requirements of the American
National Standard for Permanence of Paper for Printed Library Materials, Z39.48-1984.
Binding materials have been chosen for durability.

Library of Congress Cataloging-in-Publication Data
Women in the Texas populist movement : letters to the Southern mercury / edited
by Marion K. Barthelme ; foreword by John Boles. — 1st ed.
     p.   cm. — (Centennial series of the Association of Former Students,
Texas A&M University ; no. 67)
     Includes bibliographical references (p.   ) and index.
     ISBN 0-89096-742-3 (cloth : alk. paper). — ISBN 0-89096-775-X (pbk. :
alk. paper)
     1. Texas—Politics and government—1865–1950—Sources. 2. Rural
women—Texas—Correspondence. 3. Rural women—Texas—Political
activity—History—19th century—Sources. 4. Rural women—Texas—
Economic conditions—Sources. 5. Populism—Texas—History—
19th century—Sources. 6. Land reform—Texas—History—19th century—
Sources. I. Barthelme, Marion K. (Marion Knox), 1944– . II. Southern
mercury (Dallas, Tex. : 1891) III. Series.
F391.W8   1997
976.4'061'082—dc21
                                                                    96-53089
                                                                    CIP

For Katharine, Anna, and Donald

Contents

Part I:

Part II:

Illustrations

Foreword

JOHN BOLES

 Much of the most exciting work being done today in southern history involves recovering the experience of women. Of course, even the history of southern men is being transformed through the gendered analysis that presently is being employed to reveal complexities of causation unsuspected before now. But I write here of the effort to discover and reveal the lives, thoughts, and voices of southern women—and not just members of the articulate elite heretofore dominant in historical accounts.

As we learn more about women and their roles in the past, we are forced to acknowledge that their experience cannot be confined to traditionally "feminine" topics. Southern women could not vote anywhere in the South, but this does not mean that they were ignorant of the political issues of the day or the impact of political and economic structures on their lives. Marion Barthelme here escorts us into the world of white Texas farm women at the end of the nineteenth century. After a perceptive introduction that establishes the historical context, she lets the women speak in their own words through their letters to a Texas Populist newspaper, the *Southern Mercury.*

And what words! Here are women from across Texas, initially unaccustomed to expressing their opinions in public but becoming increasingly emboldened simply by reading their own letters—and those of other women—in print. In their heartfelt letters, we feel the energy, the hope, and the aspirations of countless women—the very ones we usually consider inarticulate, because their letters and diaries seldom end up in archives—

and sense their profound frustration with "the system." These women often are cautious about casting their ideas to the world, but they nevertheless write with vigor, humor, and pungency.

The writers differ among themselves on many topics, especially the proper role of women. Should they, for example, vote? The issue is much debated, but even those opposed to extending the franchise to women insist that women should be informed about political issues and should help (or pressure) their husbands to vote for reform. These women and others like them stiffened the resolve of their husbands. The gender roles appropriate for farm women are much discussed, but these women also reveal detailed knowledge of the organizational issues of the local chapters of the Southern Farmers' Alliance and the larger issues of the Populist movement. By no means do these women quietly confine themselves to domestic concerns and leave civic problems to the menfolk.

As we read these pages, the vibrant personalities and acerbic comments of the correspondents sometimes surprise us, conditioned as we have been by the written historical canon to expect these authors to be largely apolitical, passive, and polite. Instead, they are lively, concerned, and aggressive, unafraid to puncture a myth of male superiority and quick to deflate pretension. These women clearly are glad to discover, through the letters of other Populist women, that they are not alone in their insistence on change; encountering sister protesters encourages them greatly. As one woman wrote of this "comradeship" in 1890, "The feeling that you and I are linked together by sympathy in a mutual effort . . . goes far to strengthen the effort individually made."

Marion Barthelme, by making this vivid correspondence widely accessible, has performed a valuable service: she has brought these admirable women into our consciousness and into our historical analysis. As a result, the political and social landscape of our era and the region subtly has been transformed. The development of women's history is the best thing that has happened to southern history since the emergence of black history into the limelight. We are getting closer all the time to a complete understanding of the past.

Acknowledgments

I would like to thank Thomas Haskell for his guidance, Lawrence Goodwyn for his infectious admiration of the Populists, and Robert Calvert for his thoughtful advice early in this work. Michael Berryhill and Marsha Recknagel gave insightful comments about women and their voices. Thanks go as well to Jeff Fort for all his encouragement.

Part I
An Introduction

Introduction

✤ To most Americans, industrialization was a painful process. In the last quarter of the nineteenth century, many of the nation's groups developed alternatives to the emerging design of American industrial society.[1] The farmers' effort—the brief but powerful Populist movement—was the largest and most significant endeavor of the era.[2] It originated on the Texas farming frontier in 1877, as farmers, trying to improve their lot through cooperation and education, created the Southern Farmers' Alliance. In 1892, they turned to politics and formed the Populist party. The movement had peaked by 1896, but not before it had swept like wildfire through the South and West and out into the Great Plains, igniting the hopes of followers one to three million strong.[3]

Populists of the Gilded Age sought to shape the developing economic structure through political and economic reform—specifically, reform of railroad monopoly, land scarcity, mortgage foreclosures, and the U.S. monetary system based on the gold standard.[4] They proposed far more sweeping changes than either major party accepted; for a moment, it looked as if the movement might alter the shape of Southern, if not national, politics.[5] The Populist challenge had heroic and humanistic dimensions that appealed to women as well as men. It was a moral revolution designed to lift the nation to a higher plane.[6] The Southern Farmers' Alliance stressed the harmony of interests among producers and wished to de-emphasize the spirit of competition so dominant in the late nineteenth century. It promised greater democracy and "equal rights for all and special privileges to none."

It sought to "elevate to higher manhood and womanhood those who bear the burdens of productive industry." Productive industry meant the efforts of those who actually made or grew useful things. Profitable farming required physical stamina, reliable work habits, and efficient financial management, and the Alliance hoped to shield the agrarian work unit, the family, from potential harm by teaching sobriety, benevolence, and the avoidance of conduct that would bring reproach upon an individual or his family.[7] With heartbreaking optimism, the Populists advanced an image of America in which wealth accrued to those who produced it with their hands, and power accrued to those who best served the interests of all the people.[8]

Alliance and Populist Women

In pioneer agricultural states such as Texas, women often worked alongside men as equals in the business of farming, shouldering burdens traditionally deemed unwomanly. The Alliance recognized this and offered membership to white rural women over sixteen years of age. "Our female membership should be recognized as a very powerful element of strength," said R. A. High, president of the Farmers' State Alliance of Texas, in an annual message to the "Brothers and Sisters." "Where[ever] there is an active woman element, there is [also] found the greatest activity among the membership and the greatest prosperity of the order."[9] Significant numbers of women, perhaps as many as 25 percent of its membership, joined the Farmers' Alliance and later supported the Populist party.[10]

To encourage their participation and interest, the *Southern Mercury,* the official organ of the state order and eventually of the Texas Populist party, solicited and published letters from rural women. The many—often short-lived, rarely self-supporting—journals that grew up around the Alliance movement and helped build its audience were critically important in the dissemination of the order's programs and other information. They were state Alliance publications—the National Alliance leadership wanted one in every state—and tiny regional newspapers. Texas alone had at least one hundred such local journals. They all borrowed editorials, accounts of national political news, legislation, speeches, and presidential events— paying particular attention to farm, currency, and tax issues—from the Washington-based *National Economist,* the official organ of the national organization and the only paper to be subsidized by it. Then they added regional politics, letters, and accounts of the activities of the local suballiances.[11]

At the heart of this reform press, and the least troubled of the state Alliance newspapers, was the sixteen-page *Southern Mercury*, a Dallas-based weekly under various editors and publishers: Harry Tracy (an early Alliance lecturer and *Mercury* founder), Evan Jones, J. R. Bennett, Sam Dixon, and Milton Park.[12] The paper was published between 1884 and 1907. It became the official organ of the state Southern Farmers' Alliance in 1886, after the editor of the previous officially sanctioned newspaper, the *Rural Citizen* (Jacksboro), disagreed with the Alliance over its support of the Knights of Labor. In 1887, the name changed from the *Dallas Mercury* to the *Southern Mercury*, and from 1890 to 1892—its peak years—the paper had a circulation of twenty-six to thirty thousand. Although most subscribers lived in Texas, the large number of letters from elsewhere indicates that the *Mercury* had a sizable readership in other states.[13] It cost one dollar a year.

From 1886 to 1907, with varying intensity and dedication, the *Mercury* singled out correspondence from women by devoting one page (usually the second page) of each weekly issue to their letters and concerns. In 1888–89, women's letters comprised 21 percent of all those published. The editor labeled page two "The Ladies' (or Lady) Department" in 1888, "The Family" in 1889, and "The Woman's Column" in 1890. That same year, the editor moved the women's page to page six, and in 1894 it became "Our Household." Women's letters were not segregated completely from those of men: 11 percent of the female correspondence was published in parts of the *Mercury* other than the women's section.[14]

A prodigious amount has been written about the Farmers' Alliance and the Populist party, but until recently historians have neglected the part played by women in the agrarian movement. Walter Nugent, Richard Hofstadter, John Hicks, and Lawrence Goodwyn have acknowledged contributions (or eccentricities) of nationally prominent women worthies such as Mary Elizabeth Lease, Annie Diggs, and Sarah Emery. Robert McMath's history of the Southern Farmers' Alliance credits women with a positive role, but references are brief.[15] Recent efforts to write women back into history have illuminated the women's story but also have emphasized urban reform activities and concentrated on the North.[16] Robert Swierenga has noted the absence of research in rural history, arguing that "as a counterpart to 'urban history,' it has no recognized place as yet in American historiography or academic curricula."[17]

In the 1960s, a handful of historians began to take a look at old records, creating a "new history" of Southern women. It was a "brave beginning," said historian Anne Firor Scott, yet on the subject of women and rural reform in the 1880s and 1890s, this sort of brave new work consists for the most part of a few biographical studies, two essays, one doctoral dissertation, and a master's thesis.[18] Joan Jensen's collection of documents of women farmers, *With These Hands,* includes a brief overview of women in the Grange, the Alliance, and the Populist party.[19] In her essay "Women in the Southern Farmers' Alliance," Julie Roy Jeffrey documents the role of women in North Carolina.[20] MaryJo Wagner's "Farms, Families, and Reform: Women in the Farmers' Alliance and Populist Party" takes a thorough, thoughtful look at women's roles in agrarian reform, focusing on national leaders and on grassroots participation in Kansas, Nebraska, and Colorado.[21] Two other contributions are Sandra Myres's *Westering Women* and Melissa Wiedenfeld's "Women in the Texas Farmers' Alliance."[22] The first of these is an excellent view of pioneer women and women in the West, but it discusses Populist women only in relation to women's suffrage. The second is an overview of Texas women's contributions to the order, with additional short biographies. It does not attempt to include the many diverse voices.

The women of Texas, among the Southern states, were the most active and influential Alliance participants. A number of them—such as Fannie Moss of Cleburne; Fannie Leak, a physician in Austin; and Mary Clardy of Sulphur Springs—held offices in the order. Bettie Gay of Columbus and Ellen Dabbs, a physician also from Sulphur Springs, represented the state at national conventions, while Bessie Dwyer from San Antonio was a staff writer for the *National Economist.*[23] While these women were not prominent nationally, their names are known, as are the names and histories of the more active Alliance leaders, previously mentioned, who organized, campaigned, and attended conventions. But the Alliance movement was a mass movement, a grassroots effort, made by rank-and-file "plain" people. These people were marginal farmers and their families—tenants, landowners, teachers, preachers, and doctors operating farms in economically depressed sections of the country.[24] Among them were ordinary women. Their voices have been lost.

Perhaps the most serious problem facing historians of women is the paucity of available source material, and rural women—particularly those affected by illiteracy, long and exhausting work, and lack of leisure time—are among the members of American society least likely to keep or maintain records.[25] When women are literate, however, they are apt to write letters, and apart from their essays, newspaper articles, and speeches, the most important sources for the study of Populist women are the Alliance minutebooks and their letters.[26] "Since these long forgotten farm women

... left virtually no other personal records, their letters ... provide a crucial insight into the grassroots level of the Alliance," says Jeffrey.[27]

What are those insights? What did this grassroots movement for economic, social, and moral elevation mean to rural women? How bound were the women by the idea of a domestic sphere? What did the Populist promises mean to them? What were their concerns? "In Southern history are thickets and swamps of ill-perceived, half-forgotten myths, and many kinds of women," says Shirley Abbott in her memoir, *Womenfolks.* "They bear witness to something buried, unvoiced, powerful."[28]

Women's letters to the *Southern Mercury*—excerpts from one hundred and eighty are included here—provide a rare look into the thoughts and daily life of rural Texas women. One comes away from a reading of the letters with a greater understanding of rural Populist women and a tremendous appreciation of their resilience, their attention to detail and duty, their light humor, their strong convictions, their compassion, and their growth. The letters do not have the intimacy of private letters or diaries, but nonetheless they often are sensitive, open, courageous. Many are basically well written, sprinkled with ironic understatement or earthy pragmatism. Others are didactic. All of them recount the worries, chores, joys, and complexities of life in the 1880s and 1890s. They tell how women regarded their separate sphere and how they moved through and around it. They give us some idea of how passionately these rural women cared about Populism. In the main, it is a grassroots perspective, although a few of the letter writers became small-scale leaders and stepped above the rank and file to attain some degree of visibility. Some of the texts, for instance, are reprints of actual lectures written for and delivered by the women to suballiance audiences. Other writers seem bound in the direction of leadership, then disappear without a trace. One misses them.

Over the six years in which the women correspond, they undergo political and personal growth, due in part to their participation in the movement and in part to the act of writing and communicating in the *Southern Mercury.* The letters suggest that many of the women emerge from the experience with a stronger sense of self. Their individual and collective self-esteem is augmented by the act of writing and by the mutual reading of each other's written words. The letters also reveal, among "conservative" rural women, far greater enthusiasm for suffrage than generally has been attributed to them.[29] Scholars looking for the roots of the suffrage movement in Texas have overlooked suffrage sentiment in the countryside and have theorized that urbanization was an essential precursor.[30] In terms of establishing a critical mass, undoubtedly this is true; but a lot of energy, fervor, and early paradigmatic shifting, or reevaluating prior beliefs, has been missed in bypassing rural women. Having gained a stronger sense of self, many Populist women were able to move on to the idea of self-empowerment via suffrage. They did not wish to negate the responsibilities and special endowments that derived from their separate sphere, but did wish to add to them full citizenship.

The Alliance's stated expectation that women would join as equal members did much to bring these women into public life, even while they remained linked to a domestic setting. They entered the public arena as representatives of private life, bringing private-life concerns such as education, morality, and temperance; but they also entered with broader public-life issues, such as equal representation and the fairer division of the young nation's resources. If the order allowed women to enter what historian Sarah Evans posits as a good synthesis of the "political theorist cum feminist" definition of the public sphere—an arena which offers women and men the possibility of power, visibility, respect, and achievement, all basic to their humanity—it nevertheless was a compacted and idealized place. It was the public arena of a world within a world that grew in response to the exclusionary market economy; it was a civil society that created new possibilities for public action (such as voluntary associations, clubs, churches, charities, and reform movements) outside of formal politics and government. Nevertheless, according to Evans, it was the enormous energy generated by voluntary associations and reform movements that provided a new arena for citizenship and collective decision making—an arena that ultimately reshaped (or, as in this case, failed to reshape) the state. That energy was at least as much female as male. Women in these associations and reform movements were expected to practice the basic skills of public life—to speak and to listen, to analyze issues in relation to structures of power, and to develop agendas and strategies for action.[31]

Southern Farmers' Alliance

In the 1870s, caravans of beleaguered farmers—almost 100,000 each year—migrated across plank roads and rutted trails into Texas in search of fresh farmland and a better life. From 1870 to 1890, close to 1,500,000 newcomers flocked in, some from Germany and Mexico but most from Alabama, Arkansas, Louisiana, Mississippi, Missouri, and Tennessee. By 1890, approximately 15 percent of the state's population of 2,235,523 was foreign-born or of foreign parentage, 22 percent was black, and 63 percent was of native stock. Two-thirds of the churchgoers were Baptist or Methodist.[32]

Women who joined the Alliance formed part of this amalgam. In carving homesteads and farms from the unsettled forests and prairies, they and their families faced the vicissitudes of uncertain rainfall, primitive housing, vicious feuds, cattle rustling, loneliness, and economic dislocation.[33] Although Texas fared much better than many Southern states after the Civil War, its banking system was inadequate to the task of financing cotton and grain marketing. The amount of money in circulation, already deficient, was declining. [34]

Beginning in 1870, the price of cotton—the farmers' economic mainstay—began to drop steadily in price. Many cash-strapped farmers turned to the crop-lien method of financing, by which a furnishing merchant or landlord would advance supplies and goods to the farmer in return for a lien on the future crop. The farmer was given a certain amount of credit, legally at 8 percent interest. However, the actual rate charged was considerably higher, frequently well in excess of 100 percent annually. The effect of the crop-lien system was to establish a condition of peonage, for women as well as men. Appreciating money and diminishing returns, drought, depression, or northers often meant loss of ownership, and the number of landless tenant farmers began to rise. Even those who fared well enough to avoid lien financing and debt complained bitterly about the agricultural depression. Some farmers formed organizations of economic self-help, such as the National Grange of the Patrons of Husbandry, a secret society that officially eschewed partisan politics but called for cooperative endeavor and state railroad regulation. Other farmers pioneered new political institutions, such as the Greenback Party or the Union Labor Party.[35]

The Farmers' Alliance originated in Lampasas County, Texas, in 1877, to thwart cattle rustling. In 1880, it was moved to Parker County and chartered as the nonprofit Farmers' State Alliance organization. In 1884, the Alliance happened to select S. O. Daws, a Mississippian and farmer from Wise County, Texas, as its traveling lecturer. He provided the reactivated Alliance with a philosophy of cooperation and political action.[36] Thereafter, the Alliance experienced dramatic, spiraling growth as a result of its determination to go beyond the cash stores of the Grange and make significant efforts in cooperative marketing as well as purchasing. By 1885, it had been forged into a cohesive system of approximately two hundred thousand members in more than two hundred suballiances. Articulate, indignant lecturers traveled the countryside decrying exorbitant prices charged by monopolistic trusts and the evils of the crop-lien, and exhorting farmers to find their salvation through cooperative buying and selling.[37]

In 1886, the Alliance recruited in Louisiana. The next year, representatives from Texas and Louisiana organized alliances throughout the South. In 1888, these alliances merged with the Arkansas Agricultural Wheel, and membership spread across ten states. With its frequent suballiance meetings, at which the order's growing corps of lecturers addressed attendees, the Alliance also provided families on the lonely prairie with a group educational effort and opportunities for social gatherings.[38] The movement expanded into Kansas and in 1889 merged with strong state agrarian organizations in North Dakota and South Dakota. Lecturers toured in Colorado and California. In December 1889, farmers' organizations met in St. Louis to constitute a truly national alliance called the National Farmers' Alliance and Industrial Union. In the next four years, it attained a strength of between one and three million members.[39]

Throughout its lifetime, the Alliance struggled with the issue of political insurgency versus nonpartisanship. As early as 1886, a series of political demands was formulated, then modified by conservatives who hoped to avoid political divisions and promote harmony. These were the Cleburne Demands, and they became the agrarian gospel that organizers preached throughout the nation. They included calls for: legislation against alien land ownership, laws to prevent trading in agricultural futures, the immediate forfeiture of railroad lands, the removal of illegal fences from public lands, tax reforms on corporate holdings, unlimited coinage of both gold and silver, an expanded money supply based on legal tender notes issued by the federal government, passage of an interstate commerce act, and abolition of convict labor. All of these demands were to be presented to state and national legislators.[40]

In many ways, the Alliance was an ideal movement for women. "No other movement in history—not even the antislavery cause—appealed to the women like [Populism]," wrote novelist Hamlin Garland.[41] The doctrine of "separate spheres" gave women responsibility for morality and a higher purpose in life, a leitmotif clearly sketched in and by the order's teachings concerning sobriety, morality, benevolence, and cooperation. Its constitution announced the need "to develop a better state, mentally, morally, socially and financially," and placed much stress on the moral conduct of its members. Protection of the family was another goal. Women were a valuable component of these aims. Harry Tracy, a national lecturer, told Alliance members: "The ladies eligible must join the order before we can succeed."[42]

The women who reached the upper levels of the Alliance hierarchy shared some very general social characteristics. Nearly all were white, middle-class Protestants and had received at least a high-school education.[43] (Self-education was common among male Alliance leaders; of the twenty for whom educational data are available, only five received more than a common-school education.)[44] Little is known about the formal academic training of the rank-and-file Alliance women, but many of their letters are quite eloquent and accomplished. Some of the women who joined the Alliance had belonged to other "third" political parties, participated in temperance and suffrage societies, taught Sunday school, or served as county school superintendents.[45] Others were enlisting for the first time. They acknowledged the order's draft and urged each other to join. "Our moralizing influence is such that no good Alliance man ever wants to meet unless the sisters are there. That is what I have heard many other brethren say," wrote Mary from Limestone County, who used no last name, in a letter in the *Southern Mercury* of May 10, 1888.[46] The women felt it their duty to report, often with great enthusiasm and excitement, the various local suballiance activities and growing industry. "The new Alliance and co-operative store house [at Halletsville], is very near completed and will soon be ready for business," wrote one woman from Lavaca County in April 1888. "My husband was sent as a delegate to the county Alliance and says it is fast gaining members and interest all over the country, that it has twice as many members as it had at this time last year. I am glad that the farmers have awoke from their slumbers and see that it is high time that they were up and doing something that will break the yoke of bondage which they have so patiently carried for so many years."[47]

The county suballiances were the heart of the organization, providing its prime resource—a committed, initiated membership.[48] Ida Jones from Mansfield, Texas, understood this. In the spring of 1888, she reported: "The sisters are attending and seem more interested than at first. . . . Let us strive to use all our influence to persuade all good farmers, their wives and daughters to join the Alliance. We have slept on our rights till they are nearly gone beyond our reach; yet it is not quite so late that all hope is lost. . . . I would not give a copper cent for a man who will object to ladies joining the Alliance."[49]

Men in the North Carolina Alliance discouraged female membership in subtle ways by holding meetings in public places, such as a courthouse, where women would feel uncomfortable.[50] There is no indication that this occurred in Texas, or that Texas women would have let such behavior bother them. On the contrary, they felt needed. "We have a cooperative store in Henderson, and it is just booming," wrote Mrs. S. E. Redwise in May 1888, "doing more business than two or three stores put together, although the merchants have put [the price of] their goods down to almost nothing [in order to break the Alliance]. . . . I will say to the sisters, attend every meeting of your Alliance. If you become disinterested you need not expect your brothers, fathers and husband to be very interested."[51] And, in June 1889, Hannah Bryant from the Kelso Alliance wrote, "I think it is every sister's duty to attend as often as they possibly can. If we go oftener, it would encourage the men. We must all go to work with all our might. Let us take hold and give a long pull, a strong pull and all pull together."[52]

A Separate Sphere

It was disconcerting at first for these early letter writers to have their words and names appear in public print. Nineteenth-century middle-class American society was based upon widespread acceptance of a particular image of the "ideal lady"—modest, submissive, educated in the genteel and domestic arts, supportive of her husband's efforts, physically weaker, probably mentally inferior but morally superior to men, uncomplaining, a perfect wife and mother, and, most certainly, private and never public. Good women were not to be seen or heard outside the sacred confines of the family circle.[53] But the traditional view of the submissive, virtuous Southern lady, set apart in her "woman's sphere," had begun to crumble under the impact of the traumatic Civil War and post–Civil War conditions. As well, these were farm women who, for the common good, often were required to undertake tasks outside the circumscribed sphere of woman's place. Despite literature produced in the East, which promoted the woman's sphere, many farm women continued to work in the fields and pastures and to exchange their domestic produce for essential goods.[54] Doing so created contradictions for them, and their letters reveal their struggles to reconcile their actual roles with the feminine ideal. Paradoxically, the separate sphere also gave them a special identification with Alliance goals.

Initially the women were hesitant to appear in public. Some used pen names. Again and again, they apologized for their correspondence, their presumption of a place in the public eye, but they clearly felt that it was a duty required by the Alliance. "I have waited to see if anyone of our Union would write to the *Mercury*," Ida Jones explained. "Some member could write a much better letter than I but I will see if I can inspire them to write."[55] The letter writer from Lavaca County began: "As you have so kindly offered us space in your valuable paper I will try and write a few words, hoping to be pardoned for the errors that I may make as this is my first attempt to write for a newspaper. As some of our sisters have said, I have been waiting and wishing that some of our 'big-brained' brothers would write who are better able to write something that would be more instructive and interesting."[56] A Waco woman who signed herself "Farmer's Daughter" explained why she was compelled to write: "I can't see why some of the brethren don't write to the *Mercury* and tell how our lodge is progressing for the weather has been so bad the ladies haven't attended as regularly as the brethren. Also I think they have not written for want of confidence in themselves. . . . As this is my first attempt for the press, I will close, for fear of the waste basket."[57]

Nonparticipation was explained by Fay Forestelle, somewhat guiltily and at great length, as due to the press of domestic responsibilities. In August 1888, she wrote from her home in Wilson County: "I am not a member of the Alliance although the movement has my warmest sympathy and best wishes. Why? . . . I fear I should be a dead weight because I am the mother of seven children, most of them mere babies; we live a long mile from the place of meeting and I do not think 'twould be right to leave my babies at home, nor yet to bring them to the lodge. My husband is a member, has belonged since the order was first organized in our neighborhood. . . . The *Mercury*—has no more eager and interested reader than myself."[58]

The women clearly were accustomed to being part of an agricultural unit and pulling their own weight. "Many of our ablest men are urging the ladies to take a more decided stand in the great cause we have espoused," said Addie McCaskill from DeWitt County. "If by doing so we can wield a greater influence, it is our duty to do so, and modesty never required anyone to neglect a duty." Then she added: "So keenly do I realize my inability to write an article to be read by so many people that nothing but a true devotion to the cause could prevail upon me to attempt it."[59] The brave Mrs. S. E. Redwise from Henderson confessed: "It is with a great deal of embarrassment that I attempt to write this letter, for I feel my incompetency. . . . I will do the best I can. It is not my disposition to say I can't. . . . I intend to perform every duty the Alliance sees fit to put upon me to the best of my ability."[60]

As time passed, the women became less timid and less self-effacing. The painful apologies ceased, and confidence in their public stance grew. Their increasing numbers fortified them. "I have never written anything for publication but other sisters writing in the *Mercury* from different places, induces me to write too," said Eddie from Round Pound Alliance. "My mother and myself are members of the Alliance, which numbers about forty or fifty members."[61] They began to relate fondly to the *Mercury* as a friend and mentor—"our swift-winged messenger of truth and peace," said one letter writer from Belton County.[62] "If you have not got the *Mercury,* send for one," urged Mrs. S. E. Watkins from Centerville. "It is one of the best guides in the world to the farmer. We have no crop mortgage this year, neither any stock; so it has stirred us up and caused us to keep out of mortgaging this year."[63] The women were nourished by the act of publishing. Reading smart articles by other women heightened their individual and collective self-esteem. "Miss Lula Wade's essay on 'Usury and Mortgages' is the best and most logical I have ever had the pleasure of reading from the pen of a lady," said another writer, "Homespun Dress" of Travis County. "She is certainly a deep thinker. I see other interesting letters from ladies too numerous to mention. I am proud to see so much intellect among farmer's wives and daughters. I believe, according to our opportunities, we do equally as well as the men."[64]

Class Consciousness

If contradictions existed concerning womanhood and women's roles, additional contradictions involved the farmers' self-image. The agrarians accepted the Jeffersonian view of the primacy and virtuousness of farming, as the ideal and fundamental employment of man, and the superiority of the farmer in society, as a key figure in civilization, a crusader for truth and right.[65] Yet, farmers of the Alliance had spent much of their lives in humiliating circumstances, locked in the drudgery of the lien system, crushed by a mountain of interest. Farming people were ridiculed—called "hayseeds"— for their poverty and country ways, and they knew it. As times got tougher, in an occupation noted for hard work, they worked even harder. When this failed to ameliorate their plight, they began to feel that they were being duped, that their hard work was naïve and foolish.[66] This concern surfaced frequently in their letters. "I hold vanity as an excellent quality," wrote "Corn Bread" from Bexar County. "It stiffens the back, holds a man up and reinforces that prime element, pride. . . . It matters not that we be highly cultured: for many a man who cannot read has more gumption than the average statesman, scientist and professor. . . . We ought to feel our worth and weight. We are not near so smart as some but the smart ones are mostly shallow. Raw statesmen, small-bore lawyers, chronic office-seekers, snobs, toadies, fops and railroad wreckers are not as good as we though immensely more showy."[67]

In *The Age of Reform*, Richard Hofstadter portrays Populists as reactionaries attempting to halt national development. He suggests that being a yeoman in theory but an entrepreneur in practice created a double personality in the farmer. The Populist was a frustrated small capitalist attempting to recover his prestige and profits in the face of exploitation and unfavorable markets. Hofstadter contends that farmers were downwardly mobile and suffered from status resentment, were retrogressive, viewed history as a conspiracy, and used anti-Semitic rhetoric.[68] These women's letters do not support Hofstadter's depiction of the Populist as conspiracy-minded and anti-Semitic, although one writer expresses support for the nativist Know-Nothing movement and another for segregated train cars. More than that, these letters strongly suggest that farmers experienced high anxiety about their status while at the same time feeling themselves to be superior.

In the December 12, 1889, issue of the *Mercury*, Margenie in Angelina County asked indignantly:

> What is the use of poor farmers' wives and daughters buying fine clothing, trying to look or dress as fine as those who hold the farmers' money purse? If they want to turn the cold shoulder to us and turn their noses up, or give us the back seat at church because we wear calico, five-cent lawn, or perhaps twenty-cent worsted, it should not hurt us. Let them stick their heads in a flour-barrel and put on their silk and satin and sit in church pretending to swallow every word the preacher says. When they go home, ask them what the text was and they will most likely tell you they don't know for Miss or Mrs. Somebody was dressed in her old five-cent lawn, which has been washed a half-dozen times. But dear sisters, do not let it bother you, for there never was a bird that flew so high but it had[n't] to come to the ground for water.[69]

The farmers found sympathy among other laborers of low status who also held the rich in contempt. They shared some of the same pragmatism—if not outright hostility—regarding the clergy, which was perceived, correctly, as conservative, favoring the status quo, and against the idea that agrarians should receive an equal portion of material wealth and political power.[70] Sally Beck, an Alliance sympathizer who described herself as "cooking, washing, ironing and playing maid for Widow Skinner and her three fashionable daughters," on May 3 wrote, alluding, undoubtedly, to *Pilgrims' Progress:*

> I heard Parson Smallsoul say at the supper table (I fried two chickens for "tea" that evening), that he attended the circus with a long string of school children and while they were gazing at the animals in the menagerie, he found interest in studying the faces and appearance of the country people who clustered around the different cages. Mrs. Skinner loftily said, "Humph! Country people have so little style, I don't see anything interesting about them." Parson Smallsoul said he didn't doubt that it was unavoidable for her to feel that way, it being the opinion of Alexander Hamilton and great men of our own times that people are naturally divided into two classes, the one, the well born, the rich, the other the laboring people, and the laboring people are most numerous and necessarily the foundation or broad base of the pyramid of society and being one of God's shepherds he felt interest in all his flock and with that the melancholy man helped himself to a third big spoonful of peach jam which I worked so hard to make last summer.

She continued, "Sometimes my blood boils at sentiments I hear expressed by these dead souls, these butterfly, frivolous society folks who come and go, chattering like magpies. I often wonder . . . do 'hired girls' belong even to the less considered lower class or to one even lower, too insignificant for consideration. . . . The complaints arising from the farmers of this land strike a responsive chord in my heart so that I find pleasure in reading of their high resolves to kick; for to hear that they will kick is sure evidence that their legs are not yet tied."[71]

According to historian Lawrence Goodwyn, democratic movements are initiated by people who have managed to attain a high level of personal and political self-respect and who are not resigned or intimidated. Their sense of autonomy allows for defiance and permits them to view a new plateau of social possibility and to dare to change things by seeking to influence others. In the growing solidarity of the Alliance, a collective self-confidence was beginning to form, an individual and group self-respect that Goodwyn calls class consciousness.[72] "We [farmers] may be fools and unsuspecting," said a woman from Weimar, "but we are not such fools as not to see the rottenness of a government that is scorching us to death by the sirocco breath of class legislation."[73] S. L. S. Waelder from Colorado County was in agreement: "We know that our greatest public men have come from the farm and if we would have justice done the laboring class, our public men must in the future be chosen from among the common people."[74]

In September 1888, Dianecia Jones of Dallas County challenged farmers who had not yet joined the Alliance. "It may not interest you free farmers, who never lose a day to go to a speaking or a picnic," she said. "You and Jeremiah can't see any good in the Alliance. You sit back and let the dude spit on you and laugh at you for taking it. Listen to the big bosses; We ain't scared; The poor old ignorant farmers won't stick together; They can't do anything. Now come out, you farmers, and don't have that flung in your face any longer, and show them that you stick as tight as old Aunt Jemima's plaster."[75]

In the August 14, 1888, issue, an essay by Mrs. H. M. Calmes of Elm Springs Alliance, Farmers Branch, Dallas County, asked: "Why have we so blindly staggered on in darkness? Why have we so long paid such exorbitant rates to middlemen for transacting our business which we are in every way qualified to take charge of . . . But no longer are the ignorant farmers to be deluded, duped and gulled. We have no need of shipping our cotton and wool thousands of miles to be manufactured when we can manufacture them ourselves, no need of shipping our grain or selling at half price when we are capable of grinding it ourselves; no need of paying [an] agent one hundred per cent on our farming implements when the material for their construction flourishes on our own land. What grander, nobler achievement can be conceived than our Alliance Exchange?"[76]

As farm women began to see themselves as part of a class, they expressed concern for urban working people and organizations such as the Knights of Labor. The Knights encouraged the participation of women in its own ranks and supported women's suffrage in ways not unlike the practices of the Alliance.[77] The women were aware of the activities of the labor movement and its demand for an eight-hour day and national events such as the 1884 Haymarket Square Riot in Chicago and the Great Southwest Strike of 1886.[78] Some were radicalized and spoke of the brighter future that could be created by an organized working class. "I hope the day is not far distant when the downtrodden farmer can look back and say, we have gained the victory at last, for if any class of people have been slaves it is the farmers. If ever there was a time when the farming and labor elements should stick together it is now," wrote Ida Jones from Mansfield in May 1888.[79] A few months later, in July, "A Western Reader" reported:

A grand revolution is going on . . . a remolding of social and political institutions will enable the working classes to enjoy the advantages they create, but [these] are now wrested from them by licensed avarice. The agricultural classes, usually the most patient, have at last been touched by class consciousness, and are realizing their capacity for organized resistance . . . The system of competition now so generally practiced by our modern corporations is slowly murdering democracy and establishing economic slavery. The *News,* while applauding the New York courts in deciding that the laboring men have no right to use the boycott, should also suggest some defense for the employee of railroad corporations, against whom the blacklist is used. . . . The domination of capital in this country with its attendant evils such as an army of Pinkerton "thugs," truckling satellites, a subsidized press, extreme poverty (and its inevitable sequence, intemperance) is so grave as to threaten democratic life.[80]

At first the Texas Alliance focused on economic strategies of protest. It attempted local trade agreements with merchants, local cotton bulking, and local cooperative stores which could lower the costs of goods to the farmer. In 1887, when Alliance President Charles W. Macune realized that such disjointed efforts would not improve the position of the farmer in the market, he proposed the Exchange, a statewide Alliance-owned cooperative, based in Dallas, in which farmers would unite to buy supplies, store their crops in giant warehouses, and send them to market when the price was right. The exchange was to have the dual effect of increasing the supply of money at harvest time, when it usually was scarce, and granting the farmer credit at a low rate of interest, thereby breaking the grasp of croplien.[81]

It was a breathtaking vision—the largest and most dramatic effort to build a counter-institution ever attempted by a protest organization in America—and it fired the imagination of farmers across the South.[82] In 1887, hopes for the order were high everywhere.[83] Passionate and articulate Alliance lecturers were sent from Texas to Mississippi, Alabama, and Tennessee; to Missouri, Arkansas, and the Carolinas; and to Georgia, Florida, Kentucky, and Kansas, enunciating the aggressive antimonopoly oratory of the movement. The Macune formula for a centralized buying and selling cooperative and the establishment of the trade-store system on a county level was outlined to gatherings at hundreds of southern crossroads from the Gulf of Mexico to the Ohio River.

"The Alliance is fast assuming gigantic proportions whose influence is felt all over our country and the great monopolies of the land are trembling when viewing its increasing power," proudly proclaimed Jennie Scott

Wilson in a speech before the Texas state Alliance that later was published in the *Mercury*. "The headquarters at Dallas already do a monthly business, I believe, of over $200,000 in filling cooperative orders. The order is now running large flouring mills and ginneries and expects to establish many more local ones throughout Texas. There are over 200,000 members in Texas today and the membership is experiencing a healthy growth. Some say that women have no business in the order," she added. "When Columbus braved the perils of unknown seas. . . . whose hand was it that fitted him for the voyage? I would suggest to all those who think that ladies are out of their place in the Alliance . . . and are given to telling all they know or hear, [that they] had better read up a little."[84]

"Hear you not the anvil ringing?" asked "Aunt Huldy" of Polk Creek in that invigorated Alliance summer of 1888. "Awake! Is life so dear or peace so sweet as to be purchased at the price of chains and slavery . . . ? We will resurrect liberty, justice, and equality which the monopolists have crucified and buried. . . . They will arise at the sound of the Alliance trumpet call, Phoenix-like from their ashes, and restore our downtrodden and beloved country to its pristine glory."[85]

If one accepts Goodwyn's argument that no mass movement can exist without self-respect, the women's role of booster and supporter was vitally important. Macune had given the farmers a program for economic emancipation, and the women would ensure participation and keep up morale. "Let's have singing in our Alliance meetings, and have the ladies and gentlemen read essays," said "Aunt Slow and Easy" from Luling. "Let's gain all the information we can, strengthen our order, stand by our leader, beat down every obstacle, put confidence in our chosen ones so when victory is won it will be ours as well. Let's have truth, honor, justice, and charity for our leader, and join in the cry, 'hallelujah.'"[86]

"The plundered plowmen are now feeling the strength of this great restorer," wrote another from Morris County. "We have been plundered of all that we have made for many years by the monopolizing merchants. Monopoly has had a long turn at the grab game but many will soon be at the plow handles, or make up a club of tramps. Some are selling now at cost. We regret that any Alliance member will trade with them. . . . We hope ere long they will learn cooperation, and trade only through the Alliance."[87]

More urging and support came from "Farmer's Daughter" in Waco. "I am glad to say that our lodge [Concord Alliance, No. 912] is getting along splendidly," she offered. "I have never seen the brethren more wide-awake to their interests, for we have been slaves long enough for the rich, and I hope to see the day when we will be free; and now we see a way out, let us all pull together."[88] "Keep the ball rolling," said Mary from Limestone County. "Your words of encouragement will assist the weary toiler to bear the burdens and crosses of life. He will feel that he stands not alone, but that other brave hearts and perhaps more fertile brains are trying to pave the way for the emancipation of the toiling men and women from slavery. If we trust our leaders and heed every call, soon we may see prosperity again smiling on our now poverty stricken people."[89]

Farm Life

The letters, ostensibly about Alliance activities, describe much of the rural world. Some women appeared fully content with farm life, waxing rhapsodic about its beauty and healthfulness. "What can be more pleasant than a nice country home?" asked "A Country Girl" from Belton. "There is nothing mean and debasing in farming. It leads a man forth among scenes of natural grandeur and beauty; it leaves him to the workings of purest and most elevating of external influences. City gentlemen are glad to lay down their city enjoyments and wander out into the country where vegetation puts forth all its magnificence and the merry songs of the birds inspire within him an admiration and love for nature and the honest, heart-felt enjoyment of country life."[90]

On July 12, 1888, a spontaneous soliloquy on the joys of farm life was provided by "Birdie" from Corn Hill, Williamson County:

> Although my last communication did not make its appearance in your columns, I will not despair, but will try again. As I am now seated, pen in hand . . . I hear in the distance the sound of the reaper, reaping the golden grains as now and then a gentle breeze is wafting to my window. Waft on, ye breezes. You are welcome this warm June evening. Oh, these showers, these perpetual showers that cause the farmer to wear a long face now that he is trying to save his grain. It rains, it showers and still it rains. No more do we hear the cry of dry weather.
>
> Once more bright anticipations are filling the farmer's breast of a glorious harvest and successful crops. He walks more briskly, smiles more brightly and holds his head erect. And the young men, oh, they are far more handsome; how bright and cheerful they look when they enter our lodge. I wonder how it is that the girls are smiling. Oh yes, by the way, it is leap year; perhaps, girls, some of us may make our fortune this year,

who knows? . . . I feel we should be thankful. The cool breeze is softly coming and going, laden with the perfume of sweet flowers and the songs of birds . . . The Alliance here is booming, members being initiated every meeting. The ladies are coming in quite briskly, both married and single.[91]

Texas farmers, working newer and less exhausted land, were marginally better off than farmers in Georgia, Alabama, or Mississippi. However, conditions varied. The less fortunate on small farms in the broken country of West Central Texas or on the poor soils of heavily timbered East Texas might find themselves bankrupt, their mortgages foreclosed, while those in the less-favored portions of the more prosperous counties of Central and North Texas might be living on credit with mortgaged farms.[92] In general, Texas Populists tended to live on less desirable land, although, to judge by the women's letters, some had no debts and were doing well.[93]

For "Aunt Belle" from Pilgrim Lake, farm life was moderately good. "We are enjoying a fine rain today," she wrote on September 4, 1888. "Some think that cotton will make the second crop if worms do not come. Some have picked a good deal of cotton already, in spite of the extreme hot weather. We have had a great deal of sickness in our county this summer, mostly of a malarial type; some congestion. Our Alliance is not so energetic in its actions as a great many others we read of in the *Mercury,* but we hope to do better in the near future. Our membership increases at every meeting. It seems that the ladies are taking a great interest, as they are joining rapidly now. Our alliance has about forty-five members."[94] On Lucretia M. Dunn's father's farm in Live Oak County, Oakville, everything seemed abundant and prosperous. Sixteen-year-old Lucretia recently had joined her town's Alliance, which the year before had had thirteen members but which now numbered sixty and was still growing. "Our neighborhood can't be beaten in this state, either morally, socially or religiously," she told the *Mercury* happily.

> We have no lawyers, gossips or other chronic disturbers of the peace among us and harmony reigns supreme. In the first place, . . . none of us are rich enough to excite envy, and none so poor as to create suspicion. When we go to church we take our dinners and are as social between religious services as though we were at a picnic; but when the hour for service arrives, we all gather into the church house and listen to the sermon; none stays outside to gossip. . . .
>
> Crops, corn and cotton, are very good here; so nearly all the girls in the neighborhood don their sun-bonnets and gloves and spend the day

picking cotton. Our cotton has averaged a thousand pounds per acre and there are a great many matured bolls in the patch now, but I'm sure that my cotton picking will be finished when they have opened, for within the last ten days worms have appeared and completely destroyed the leaves.[95]

The next year, Lucretia Dunn wrote to the Mercury again:

I don't know of one member who has ever mortgaged his crop before it was planted, though I suppose many of them do buy on a credit. But that is not papa's plan at all; he has always made it a rule never to buy anything unless he could pay cash for it, and although there are twelve of us in the family, not one of us has ever starved to death yet. We raise almost everything we eat at home. We have lived here eleven years and our smokehouse has never been empty, nor have we bought five pounds of bacon or lard. Papa killed two pigs less than eight months ago, one weighing 205 and the other 195 pounds. I don't know whether they would be called fine hogs or not, but they are fine enough for me.

Papa plants cotton only as a surplus crop and never more than we can gather our selves. . . . We have never hired a lock of cotton picked. Our land is very fertile. I don't remember that we have ever gathered less than 1,200 pounds per acre, but one year, and then the best part of the crop was blown out by a storm.

In your letter you alluded to men who go to town and spend all their money for whisky and then growl about monopolies. I can say this much for our Alliance, in fact, for the entire neighborhood. I don't know of but one man in this vicinity who ever gets even moderately drunk. I don't remember having seen a drunken man in my life, though I've always lived in a local option county, and if whisky is the horrid thing it is represented to be, I never want to live out of one. . . . We have had a lot of rain this winter but the ground is not muddy. Several farmers are planting corn now. The soil is mostly black sandy loam and doesn't get very muddy. The fruit trees are in full bloom.[96]

A month later, Lucretia Dunn wrote once more.

We raise corn, cotton, hay, sugar cane, both Irish and sweet potatoes, and melons of all kinds in abundance. I don't think small grains will do very well here, as a rule. Vegetables of almost every kind thrive splendidly; plums and grapes do better than other kinds of fruit. The health of the country is unexceptional. Our timber is mostly mesquite and live oak; there is plenty of it for fuel and fencing. We depend upon tanks and wells for water; the well water generally contains so much mineral that it is used only for household purposes, though some of it is good. Fish are not very plentiful. They can sometimes be caught in the Nueces river. Deer and wild turkey are still to be found but not very plentifully. The county is mostly thickly settled and almost every man has his land fenced, so you know there is not much land common.

There are but few negroes here and they congregate in the towns. Mexicans can be found out on the ranches, wherever they can get work. The country is generally rolling and has a good supply of chaparral and various other kinds of thorny brush. Unimproved land can be bought at two dollars per acre. Crops are in fine condition, corn is tasseling, and I have seen some silks; cotton is ten inches high and forming squares.[97]

Earlier in the year, however, conditions had not been quite so good in Colorado County. "This has been a wet, dreary winter," a stoic Mrs. Maner wrote in February 1889.

There is some cotton to pick yet; very little plowing has been done. Many cattle have died, I think more from disease than hunger, as we lost some and ours had plenty to eat. We have corn, potatoes and pork for our own use and some to spare. We keep our cotton seed to feed the cattle, and have milk and butter all year. We have several acres of Johnson grass from which we get more hay than we need. During this gloomy weather I've been busying myself repairing old garments, making quilts and getting better acquainted with my husband, who, by the way, is not near so attractive since he sits in the house and whittles, as he was when he only came in at meal time. The sum of human happiness is made up of little things.

Men must work and women must weep. Men will whittle and women must sweep. I'm going to have my share of happiness. I fill my lamp of love with the oil of patience and keep it burning brightly. Last night was Saturday night. After the work was all done, Ben sat before a cheerful fire drying the dampness of his clothes. Georgia in her own corner busied herself with some lace work, while I, too tired to knit, drew my low rocker nearer the lamp and sat down to rest and read. I selected a volume of Alden's Cyclopedia and read aloud extracts from the writings of Heroditus and poems by J. G. Holland.

Mrs. Maner used a wonderfully domestic metaphor to describe the work of the order: "The Alliance has brought its knitting and come to stay;

the clicking of its needles are heard in every neighborhood. We're winning, too. Outsiders have left off scoffing at us; that helps some. Our enterprising brothers started a co-operative store here which is a sure success. We are beginning to trust God and help ourselves."[98]

Texas Populists lived in relative isolation from the cultural mainstream. Populist counties had few towns, and those communities that did exist had small populations.[99] Farm life could be very lonely, a fact to which the women attest. The Alliance provided many opportunities for families to socialize at meetings, suppers, rallies, and picnics. *Mercury* readers also found companionship and comfort through the women's page. "It is raining to-day, part of us are gone, myself and smaller ones are alone," wrote "Aunt Slow and Easy" from Luling. "We who have a house full of little ones and an empty purse know how hard it is to get off and when I tell you I have been in the Alliance but once this year, you will not rebuke me but sympathize."[100]

"I have been attending school at Hope Institute, Italy, Texas, for the past three years, but circumstances prevented me from attending this year," wistfully said the eldest of six siblings, sixteen-year-old Lula Thompson, who found herself back on the family farm in Grandview, Johnson County. "I love my books," she admitted, "never tire of devouring their contents. I often while away the weary hours by reading and rereading the pages of some favorite study which brings back to me the dear familiar faces of old—I speak of my classmates. . . . How I would enjoy another bright season with them! . . . Perhaps when we have gained the victory over our many oppressors, I will be able to go back to the dear old spot."[101]

Others spoke frankly of the seemingly endless work of farm life, of fatigue and poverty. "Birdie" from Corn Hill asked:

How can we be happy when we toil so from day to day? . . . Fathers and brothers toil until when they come in from work they are too tired to talk or enjoy home with its softening influences. Mothers and sisters cannot bring any hope to the taxed and overworked brain. Mother thinks, how can I tell him there is no meat in the house, lard or coffee when he has no money and don't want to go deeper into debt? She looks at the children and wonders how shall we support them, educate and clothe them? The daughter wants a new dress as she has been making out with her old one but she looks at her father and thinks she must wait longer before she asks, and still she waits. There are hundreds of families in this condition, dear readers. What is the cause? Not idleness. What is the remedy?[102]

Women's Concerns

Alliance leaders believed American democracy to be in moral and political decay, corrupted by the professional politician and slick financier. The farmer was the last repository of the true values—the very humanity—of American culture. Education was needed not only to bolster agrarian self-esteem and to protect the unschooled farmer against merchandising fraud; it also was central to an understanding of urban, financial, and industrial capitalism and to the creation of a sophisticated political movement based upon unity, cooperation, and independence. Educated citizens not only could read, write, and understand contracts and ballots, but also they could fathom structural inequities in economic power. They could choose a government whose actions served the greatest good for the greatest number. The farmers had allowed political power to slip from their grasp because they lacked a political education.[103]

Education also was a logical extension of women's traditional roles as child rearers and as moral and cultural guardians. Children constituted the next generation of voters and politicians, and they needed to be trained at the earliest age. Women were expected to shield home and family from the rapidly changing values of an increasingly materialistic society. Alliance and Populist platform demands included a uniform, inexpensive system of textbooks and free public schools.[104] The women also worried about young people leaving the land and moving to the city, a place which, like ignorance, fostered political corruption and personal degradation.[105] Farm life was morally superior. While migration to urban areas was not yet widespread, it had begun. In 1870, approximately 70 percent of all persons gainfully employed in Texas were engaged in agriculture of some form; by 1900, the figure was 65 percent.[106]

In the April 19, 1888, issue of the *Mercury,* "A Country Girl" from Belton wrote that there was one thing farmers "could go into debt for if we cannot obtain it otherwise, that is an education. Knowledge is power." She believed that children should be taught the value of an education because "they can never be swindled out of that. . . . Educate your girls that they may be independent. Educate your boys that they may perform the work assigned them through life with intelligence and then our country homes will be a paradise surrounded by the beauties of nature and enlightened sons and daughters of toil and prosperity."[107]

In May of the following year, P. D. Ellis from Gonzales County wrote:

Ask the farmer's son what he intends to do and he almost invariably answers, "I don't know but certainly not farm." Nothing is done to make the farm attractive. We must educate our sons, send them to college to learn farming as a science, all the best methods and improved implements. He should also read literature; pure, high-toned books and papers are the best educators. Do not let him complain after following the plow all day he is too tired to read or study. Give him a bath and a slice of mother's snow flake bread and golden butter and a goblet of rich buttermilk to refresh him and he will not miss from sleep the hour spent in study. Study every feature of farm life—the most free and happiest on earth in its sweet intercourse with nature. For those who crave the noise and din of the city, the close, dark counting room, there is weariness beyond expression. Those poor oxygen starved creatures would give half their life for your happy privilege of roaming carefree and contented through the cool dark woods, inhaling pure air. Stay at home with mother, who gentle hands are ready and quickly soothe your slightest pain. How can the stale bread and reeking hash of the boarding house compare to her puffy rolls, nice new eggs and savory tempting ham? Come back to mother after your college course and enjoy the happiest life on earth, on the farm.[108]

In the June 6, 1889, issue, Mrs. Blanch McGarity wrote from Leesville that "each farmer ought to have his own private library and every community its circulating library and reading rooms where the best literature and information about farming can be gotten. Rouse yourself!" she urged. "Be alive, wide-awake, build up and improve constantly, not so restless and always planning to leave the farm. . . . On the farm are modeled some of our most noble characters, instilled with the best principles. Father, see that you make the farm what it should be by honorable example of honest industry, judicious management. Mother, who can estimate your influence? Make it a cheery, joyous home, full of sunshine and pure pleasure."[109]

S. L. S. Waelder from Colorado County, too, was inspired to speak to "those poor farmer's wives who like myself, have to depend on poorly conducted public schools, or where we have only three or four months school in a year . . . I have as much work as any woman who does all her own work, with a family of six to care for and yet I should like to tell how I have succeeded as it might encourage some other poor mother to teach her little ones at home. My oldest one is seven years of age and in the time I have had to teach her—about a year and a half—she is writing and spelling and is ready for a fourth reader. I have heard people say they did not wish their children to learn more than they knew. But why should we deprive our offspring of a thing so essential to their prosperity and happiness?"[110]

As the women continued to write letters and to exchange information, thoughts, support, and comfort, a mutuality began to develop. Laura Oakly of San Saba expressed it well as she responded to a letter from Charitie:

This is such a rare golden afternoon that I cannot refrain from calling on you all. Our Alliance is in a prospering condition. The sisters think they have missed a grand treat if anything happens to prevent them from attending. Charitie, I want to tell you how glad I was to read your letter. I like your idea of comradeship among women. This feeling that you and I are linked together by sympathy in a mutual effort (if you will permit such an expression) goes far to strengthen the effort individually made. What has become of Rebecca? Come again Rebecca, with your brave, true words. Will Charitie and Ann Other tell me through the family if we are responsible for our thoughts to one? Dear family, we never made a greater mistake in our lives than when we judged "Rural Widow" by her letters. I expected to meet a woman past her youth and extremely cold and haughty. What I did meet was a girl lovely in face and manners—and those blue eyes, they were beautiful enough to make captive every heart.[111]

Ellen D. also was moved by one of these letter writers. "Dear Charitie, what are you doing these beautiful autumnal days," she asked. "Are your motherly cares so oppressive that you cannot find time for one of your comforting, helpful chats with the sisters?"[112]

The women shared advice of all sorts and took many opportunities to moralize and talk temperance. Ann Other from Ennis, Texas, spoke quite severely and at length to the "boys," saying:

Where are you drifting and what kind of old man do you intend to be? I dare say you will be fully good enough for those young ladies who you think are 'sticking up their noses' at 'farmer boys' and looking for the 'ten cent dudes.' Let us consider. Are you always as choice of your company as you would require them to be . . . ? Is there never any time when you are out with the boys smoking, drinking and indulging in low class stories . . . ? Is your mouth always clean and the breath sweet as nature intends it should be, without the assistance of cloves and cardamom seed? Do you know that tobacco is, according to all our best scientists, to be one of the strongest leaders to strong drink? It destroys in a great degree the vigor of the mind, dulls, by its narcotic poison, the quick sensibilities for purity and virtue; makes a slave of the appetite and a filthy casket for the soul. . . . Instead of spending forty or fifty cents for that pound of tobacco . . .

[or] that "yellow covered literature" . . . look instead for the "Alta editions," beautifully bound in blue and gold, of the lives of our greatest men, Washington, Jefferson, Patrick Henry, Clay and Webster, and also at the books of travel, of foreign lands. . . .

I hear you say, "but I don't have the time to read." But stop and think: Where and how do you spend your Sundays? Of course you will say you go to church, but does church last an entire Sunday? How is the rest of the day passed? Do you pay attention to what is said? I think there is not a clergyman in our land who would not prefer to have you stay at home and read and study one of the books I have mentioned to having you attend church simply to cast your eye over the audience to pick out the best looking girl and wonder if Jim could cut you out with Annie since he had this new suit of clothes.[113]

Intemperance and the errant ways of men were frequent subjects. "Is the farmer's wife a miserable woman?" asked a writer from McKinney, Collin County.

Not all. There are thousands of happy country homes where husband and wife work for each other's happiness. I, for one, believe that most of those who are miserable are to blame because they do not exercise their own common sense.

So many are seemingly in a great hurry to get married. Girls will marry men who are drunkards and know all along they are not going to quit. Girls will marry men who have been at work for themselves, or should have been for years and have nothing but a few clothes. Now if they can't support themselves, how under the sun can they support a family? I think that the girls who marry this sort of man are they that plod about in coarse shoes, go to church under sunbonnets and ride in the farm wagon with the rusty plow gear. Farmers' wives have a great deal of work to do in the house, and it is not a woman's place to work in the field. . . . They will gain very little if they commence it.[114]

Lettie Reynolds of Tarrant County wrote that she was glad women were sensible and not "blindfolded by folly and fashion." She longed, however "for a reformation in the ways of some of our country boys, who work hard all week, probably for fifty cents per day, just for the satisfaction of sporting a cane and wearing a Prince Albert on Sundays. If they would only save their hard-earned money and buy homes and educate themselves upon their own interests, we could look forward to the time when all shall enjoy equal rights with special privileges to none. . . . O! for another Cincinnatus, that can leave the plow and rule a nation, and return again to the humble farm without any feelings of mortification."[115]

"Rural Widow," from Harmony Ridge, had the gumption to get into the love and marriage question, although only because she was prompted.

> I would that I could answer your first question, sweet Laura, but it is beyond human ken to say whether one will be happy after marriage. Love in marriage is desirable, but I don't think positively necessary to happiness. Some of the happiest marriages that I know of, the persons were unacquainted save by a letter, until a very short time before marriage. I am persuaded that if all the women who have married men who professed to love them could but lift the veil from the hearts of their husbands, three-fourths of them would find there a face not their own, on which was written "my idol," in burning letters of love. Love need not necessarily be "woman's whole existence" in this day when the wife may have to work as well as the man.[116]

The women discussed the propriety of working in the fields, an activity that conflicted with the notions of woman's sphere. In April 1889, Frankie Bradford of Luna Vista had written:

> Spring, the most beautiful season is now here. . . . The farmers are busy farming. Papa has no boys large enough to help him, and therefore his girls must help. I am not ashamed to confess that I work on the farm, for I am sure it is no discredit to do so; and whoever thinks so, have some lack of knowledge. I believe a girl can work in the field and be so full of grace as one that dwells in a palace. . . . Let those who say it is a disgrace to a girl to work in the field take heed . . . A girl can live a true Christian while working in the field as she can at any other kind of work. She may plow, hoe, plant, pick cotton, etc. yet, while doing any of those things; she can have her heart full of love and grace; speaking to herself in psalms and hymns and spiritual songs, singing and making melody in her heart to the Lord.[117]

The issue apparently was raised again by Jennie Dixon, who, with a somewhat prim, conservative voice, edited the "Woman's Page" of the *Southern Mercury* from September to November 1890. Mrs. Dixon, who also edited the *Texas White Ribbon*, the official publication of the Women's

Christian Temperance Union, was the wife of Allianceman Samuel H. Dixon, a Baptist and the *Mercury*'s managing editor.[118] The *Ribbon* and the *Mercury* often reprinted each other's material.[119]

In the October 30, 1890, issue of the *Mercury*, Mrs. Dixon was answered rather defensively by Alice E. Miller, a reader from Wortham.

> If I was a farmer's daughter and had three brothers and seven sisters, you may know my education is quite limited. I agree with Mrs. Dixon in regard to women working in the field, although every woman I see has been picking cotton. It seems that they are just bound to work in the field to help make a support. I do not think it is a disgrace although I do not think we were made to do hard field work or we would have been as stout as men. If it gets much worse, I think women will have to take the lead in the field. This is one thing that is ruining the women's health of today as well as tight lacing. Let us work, watch and pray and perhaps we will see the day when we have more time for reading and brightening ourselves up.[120]

In that same October issue, Jennie Dixon defended her earlier statement, saying that honorable work was never disgraceful, but that she thought farm work was too heavy for delicate women. "I, for one, wish to see other employments open to them where they will receive equal pay for the same kind of work that men perform. A reform of some kind is needed to improve the affairs on the farm but . . . I feel sure that it is not more work or better management or more scrupulous economy on the part of the farmers' wives."[121]

Writing in the "Boys and Girls' Department," she went on to correct a young and apparently too impetuous Maudalene from Willow Creek, who had asked if corresponding with an unknown person was proper. "We feel no timidity in stating our views on any subject," Maudalene had said boldly in its favor. "We can give our imagination unbounded sway; we can discuss books, music, and any and all sentiments of the human heart and feel no fear in treading on any personality. I have books, music, flowers, shell[s,] and rare specimens of writing which have been sent by persons whose faces I have never seen; still, they are dear to me. I feel we are kindred spirits."[122] Jennie Dixon severely cautioned Maudalene against such behavior, and in doing so passed on the insecurity that her own generation felt about women writing. "When they come to Maudalene's age, girls cannot be too particular in their intercourse with boys whether in their company or through letters," she warned. "My dear girls, you do not know whose eye your letter might fall under, and to have it criticized, even the spelling, and picked to pieces by a thoughtless and may hap, vicious crowd of boys, would cause a painful blush of wounded pride to mantle your cheek. And oh, Maudalene, we should never give our imagination 'unbounded sway' in writing, for sure the world is so that it will all come back to us, a mass of silly gushing nonsense, which, like a ghost, will rise to distress us in later life. Don't do it."[123]

Others spoke of sickness and death, and reached out through the *Mercury* for support from sympathetic, kindly readers. In such letters, the character and the sources of strength of the women emerge, as does their sense of their helplessness as they experience one loss after another. Death "has visited my home circle this summer," wrote Ann Other in October 1888.

> After weeks of patient and prayerful watching and faithful nursing, I have seen the little bud slowly fading, fading, and feeling that its little spirit was unavoidably passing from our care and skill; and then . . . to realize that another one of our home circle just putting forth the foot of manhood . . . to see such a tree of Lebanon drop its branches and fall to the ground with the crushing weight it must bear to all hearts that love it; to go and witness the last sad rites the living can pay to the dead, then to return and still see the death angel perched above your door, and to hear your sad heart cry for the return and know the answer of "nevermore," and then after another week's anxious waiting and prayer to lay another loved form in its little white casket . . . this calls forth the heroic strength of a Christian nature.
>
> We find comfort in the thought that where they have gone will be no hindrance to the full development of the beautiful minds with which God endowed them. They shall behold the beauty of the Lord . . . who can conceive the beautiful lessons they shall learn as they wing their way from star to star, from one planetary system to another, to there drink in all the mysteries of astronomy with God's angels for guides and teachers, or to stoop to the lowly flowers of our fields and penetrate all the unacquired problems of botany and chemistry. . . .
>
> In these hopes perhaps the waiting hearts may find solace and while each token that tells of the departed—the straw hat with its broken crown through which a stray curl once peeped, the violin and harp that once awoke sweet echoes in the old home corners, the locked chest with its boyish treasures, the chest of tools with its repaired knives and other mechanical inventions with which the dear hands last worked, to school books here forever closed for the studies to be taken up higher, or the tiny

shoe which baby feet never soiled and the little white robes folded away as a mother's shrine, to be replaced by brighter, fairer robes to be worn in an immortal world. . . .

If to any other homes of the sisters such grief has been sent, let us clasp hands over the space that separates the readers of the *Mercury* and with firm resolve, take up our burden and use every opportunity given us to improve our minds, realizing that is the immortal part.[124]

Laura Oakly, from San Saba, shared a similar sadness and sought consolation from her letter-writing sisters. "Since I last wrote, which has been but a short time I have been changed from a lighthearted girl who found nothing but bright, beautiful flowers in her path, to a sad, heartbroken woman," she wrote. "My mother, the one who was my sun by day and guiding star by night, has been taken from me after a short illness and I turn to the family for comfort. I know there are some in this large family who can sympathize with me from experience. I have three little ones left in my care and I feel that I need the prayers of every sister. Oh what a trial it is to try to fill a mother's place."[125]

Frugality

Times got rougher as the currency contracted. Among other things, the dollar continued to appreciate, its value rising steadily, while prices for agricultural products, especially cotton, declined.[126] The farming community, noted for its hard work and industry, worked harder.[127] The women urged each other to economize, to be more frugal. "We can be the most independent people in the world if we will only try," said Eddie, from the Round Pound Alliance. "First, we must economize. If we want to accomplish anything, raise everything that we can at home, wear old clothes and keep out of debt. . . . The Alliance . . . may continue its onward march until the farmers all over the land can shout 'Victory.'"[128]

Some sisters—as well as editors of the *Southern Mercury*—shared tips on stretching resources. "I have just learned a good lesson in economy from some Alliance people while on a trip to Galveston Bay," offered Fannie Kerley from Limestone County, who, along with her husband and their three sons and three daughters, belonged to her county's "grand and ennobling" Alliance. "It is how to make four pounds of coffee go as far as eight: Take four pounds of potatoes chopped fine and dried, mix with an equal quantity of coffee, parch together, and the oldest Texan cannot de-

tect the difference. Sisters, lend a hand and see if we can't help our husbands and sons out of the fearful bondage in which we have suffered ourselves to be placed, as slaves to the mercantile class."

"We tried potatoes alone from '61 to '64," added the *Mercury*.[129]

In June 1888, Bettie Gay from Columbus suggested boycotting coffee
until the price fell, something she had done during the Civil War. She had
a blunt response to a contributor's suggestion that women return to the
spinning wheel and loom. "I am in sympathy with every economical move,"
she said, but

> in the first place, it is killing on any one to card and weave. I speak from
> experience, for we had to do it during the war. It will take three days
> to weave one yard of cloth; at twenty-five cents per day, it would cost
> seventy-five cents per yard to spin and weave a yard, besides the expense
> of the machinery, so you see there is no economy. It would be more
> healthful to raise a cotton patch, work in the open air and buy calico or
> muslin for five cents per yard. You would have more and play half the
> time; besides one pound of cotton will make five yards or more of goods
> and you might drudge your life out and not accomplish anything unless
> the men will unite and vote in a solid body of men who will represent our
> interests. You might spin, weave and work until you would faint by the
> roadside and the evil would be the same.

"I saw some sister writing about dress making," this writer continued
helpfully. "Anyone can make a full skirt, with body or redingote, and we
farmers do not care to put on style till our independence is declared. What
should we care for style? If we are not able to buy fashionable bonnets or
hats, get a nice piece of gingham and make a neat bonnet. They are very
becoming."[130]

Others were becoming tired of being instructed on money-saving
measures. "Sisters, why don't you preach economy to one who has the
power to economize?" asked A True Friend angrily from Eagle Cove,
Callahan County.

> One sister says, let us help our husbands by patching old clothes. . . . We
> have been in the habit of patching as long as we could make things re-
> spectable. Another sister says, let us make over our old clothes. We have
> been in the habit of doing this also. And by the way, we have sold butter
> and eggs to buy the dye to color them and for a while in the spring, we
> got fifteen and twenty cents per pound for butter, but very soon they

began to say we can't give but ten or twelve cents. Now that is poor encouragement for we are at the cow-pen late at night, and work our butter every morning to have it nice.

Now a farmer's wife has a heart and wants to see her family look nice at least once a week to go to church, and if one has a flopped hat and another a patch on the knee and a third has his toes out, must we still economize and work so hard all week that we can't enjoy the sermon on Sunday? . . . I think the Alliance is to help the oppressed as who is more oppressed than the farmer's wife? Now, if some good sister can tell us how to keep our house neat and clean without so much hard work, so when our husbands come in we will not be too tired to talk and can have more patience to teach our children, I think most of them would appreciate this, much more.[131]

Mrs. Maner from Colorado County wrote again with her thoughts on the subject:

Most women (I mean the middle class) do too much unnecessary work. This everlasting stitch, stitch, cook, cook, wash, wash, iron, iron, is killing our women. It is costing lots of money for doctors' bills and patent medicines; it is making women prematurely old, husbands unhappy and the young folks discontented, driving the boys away from home and making the girls want to go. When will mothers learn that there is something more beautiful in life than tucks and ruffles, lace and embroidery, something more enduring than the pleasures of the palate?

Mothers, dress the little ones in plain comfortable clothes and do away with so much machine and laundry work. . . . Don't waste your time, health and life in non-essentials. Cold bread, butter milk, tea or coffee, with a smiling mamma at the table are more enjoyable than hot biscuits and fried chicken with a tired, fretful, unresponsive mother, whose presence chills the warmth and glow of childish joy.[132]

She did not mention Mr. Maner this time, so perhaps he had returned to work in the fields.

Frugality did not change things significantly, of course, and some women reacted with depression and a sense of futility. "Justice," a farmer's daughter from Albany in Shackelford County, said of the workingman: "He is no longer content to do all the work and let others do his thinking. He is asking, 'why is it I toil early and late, live on the poorest food, wear the cheapest clothing, only give my children the advantage of the free school, model my house for the least cost and shelter my stock with the heavens; yet after all this close economy, when I have lived my three score years, I shall perhaps be laid in the potter's field, my children doomed to be hewers of wood and drawers of water and meet the same fate.'"[133]

For others, the hard times were galvanizing. The farm women, gaining confidence, began to get angry. "Corn Bread" from Bexar County said, "There is a monster in our path that is not a bugaboo but a real devourer, worse than the devilfish with thirty-foot tentacles. Protection stands before us, brazen and audacious, demanding that the poor whom it made poor shall protect the rich, the same as the lambs protect the wolves. And the working people protect the band of greedy rascals who have robbed us twenty years or more. It has hordes of gold gotten from us through unjust laws that it worked upon us through Congress. Members go up to do our work, and the cunning men beguile, bribe and seduce them to give them laws to take our earnings. So brothers, be careful what you are doing at the polls when election comes off."[134]

Apologizing for her "coarse language," "Poor Gal" from Red Oak, Ellis County, lashed out furiously: "I feel, see, and hear so much about the downtrodden farmer that I sometimes wish I could split myself up and make a dozen men out of myself and join the Alliance that many times, and that my tongues were loose at both ends, so that I could cry out, down with monopoly and the middle men! If it came to the worst, I would have fists enough to hit extortion, strike monopoly, punch the middle dude who gets what we ought to have, plug a dart at the cotton buyers, who say, 'I will give you seven and a half cents a pound,' and punch the ignorant farmer for letting him have it, and with one mighty jump, leap square down on debt, doctors, and lawyers, and there hold them like grim death to a dead nigger, until they were willing to practice for farmers in the neighborhood of living reason."[135]

Religion

In 1890, more than two-thirds of all Texans did not belong to any church, in part because of frontier unorthodoxy but also because of the state's overwhelming emptiness (8.36 people per square mile). However, almost 30 percent of the population, or 677,151 souls, did profess membership in some religious group. Of these affiliates, two-thirds were Baptist (37 percent) or Methodist (32 percent). Catholics comprised 15 percent of the other churchgoers, while the Disciples of Christ and Presbyterians had 6 percent each.[136]

Texas Populists shared an essentially religious view of society, and this influenced their political behavior. McMath maintains that the universal idiom of the rural South was neither Jeffersonian nor conspiratorial but rather was evangelical Protestant, because the ethnic and religious groups who comprised so much of the Alliance were Anglo Baptists and Methodists. At a time when many of the Populists were finding prevailing myths of Southern and American culture inadequate to explain the conditions of life and the increasingly skewed distribution of the nation's wealth, the religious rhetoric of the Farmers' Alliance helped render their situations and their movement more intelligible. Significantly, leading churchmen used the religious tradition to support the economic and political status quo while Alliance members employed the same tradition to advocate change.[137]

In county after county, Alliance meetings began with prayers for the humble tillers of the soil, included hymns and Bible readings, and ended in political speeches, many of them delivered by the suballiance chaplain, who frequently doubled as lecturer and organizer in spreading the new Social Gospel. Picnics especially were popular, and some camp meetings in the groves—filled with lectures, speeches, songs, camaraderie, and lemonade— lasted two, three, or four days. Whole families came for twilight suppers and gathered by the thousands at encampments, their long trains of wagons emblazoned with suballiance banners. Men and women listened to lecturers speak about the "money trust," the gold standard, and the private national banking system, or plan the mass sales for the bulking of cotton. The lecture format somewhat mitigated the problem of adult illiteracy, while the gatherings enhanced group identity and commonality.[138]

Mrs. V. A. Taylor from Americus, Marion County, happily recounted such a propitious event:

First there was the hurry and bustle of the morning's packing provisions, placing baskets and children in the wagon so as to consume as little space as possible for we must take in friends on the way until we are pretty thoroughly jammed. No inconvenience I assure you for our sub-Alliance which had been invited to join the Lasater Alliance in a day of general boom, fun and frolic must be well represented, hence the cram in all available vehicles. A drive of eight miles over rough roads, under a blazing sun did not in the least damp the ardor and enthusiasm and we arrived there with keen zest for the enjoyments of the day, meeting old friends and forming of new acquaintances under the auspices of being united in fraternal love.

I look upon this Alliance movement as the most potent abettor of Christianity that has ever originated, but hold! I am not going to moralize just now. The program of the day was first music; second, essay on the principles, aims and possibilities of the Alliance, by your scribe; third, lecture by Brother Macready who was sent to us by Dr. Macune; . . . fourth, dinner, and that in quality and quantity all that could be desired. After dinner, music, then . . . a sort of "fill up the time talk" by Brother D. R. Hale. . . . His happy hits and telling anecdotes fill us with mirth and enjoyment while his unlimited zeal fires us with enthusiasm for the cause. Next, short speeches from the candidates for county office and there seemed to be less palaver this year than ever before. . . .

Toward the end, I allowed . . . music and dancing, to divert my attention from the graver questions of the day, but I had an excuse. I took my little ones where for the first time they might behold displays of the terpsichorean art; not that I cared to witness, oh no but like school teachers and preachers who have to carry the little ones to circuses and menageries, sacrificed my wishes in order to please and interest the children.

The sinking sun reminded us of the weary miles we had to plod upon our homeward way and bidding good-bye to friends [we] departed with the kindest of feelings in our hearts, our loyalty to the Alliance strengthened.[139]

Understanding the Politics

The Cleburne Demands of 1886 and later Alliance and Populist platforms were disseminated widely among the Alliance membership. Moreover, after 1888 the Alliance's educational campaign efforts intensified, and the many reform journals and suballiances embraced new roles as schools for education. Alliance newspapers carried voluminous eighteen- to twenty-part series on the history of democracy or on the economic theories of Ricardo, Mills, and Smith. Long and capable—if somewhat mythological—letters, such as Ann Other's earnest two-column synopsis of civilization's development, reflect a reading of Macune's similar multi-part educational accounts of history. "Away back in the twilight of time, we see mankind on Earth wandering, obtaining sustenance from such provisions as nature furnished to their land, living in caves or wild rocky recesses," she began in a July 1888

Mercury. She went on to trace the arrival and decline of the Greeks and Romans, the development of family and government, as well as the growth of vast corporations.[140]

In the suballiances, chosen individuals prepared talks on the issues of the day. According to Macune, "hard financial and economic questions are being discussed . . . now." Sarah Emery's widely read pamphlet, "Seven Financial Conspiracies Which Have Enslaved the American People," was the classic explanation of the Populist belief—not entirely accurate—that bad legislation caused disastrous monetary policies, ruining farmers and urban workers alike. Such material informed the *Mercury's* readers and provided a common language or rhetoric of needs and goals, upon which the women's political letters to the paper drew.[141]

Some of the letters were sophisticated and explicit, and writers asked important, thoughtful questions. Other opinions were abstract, as indeed the whole Populist theme could be, again with the discussion of economic issues cast in moral or Christian terms and expressed in statements filled with Old Testament imagery and Christian metaphor.[142] To some, the "money power" indicated particular individuals—for example, the legislators who had passed the bill for the demonetization of silver. For others, the phrase loosely denoted not only politicians on the wrong side but also all wealthy men and corporations—Wall Street brokers, bankers (American and British), small and large business owners, railroads, mortgage companies, mine owners, and landlords.[143] Frequently, passionately expressed concerns were combined with religion and traditional family values. Biblical injunctions against usury reinforced Alliance condemnation of money-lending, liens, and mortgages.[144] Always the letter writers urged the farmers on in the struggle.

In May 1888, a letter from "Western Reader" provided a cynical rejection of the farmers' traditional solution to problems, harder work:

It is in the interest of our masters to keep all labor so busily employed getting a bare subsistence that none shall have time to inform themselves as to the cause of our degradation, nor study a proper method of remedies. They say to us, "rise a little earlier, work a little harder, farmers, and don't meddle in questions concerning your political existence."

Farmers, ignorance and poverty are effects, effects of preventable causes!! If you continue to bind yourself to such leaders or to either one of the present two parties, to cringe when its astute leaders crack their whips, to ignore the study of politics, to try to make a cookbook out of your present organ, then you deserve to have your suffrage bought and yourselves the slaves of big-salaried law-makers who are faithful guardians of their own interests. . . . How can you expect the aristocrats of the senate, the bankers, the lawyers and peacock tricksters of the house of representatives to efface their own self-worship and be mindful of interests which you foolishly pay them to trammel and neglect?[145]

The dialogue of Annie Mims of the Wood County Alliance in Winsboro, too, was broad and fervent, a letter typical in its use of classical, biblical, and other allusions. "What has become of our glorious old bird of liberty?" she asked. "Uncle Sam is throttled. Like Prometheus, chained to the barren rock, the shylocks, vulture-like, eating the beast daily, and the old eagle dead drunk can only croak monopoly; and the whisky traffic has put us in the fix. What Herculean power can or will cut the chains that thus bind this government and place the proud eagle on its perch again? Let me answer, the Farmers' Alliance can do it, with, if need be, the assistance of other labor organizations."[146]

"We have indulged in a Rip Van Winkle nap of many years and our minds have become so thoroughly impregnated with somnambulistic tendencies that we have almost become indifferent to our condition but the time has come when we must awake from our slumber," said "Aunt Huldy" from Polk Creek. She called upon members of the Alliance to "grow and flourish and spread until they join hands and with unity of action descend upon king monopoly and beat back the invading foe to its own domain. Then we will resurrect liberty, justice, and equality which the monopolists have crucified and buried."[147]

On August 22, 1889, Mrs. Garrett from Delta County dramatically asked: "Where is the proud American eagle? You left liberty's golden bowl unguarded at the political cistern and your proud bird swooped down to drink; designing politicians came and by wiles and art have stolen him and made him a prisoner in the congressional halls of these United States, and he will remain there until the farmers and laborers rise up in their might and demand its release. I will tell you where the gold is that should be in circulation among the working people. Railroad kings own about ten millions."[148]

Religious rhetoric had a powerful appeal. "The great civil revolution is to be supplemented with a great social revolution. God has so written it down," said Mrs. Louisa Crowder from Armstrong, Erath County, in June 1888. "No man or combination of men can stop this labor move. . . . Upon the white crest of it thousands will be lifted to virtue and honor, and thousands more who are before it will be submerged and swept away."[149]

"Old Maid" Sallie Beck announced her particular method of analyzing the existing world system and, in doing so, added a refreshing culinary metaphor to the study of social and political science. "Human misery will be apt to disappear with good cooking," she wrote. "It is highly probable that men fed on sodden bread and watery turnips are capable of wife-beating and conspiracies against even the democratic government of the present day. . . . A nation's civilization, it is said, can be judged by the bread it eats. Liberty bread is light, spongy, untaxed and nutritious. . . . This bread always rises and is always a brown success. The heavy, black bread of the protected Russian peasant, mixed in tears and weariness, kneaded in hopeless sadness and despondency, suggests the cruel, despairing bondage of those who subsist on it. Tortillas engender monthly revolutions, as our child-loving neighbors, the Mexicans, will testify."[150]

The women's letters reflect their awareness of national events. Ann Other, who came from Ennis in Ellis County, wrote in her lengthy letter of the late summer of 1888:

> When we see with what greed those in high places are grasping the wealth of the nation; when we see vast corporations fostered and protected by the nation; when we see the bonds issued by the nation and bought up by the capital at sixty cents on the dollar and then so protected that the nation has retained no power by which she can pay them off at their face value at such time as it may become convenient, when we see these same bonds now demanding one hundred and twenty-five cents on the dollar of the producing population; when we see this same population stifled and clogged in their efforts to alleviate some of their hardships by this same banking system that our nation is fostering, then it is time for the people to cast their eye on the rise and fall of other governments and see that theirs does not meet the same fate.

By this time, Ann Other had sent many letters to the *Mercury*. Having informed herself, she now began asking questions and educating other readers. She had become at ease with the written word. "As the patronage of the government has increased," she said,

> the presidents have used it so as to enormously increase the power and prestige of the executive, while the legislative branch has been dwarfed almost to insignificance. When we see our senators voting $250,000 from the public treasury for themselves to visit Paris, it is time the common

people inquire how that would benefit the people whom they pretend to represent. When we see them voting to Mrs. Garfield $20,000 of the people's money and then $5,000 per annum besides, it is time to ask how long [it will be] before we will have the aristocratic title added.

The war is soon to be fought over again against centralization of wealth and power in government, against railroads and all other combinations, a war with ballots, not swords. Where will you fight? Will you do your own thinking or give your oppressors another four years' hold on you?[151]

On the subject of banks, Mrs. N. I. Rankin said:

The tenth plank of the Democratic state platform announces that the Democratic party of Texas is opposed to rechartering United States banks. According to my understanding, there is not a single United States bank in existence and has not been since Jackson vetoed the bill rechartering the U.S. bank in 1832 and withdrew the public money from its keeping in 1833. He said it was a power too great to exist in a free government, for its wealth would become so great that it would buy, bribe and force all legislation, both national and state to act in the interest of the bank which is just what the present banking association has done. . . . Is it not more probable that it is a scheme originated expressly to deceive a trusting people, for they know well enough that Cleveland has never uttered one word against the banks and cares no more for the Democratic platform of Texas than he does for the croaking of a frog in a mill pond. . . . The people are tired of paying fifty millions a year on bonds that are past due and hold our present Congress and President and Secretary (of the Treasury) responsible for the great robbery that is robbing our little ones of every comfort which childhood should know. Yet the democratic convention attempted to deceive the people by saying they were opposed to rechartering the U.S. banks knowing full well there were no such banks in existence. If my position is true, surely this is sufficient to drive all who are in favor of reform from the ranks of a party which deceives a people and which is supporting a president who, for four years, has never by word or deed shown that his sympathy was with the people.[152]

Because of federal restrictions against national bank loans based on land and because of the scarcity of state banks, farmers having difficulty with debt payments could borrow funds only from a limited number of private banks or from out-of-state loan companies. Fewer of these companies operated in Texas than in the Northern Plains states, and they usually charged higher interest, 10 to 12 percent, because of the greater risks and the legal complications of their Texas business.[153]

In March 1889, Ann Other wrote again about the scarcity of currency: "As for the laboring people, they are now so crushed and crowded for money, that votes can be bought for half a dollar or a pair of shoes for the little ones. As long as our currency remains in its present contracted state and a few individual bankers can convulse the whole nation in its finances, as long as we live with our present banking laws, there is no power on earth that can destroy our railroad monopolies and monopolies of all kinds. As to issuing bonds on the counties to build our roads it seems to me no thinking man can contemplate what our national bonded debt has done for us and then authorize the issuing of still more bonds for the present and rising generation to pay."[154]

The land belonged to the farmer—not the government, the speculator, the banker, the London financier, or the railroad magnate.[155] "It is good to discuss the why's and wherefore's of the exceeding scarcity of money but there is another question of great magnitude," advised Mary of Limestone County. "Why is it that there are so many homeless men and women, men who would till the soil for a living, and yet there are thousands of acres of land lying idle. Why did our state officials give the railroads so much of the people's land, and compel the poor to rent? Why did they give so much land to build a state house? Would it have not been better policy to have given that 3,000,000 acres of land to the poor renting farmer and built a less palatial house by direct taxation?"[156]

The women articulated economic theories and financial legislation well, but in their personal analyses and final conclusions, they emphasized the human aspects of poverty among all classes and its effects upon the family and home. They never doubted that impersonal industrial capitalism caused family poverty and the poverty of single women.[157] "Aunt Slow and Easy" of Luling questioned pensions for public officials in this light: "I am very much opposed to Congress allowing pensions to Mrs. Logan or Mrs. anybody else just because their husband figured largely in public. Our big men in Congress and Senate have done enough to rob the poor farmer, and Congress would tax our poor, half-fed and thinly-clad farmers to pay these pensions while our farmers' wives are left helpless with large families to support and perhaps no home, are passed completely by with silent contempt, only the tax assessor and collector gives them notice if they have anything they can tax."[158]

The February 28, 1889, issue of the *Mercury* contained an astute letter about the electoral process from "Corn Bread." She discussed the Haymarket Square incident in a way that suggested unconscious ambivalence about the event and a tacit understanding of the anarchists' politics. Farmers were having to justify their loyalty to a country which was, in their view, developing an increasingly unjust and insupportable economic and political system. "In this government by the people, the majority of men take no real part in governing," said Corn Bread. "The government is chosen by the caucuses, and people never attend the caucuses—only politicians as a rule do this. . . . That the caucus and not merely the polling place is the direct point of contact between the government and the people [is] the first great lesson of citizenship. . . . Our system of government is menaced by tremendous forces of socialism, anarchism and other disturbing elements," she continued. "The disciples of the systems are not . . . ignoramuses and half lunatics. They are members who have made a lifelong study of the world's social and political problems. The anarchists recently hung in Chicago were learned men, doctrinaires, well-drilled specialists in the social problems of the day. These men are dangerous because they think they have found a tremendous injustice at the bottom of society, and they are doubly dangerous because in this belief they are right. It is the duty of all good citizens to recognize this truth early and to set about finding remedies for this injustice before these dangerous men find it in the firebrand, the dynamite bomb."[159]

Alliance women understood the importance of the Exchange. If successful, it would have freed the farmer from the control of the local merchant-landlord and from the terrifyingly exorbitant interest rates of the crop lien.[160] A speech by "Little" Jennie Scott Wilson was published on the front page of the *Mercury*. "Thousands of friends and enemies to the Alliance have prophesied that the Alliance would suicide," she wrote.

> One fearing that it would; the other, hoping and confidently believing that it would. But today the mists have cleared away and every intelligent Alliance man recognizes that it is founded upon a solid careful basis. The Alliance is fast assuming gigantic proportions whose influence is felt all over our country and the great monopolies of the land are trembling when viewing its increasing power. The Texas Alliance headquarters at Dallas already do a monthly business, I believe, of over $200,000 in filling cooperative orders. The order is now running large flouring mills and ginneries and expects to establish many more local ones throughout Texas.

There are over 200,000 members in Texas today and the membership is experiencing a healthy growth.[161]

Alliance officials claimed that during its existence the Exchange did have a favorable economic impact. According to Macune, in Texas it reduced the farmers' supply bill by 40 percent, produced a general 20 percent deflation, and saved farmers more than $6 million.[162] But often crops were already mortgaged, and noteholders determined their disposition regardless of changing market conditions. The Dallas Exchange handled its own credit operations; by March 1888, notes exceeded capital three to one. Banks refused to honor Exchange paper. As it began to falter, farmers passed hats for contributions in county meeting hall after county meeting hall. In farmhouses all over Texas, women dug into domestic hideaways for the coins that represented a family's investment in the hope of escaping the crop lien.[163]

Rena R. Scott of O'Daniel, Texas, lamented that, rather than using the Exchange, farmers were "trading with others because they are told they can do better than with their own firm. . . . I visited an Alliance not long since and a resolution was passed [where members] pledged themselves to not mortgage their cotton crop to anyone. Such a resolution should be passed in every sub-Alliance in the state."[164]

Some went further, took matters into their own hands, and on a level of independent grassroots activity not exercised before by Alliance women, began organizing their own form of financial support for the Exchange. It began in June 1889, when Mrs. A. P. Shaw from Donalton, Hunt County, wrote: "From reading the *Mercury,* it seems to me that the brethren of sub-alliances are not doing their duty and are afraid to trust our leaders, or they would pay off the indebtedness of the Exchange." She proposed "to the sisters of the Lone Star state: That we sell eggs, butter, chickens and garden stuff to the amount of one dollar by the first of July, to help pay off the debt that hangs over the Exchange. Now let me see in the *Mercury* how many sisters are willing to lend a helping hand to save our head; for the Exchange is our head and if our head be cut off, our body is worthless."[165]

Two weeks later she was joined by Mrs. Bettie Gay of Columbus. "We the undersigned sisters of the Farmers' Alliance of Texas, agree to sell eggs, chickens, butter and garden stuff to the amount of ONE DOLLAR, which amount is to be paid by the first day of August and the total amount so subscribed is to be applied to the payment of the Exchange indebtedness," they pledged.

"Action is now essential," urged Mrs. Gay. "Let us save the Exchange. Let the lecturers at the July county meetings collect one dollar from every member or fifty cents, which would more than pay the indebtedness and also assist in securing cotton bagging for those who cannot advance money for the present crop. . . . In one of our county meetings the question of taking stock in the New Braunfels mills was discussed nearly all day. Finally, one man arose and though poor, offered a dollar from his own pocket. Others followed and in less than twenty minutes, the entire amount was raised."

Mrs. Gay decried a lack of leadership and organization. "Many do not read and many do not go to meetings. If it could be arranged for every county to have a barbecue or basket dinner and have a first-class business man speak and take up a collection, I wager we'd have the whole amount needed raised in two months. I am a woman and with many more like Mrs. Shaw, we can pay out of debt and stay out."[166]

In the next week, five more women wrote from Rodgers, Benton, and Caddo Mills counties, agreeing to sell eggs, chickens, butter, and garden stuff for the Exchange.[167] In early July, five more joined the effort. By mid-July, there were yet four more, from Red Rock, New Caney, and Jewett counties. By the end of September, some fifty-five women had committed their support.[168] But the financial problems were not to be solved by such egg-and-butter efforts. By the late summer of 1889, after twenty months of operation, the Dallas Exchange went under.[169]

Bettie Gay

In many ways, Bettie Gay epitomizes the ordinary Alliance woman—the stolid, independent, strong-willed, resourceful Texas farmer who heard the challenges of the Alliance and embraced its promises. In other ways, she is different, representing a smaller group of women who were radicalized first by the movement and then by its failure to deliver on its promises. In an old photograph, she is seated in a wicker chair next to her son, James Jehu Bates Gay, his wife Juanita Green, and two grandchildren. She is wearing an apron and zigzag-striped dress; her black hair is parted down the middle and pulled back in a bun. She has a strong, handsome face and dark eyes which stare out somewhat severely. In another photograph, the one accompanying her essay on women in the Alliance in Nelson Dunning's history of the order, she is dressed in a suit, a bow of lace at her throat. She has the same direct, dark-eyed, no-nonsense expression.

Bettie Munn was born in Alabama and moved to Texas with her parents as a child in 1836. She married Rufus King Gay, also an Alabamian, at a young age. He was said to be cultivated and widely traveled, someone from whom she learned philosophy and science. Like many Southern women whose circumstances were reduced by the Civil War, she took up the unaccustomed duties of household and field work. In 1880, her fifty-two-year-old husband died, leaving her with a mortgaged farm, debts, and a half-grown son. She worked the farm, took in sewing, sold goods at market, and managed to pay off the mortgage. Her white clapboard, two-chimney, plantation-style home a few miles north of Columbus was on the stagecoach road. Over the years, she took in and raised six boys and three girls, orphaned perhaps along that road.[170] She was active in the Baptist church. In 1891, the *Nonconformist* reported that Gay was a "woman of wealth and influence"; with a plantation of 1,776 acres, she was one of the largest cotton planters in Texas.[171] Eventually she turned the management of her farm over to her son, who also was an Alliance member.

Her first appearance in the pages of the *Mercury* may have been June 14, 1888, and signed "B. G." She was urging people to boycott coffee. In June 1889, she and Mrs. Shaw proposed that the Alliance women sell poultry and dairy items for money to save the Exchange. In 1891, she angrily complained about the decline of women's letters in the *Mercury*. When Nelson Dunning published his history of the Farmers' Alliance that same year, he included a chapter by Gay on "The Influence of Women in the Alliance," which summed up the status of women. It has been interpreted by McMath, among other historians, as accepting women's conventional roles, because in it Gay speaks of woman as man's companion and helpmeet.[172] However, she did not marry again after her husband died, choosing not to become someone's "helpmeet." Read from a different perspective, her essay seems strongly feminist, almost revolutionary. "Nature has endowed women with brains," she wrote. "Why should she not think . . . why not act? If allowed to act, what privilege should men enjoy of which she should be deprived?" She looked to the Alliance to redeem woman from her "enslaved condition," insisting that "what we need is a better womanhood . . . acknowledging no master and accepting no compromise."[173] Bettie Gay strongly espoused suffrage and eventually became a Socialist.[174]

Suffrage, Yes and No

Historians of Alliance and Populist women have found that, despite the movement's official support of expanded roles for women, the meaning of equality was constricted by and to the organization's major goal of reviving Southern agriculture. It has been understood that political rights within the Alliance were not seen by women as the first step toward political rights outside the Alliance. The ideology of their roles did not change. They always emphasized their traditional place and importance in the family and on the farm.[175] Despite the equality of membership in the Alliance and its promise of democracy, Alliance and Populist women were not able to convert the party—or even each other—to unequivocal support for suffrage. National Populist conventions consistently omitted women's suffrage (and temperance) from their platforms. With a majority of the women in agreement, these issues were tabled to preserve party unity.[176] Only in Colorado in 1893 did women gain suffrage under a Populist administration.

Success, however, is not the only criterion of importance. If an accelerated transformation of consciousness among a group of oppressed people was vital to the formation of the Alliance movement, it was to the suffrage movement as well. The first promptings of collective power are often elusive, however. "Prior to a movement's emergence, before the initial problem of radical social change is solved, its coming into being is difficult to imagine," writes Ellen DuBois. The early history of women's suffrage vividly demonstrates this phenomenon. The movement started with a handful of mid-nineteenth-century women—scattered, isolated, and handicapped by the limited sphere of their sex—who began to demand political parity with men.[177]

It is precisely this moment of awakening consciousness that these rural Texas letters illustrate: the difficult-to-imagine, two-steps-forward-and-one-step-back emergence of scattered, isolated thinkers who dared to push outside the limits of their sphere, to question its existence. Very possibly these letters about suffrage represent the first articulation of feminist consciousness for many rural women. Ann Other, one of the most frequent letter writers, confessed that "when I began to study suffrage . . . I thought women's only ambition should be to read the latest novels, work green dogs with pink eyes on cardboard and other ornamental work, keep her house and children clean and healthy and 'always meet your husband with a smile' but now I am satisfied that with suffrage, she can benefit her country, keep her own womanly traits and have more just laws for herself and better protection for her children."[178]

Between April 19, 1888, and April 18, 1889, women were stirred to write to the *Mercury* about suffrage and women's rights, more than about any other topic. Fifteen percent of the women's letters focused on female suffrage or women's rights. Of the Texas letters, 56 percent were in favor of suffrage, while 44 percent were against it.[179] The viewpoints in these and later letters are diverse. Some women appear deeply saturated with the traditional thinking of the day. It is clear that Texas agricultural society was patriarchal. While the belief in separate spheres was embraced less tightly than in eastern urban communities, perhaps, it still had a strong impact, as the letters indicate. Heavy, too, for some women was the psychological weight of the Adam and Eve story. "Women under condemnation for a violated law must suffer the penalty until she is redeemed from the curse at resurrection," wrote Mrs. Ussery from Lavaca.[180] Other writers questioned it, however, and, as the women grew in confidence and political sophistication, they began to experiment with direct action and to express their views. Their debate about their proper sphere, suffrage, and other rights then becomes a compelling, occasionally heated, exchange via these published letters.

In *The Bonds of Womanhood*, Nancy Cott suggests that, by giving women a unique sexual solidarity, the woman's sphere contained a precondition for feminism. It is possible that the sentiments of mutuality and sisterhood expressed so felicitously by some of the *Southern Mercury* letter writers came from women who, for the first time, were discovering a world of true peers among their own sex. Finding value in their peers allowed these women to affirm their own value, express a new individuality, and enter into relationships as separate and distinct, rather than familially linked, human beings. This kind of group consciousness was one that could and, I suggest, did develop into political consciousness.[181]

The men and women who so heroically met at Seneca Falls in 1848 had little influence in the South. Women's suffrage entered the consciousness of Texas briefly during the 1868 and 1875 constitutional conventions. In 1868, T. H. Mundine of Burleson County proposed a declaration that electors be qualified "without distinction of sex." This was referred to committee and rejected, fifty-four to thirteen. In 1875, suffrage was extended to all male persons except minors, paupers, lunatics, felons, soldiers, and sailors. A petition for female suffrage was referred to committee and tabled. Little other interest was manifest until 1888, when the Women's Christian Temperance Union began to support the idea.[182] On May 10, 1888, Addie McCaskill of DeWitt County wrote: "I notice that some who write for the *Mercury* seem to be in favor of woman's suffrage. . . . If I am not entirely wrong we, as a sex, have no desire whatever to extend our privileges beyond what they are now. I believe in ladies attending public gatherings, and going abroad and lightening in every manner possible the burdensome cares of life; but . . . home is the field in which we can wield the greatest power of influence. . . . Kindness is our scepter, and the human heart that cannot be reached by loving kindness is out of the reach of all power of woman's. Let us look to the upbuilding of our homes; to properly rearing our children."[183]

"Homespun Dress" of Travis County held less conventional beliefs. "As I understand the Alliance, it allows the ladies equal rights with the men," she wrote in the same issue. "This, I think [is] a great inducement to them to join, as we don't have it anywhere else, some not even at home." She complimented some of the *Mercury*'s male contributors for their "exalted opinion and high appreciation" of the female sex and turned to the subject of "Mother Eve": "One thing is certain; Adam obeyed Eve, whether she was put there to rule or not. Let us not, like Eve, influence our husbands to eat forbidden fruit but climb up with them, hand in hand, step by step, to a higher, nobler plane of existence."[184]

Religion was employed to both support and denounce suffrage. On June 7, 1888, Annie Mims of the Wood County Alliance in Winsboro, Texas, published her prosuffrage essay in the "General Correspondence" section of the *Mercury*: "I am but a woman yet women have an influence, as you all well know, as in that little affair about the apple. I need not tell you I am Alliance, prohibitionist, greenbacker and know-nothing. I also believe in . . . suffrage, and as woman has the credit of leading to the fall, when she is granted the right of suffrage, she will assist in uplifting and reinstating you; and women, who constitute the best and purest part of this government, should have the right to make the laws under which we live, to help lift us from the oppression of class legislation, monopolies, and trust combinations."[185]

In *Women of the Grange,* Donald Marti wonders if hardworking rural women, uncertain that they were acknowledged to be ladies, did not assert their gentility forcefully and try to help other rural women develop ladylike graces. Or perhaps, as Karen Blair suggests in *The Clubwoman as Feminist,* they resented the limitations that propriety imposed on them.[186] Certainly Mrs. J. Morton Smith of the Bell County Alliance was intent upon teaching grace. "The true history of the world is the record of the home life," she said in an essay published in the *Mercury.*

It is to women [that] we owe the little niceties of social intercourse and to her we look as the "star of Bethlehem to light the way to a higher and better life." . . . We are thankful that the vigorously demanded woman's rights have been denied us. If it were not for the restraining influences of conventionalism, it is possible woman would never have acquired the genius . . . for adorning and refining home. The cultivation of flowers, the lavish use of the painter's brush, sculptor's chisel and artist's pencil as well as the various exquisite embroideries transform the rude hut into a vine-wreathed cottage, making it a "thing of beauty and a joy forever." Every dainty piece of fancy work speaks of aspirations for higher and nobler things.[187]

Others were outspokenly resentful of such thinking and viewed the sphere as no less than a strait jacket. "Sister Rebecca, you class the decline of patriotism with the rise of the popularity of universal suffrage and 'woman neglecting her duty in her proper sphere,'" said Ann Other, responding to another letter writer on May 31, 1888.

Now will someone kindly tell me what is her proper sphere? . . . I am obliged to conclude it is whatever the state of society dictates to her. . . . Women used to be our bakers, brewers, dry-salters, butter-makers, cooks, dressmakers, cheese-makers, confectioners, jam and jelly makers, pickle makers, soap makers, spinners, weavers, sock makers, lace makers, embroiderers, and midwives. Thus crowded out of her old fields by men's intrusion and invention, she must either accept a life of idleness, and be satisfied with such as her brothers see proper to give her, or she must demand a more useful and energetic life. . . . Society . . . has so limited her sphere of usefulness in life that there is nothing left for her to do but marry.

She quoted from Frances E. Willard's address before a Senate committee:[188] "Honorable gentlemen think that we women want the earth, when we only want one half of it." Then Other continued in her own words: "It is said that if women are given the right to vote, it will prevent their being womanly; how it is a sentiment of chivalry in some good men that hinders them from giving us the ballot? . . . It is inconceivable to me why some women, simply because they do not wish to vote, should clamor so loud against giving the right to those who do, as there would be nothing compelling any to vote who did not think they could benefit the laws by doing so."

In the same letter, Ann Other responded to another writer, who she decided was a man: "You 'fear that men will lose their respect for women who assemble with them at the ballot box.' Now I think those men who could think less of a woman because she took a judicious interest in the laws of her country would not be worth the while to mourn over; whether they respected her or not they would be obliged to respect her laws. When you hear men talking of women losing men's esteem by using the highest and most sacred right of an American citizen, you can rest assured that his esteem is not worth having. . . . If you are obliged to associate with all whom you meet at the polls, do not go there, for your soul is just as liable to be contaminated as mine." After this strong stand, she retreated, saying that she had not done justice to her subject as she was sick, her "physical machinery" out of repair.[189]

The subject of the black vote was raised only once, by Annea Yarbrough of Belton, Bell County. On June 14, 1888, she wrote: "My opinion is there are a great many men as well as women who should not vote. When we have officers to elect, to whom the safety of our whole nation depends, the most ignorant Negro, whose vote could be bought for a glass of beer, is perfectly acceptable."[190]

Later that month, "Rural Widow," a frequent contributor from Harmony Ridge, announced: "Sisters Ann Other and Charitie have sounded the alarm—to vote or not to vote, that is the question. What will befall our republic when women become a political factor? Better no government at all than that of a republic without homes and home-keepers. Women without the right of franchise cast the mightiest vote for good is a truism we all know full well."[191]

In the next week's issue, Ann Other, her physical machinery apparently in fine repair by now, responded extensively. She wrote about Kansas, where women—or at least single women and widows—had municipal suffrage, quoting from a letter she had received from Mrs. M. S. Salter, the first female mayor of Argonia City in Kansas:

A majority of the women vote and they are the very best of society; true, some of the disreputable also vote—don't the men do the same? Men are more careful in the selection of the officers for they know we vote in such affairs for the best men who will help us protect our homes. . . . Our polls are respectable places with no loitering or peddling of tickets within fifty feet of the polls. Our women come with their husbands, fathers, lovers or other friends, each casts her little slip, gives her name and passes out. . . .

Insults have been rare, if any. Kansas men have been courteous, kind, true, noble and whole-hearted.

"Are our southern men less courteous or noble-hearted?" asked Other. "I think not. As to some objecting to suffrage because they think it incapacitates her for returning to her household duties, I would say the day Mrs. Salter wrote me, she had been washing, and says she has seven boarders and four children, and does all her own work with the assistance of a little girl twelve years old. Now I would ask if the burden of office at six hundred per year is any greater than keeping boarders and doing all your own work."[192]

As Populism gathered momentum, churches across the South joined their secular Democratic counterparts in denouncing the formation of a third party and the Alliance's role in it. A rift opened between Populist and Alliance leaders and Southern white Protestant ones.[193] Traditional church leadership supported the status quo and remained loyal to the party of their forefathers. Political nonconformity and religious nonconformity reinforced one another.[194] The churches took a conservative stance toward the Alliance and also toward suffrage. Ann Other continued her letter, pointing a long finger at religious hypocrisy:

> If politics are corrupt, what is the matter with our churches that our great Methodist conference refused to seat the lady delegates sent? Is it, too, too corrupt for women? . . . Then to add insult to injury, one minister took up his text, "Behold the enemy cometh in like a flood, but I will raise up a standard against him," meaning her. When church debts are to be paid or minister's salaries to be raised, then the ministers think there is no harm in woman's counsel and woman's energetic work, but when it comes to admitting women delegates they fear this may prove a stepping stone to the pulpit and thus the salaries of men and they are frowned down. . . .
>
> Sister Charitie says she thinks the theory of only a certain class of woman voting not well founded. I know it has no foundation and no one claims it but those opposed to suffrage. I challenge anyone to bring up statistics to show that more bad or ignorant women vote than the intelligent.

One of the arguments for equal suffrage originated with the Grangers, an earlier agrarian organization. This was the "home protection" formula, the claim that women needed the vote in order to guard their domestic sphere from society's corruption.[195] Ann Other made that argument:

You say, "There are homes we must make happy, our own erring husbands and sons to reclaim." I know of no better way than to make laws to put temptation out of the reach of erring sons; and alas! dear sister, you seem to think that every sister in the Union has a home, a husband and son. 'Tis strange to me that some women never seem to realize that all are not as pleasantly situated as themselves. . . .

You speak of our educating our girls; how many of our colleges in the Union [that] are supported or aided by direct tax, think you, will admit our daughters within their walls if they knock for admittance, remembering woman's property is taxed just the same as man's for this purpose? . . . I could quote enough instances of these "just laws" to fill two columns of the *Mercury* and not be half done. Don't worry about our "usurping the duties of the sterner sex without their consent." They have the power and there is no danger of taking it without their consent.[196]

Widespread support for prohibition existed among Populist women and was linked with suffrage sentiment, pro and con.[197] "I have been reading sister Ann Other's letters and I think they're splendid," said Mary M. of Greer County in another letter published on June 28. "I can't understand why some are so opposed to us ladies voting. One good sister thinks it would be a downfall to the female sex to go there among so many grades of people. Well, have we not got all kinds of people in our country and do we have to stop and shake hands with them and tell them we are on their side? No Sir. . . . Where would whiskey have gone if women had been allowed to vote? There would not have been a drop of whisky now in existence."[198]

Eva J. Sims of Sault Creek Alliance, Indian Territory, also blamed the failure to pass prohibition on women's inability to vote: "Now Sister Ann Other, I wish I could put my thoughts in words as you do for I am of the same belief. Some of the sisters try to make us think it is a disgrace for a woman to vote, but they have failed to do so for I felt like voting last August for the prohibition for I thought if we ever voted for anything, it would be to put down whiskey. I did not feel any more disgraced to go to the polls and vote than I would to go to any other big gathering."[199]

Ann Too of Gribble Spring Alliance also held prosuffrage views, coupled with humor and prohibition sentiments. "It also seems absurd to me that voting would make a woman rough or forgetful of her duty at home," she wrote in the same June *Mercury*. "I don't believe I would forget to wash the children on election day, or forget that I was a woman either, and as for going to the bar and taking a drink, I know I would not do that for I don't love the stuff and if I had any say I would do away with it." She referred to letters from other women, including Rebecca, who "says there are corrupt women as well as men and the vote would not be materially changed, leaving the impression that she thinks good women are in the minority. Speaking for my neighborhood, I don't think we have many women who could be bought for a drink of whiskey but can't say about the men. . . . I say like what Mary Ussery says, we have a hard time anyhow; don't throw any obstacles in each others way."[200]

The June *Mercury* was full of interesting letters, including a heated antisuffrage message from Rebecca of Jefferson, Texas. "Please withhold your vials of wrath while I reassert that there are corrupt women as well as men," she wrote, in defiance of the traditional view of female perfection. "As women are neither mentally or morally stronger than men, if they are exposed to the same corrupting influences of political vice and the buying and selling of votes as men, might we not reasonably conclude that there would be as large a percent of corrupt women as men? . . . These thousands of women will always flock to the polls to defeat any measure for good that may be put forth. Would our lady-like deportment and modest refinement which suffragists say we could preserve protect us from the low and scheming aspirant for office who sets forth upon his electioneering tour reeking with the fumes of bad whisky and vile cigars?" Rebecca raised the specter of "Lady Macbeth whose unholy ambition (I think she wanted female suffrage) caused her to suggest and help execute the murder of her king, and which finally resulted in the ruin of herself and the overthrow of her family. Thus it is often the case when a woman obtrudes herself beyond her legitimate sphere." "You sit with empty heart and hands, waiting for universal suffrage before you deign to consider life worth living," she continued. "You profess to have a longing for higher and more exalted attainments, that your sphere be widened. Have a care my sister; Mother Eve conceived the idea that by enlarging her sphere she would be wiser and happier. You know the result."[201]

Another intensely antisuffrage letter, from "Rural Widow" of Harmony Ridge, appeared in a later *Mercury* (September 1889) and reflected the sense of inadequacy that society had imposed on women. While "Rural Widow" admitted that women's work was "unhappily, to some extent, depreciated," she maintained that "strict justice forces the admission that for this, women are largely to blame. . . . In time past, women unknowingly, I believe, did imperfect work. Her will was good but she had not gone into the fight rightly equipped; therefore she put before her employers a deficient result, expecting the deficiency to be supplied by consideration for her delicacy of temperament or constitution or some other such ill defined and suitable feminine quality." But things had changed, she asserted.

> Now women realize that if they are to receive equal compensation they must give in all respects an equal service and this "equal service" from the very nature of the case, must always press harder upon the women, consume more of the precious life-blood, make larger demands upon the brain and nerve force for speculate as we might, the God-favored and indestructible fact remains the same. Women are weaker than the men and less fitted for the stern and pressing work of the world.
>
> If we could return to the God-appointed order of things, all this talk about the depreciation of women's work, whether it be to save the Exchange or be president, would cease. It is the work of the plodder that is most effective in the practical world; and a large majority of men are plodders. By contrast with the quick nervous unequal effort of women, man gains much in power and effectiveness.[202]

Mrs. M. E. Ussery from Lavaca also cautioned against female ambition, begging readers to "give the hours devoted to politics to the moral training of our children; the idea of a refined lady going to the polls is absurd: if our good men can not run the government, I am sure we can not. . . . The true elevation of woman and her restoration to the place she occupied in the beginning is assured to every Christian woman and enables her to aid in restraining vice and correcting evils. Ambition will lead women to neglect wifehood, motherhood and all the nameless graces that adorn women."[203]

Others, such as Jennie Scott Wilson, were undaunted. "Some say that women have no business in the order," she said in the August 1888 issue. "When Columbus braved the perils of unknown seas to add America to the world, whose hand was it that fitted him for the voyage? Queen Isabella. Every effectual man who has left his mark in the world is but another Columbus for whom some Isabella in the form of a mother has laid down her comforts, yes, her chance, her jewels. I would suggest to all those who think ladies are out of their place in the Alliance and have no discretion and are given to telling all they know or hear, that they had better read up a little and be less explosive themselves in the lobbies of convention halls."[204]

In the same August *Mercury,* Ann Other reasoned: "If independence of thought and action is good for the development of man, why would it not be for women? Can we have the full development of mind in children when mothers are trammeled by inconsistent laws and dictates of fashion, and society that dictates to her in dress, in thought and in action. . . . When we see laws passed by men alone, have we any right to wonder they are not always just to the silenced element they govern? Have women an equal right (with their husbands) in law to their children? Have women a right to property acquired before marriage, and have they an equal right with the husband to that acquired after marriage?"

She informed her readers that Wyoming Territory had enjoyed suffrage since 1860, and that Governor Warren had written in 1885 that it had not lowered the grade of public officials there. She quoted Governor Warren: "On the contrary, our women consider much more carefully than our men the character of our candidates and both political parties have found themselves obliged to nominate their best men in order to obtain the support of the women."

Ann Other quoted a succinct analysis of the opposition to suffrage, maintaining that it was confined to three classes. The first was "that immoral element which sustains and is sustained by the drinking saloon, the gambling house." The second, "much smaller," element was "the 'high-toned' class which finds delight in the frivolities of fashionable life." To the third "small but eminently respectable element, that is bound by traditional notions of man's superiority and 'woman's sphere,' and lies curled up upon itself altogether like a chick in an eggshell who ought to hatch but doesn't," belonged "those who think they read in the Bible a divine right of man to rule over women."

The remainder of Ann Other's letter supports MaryJo Wagner's contention that women in particular emphasized the personal effects of industrial capitalism on the family, on women, and on the home.[205] "The condition of the 3,000,000 women in the United States, who earn their own living, should be considered in the light of the Golden Rule," she wrote.

> Those who are in bonds should be remembered as if we were bound with them. I beg satisfied ladies of fortune and gentlemen who boast of the perfection of "woman's sphere" and our Christian civilization to imitate Christ by going among the people of want and there learn the lessons of needed change. Go to the stores and shops where the products of woman's work is sold and watch the merchants pass the lives of women over their counters in every package of ill-paid work they sell. Go and learn how

helpless women are driven to lives of shame and then despised by the class of persons who have lived off their labor and their tears. Then sit back in your easy chairs and cry against the ballot for fear it may sully some hands too indolent to use it for the emancipation of the down trodden.

Oh, may the day hasten when all women shall understand the laws that govern them and is also grinding the faces of the poor. May the time come when men shall intelligently understand the franchise and exercise the same in an intelligent manner. When we will no longer hear of such arguments as I heard a man make a few days ago when the subject of suffrage was broached. "Let my wife go and pitch millet all day as I have and I will take her place in the house and she may do the voting." Oh, depths of logic![206]

As historian Sandra Myres suggests, there were those who feared that undertaking tasks outside their proscribed sphere might cause them to lose their claim to moral superiority, their femininity, and even their looks.[207] "Corn Bread" weighed in against suffrage with this in mind.

I have seen so much said about "woman's rights" I thought I would beg admittance to you, dear paper, to say a few words. We are the housewives, the makers of the home, and the home makes the nation. It puts me all out of patience to hear some of the ladies talk about their "woman's rights." How can any true wife and mother walk up to the polls on election day amid a crowd of gaping men, some of them perhaps drunk and some of them using slang. That is your husbands' and brothers' and fathers' business, not yours. . . . If you are to be a man's equal in these things you must help to make the living. My husband is a farmer and I think I would much rather be a housewife than be a "woman's rights" woman. . . .

Do you not know why your husbands object to your going to the polls? It is because as a masculine woman you are no longer the dear little girl whom he promised to love, honor and cherish. Be contented as we are and make the home pure.[208]

This was too much for "Poor Gal" of Red Oak, Ellis County, who in the August 21 issue took "Corn Bread" to task: "Had she seen her husband and sons, if she is so fortunate as to possess the same, after spending all day in town, being treated by so many friends seeking office, coming home totally unbalanced, reeling, staggering, swearing, thinking the wife and mother a robber, while she tries to get their clothes off and put them into a nice warm bed before any one outside should suspect the disgrace, I think she would say, woman's rights out of the other side of her mouth; vote to put down whisky, vote to keep thieves from ruling us, vote to fight the foreign moneyed cliques, vote to keep our sons from being peons; yes, she would say let me vote till I die."[209]

For Dianecia Jones of Dallas County, the discussion had gone on long enough. "Woman's rights!" she exploded. "Now sisters, let that question rest. As for my part I don't think it would improve things for the ladies to vote. Let us allow the men to make laws. We can certainly live by their laws if they can. As to woman's suffrage, that is something we will never get in this world. I say look up and trust for our rights in a better world."[210]

Despite Jones's weary surfeit, the Alliance and the Populist party awakened in other women the powerful drive to participate in the more formal realm of politics through suffrage, and aroused a discontent with purely private identities and definitions of femininity. Wrote "Western Reader" in the May 3, 1888, *Mercury:* "Universal suffrage, guided by intelligence, will be a powerful weapon, not withstanding [the fact that] some blushing, stay-in-our-own-sphere sisters, shiver with apprehension at the degrading results."[211] Women took their voting privileges seriously and looked to the Alliance to increase their political understanding. Through the order, women were able to practice the arts of participation and experience themselves as visible and effective. Many began to learn what Harry Boyte has called political "arts"—negotiating, debating, and exercising judgment.[212] Another woman named Rebecca, this one from Marion County, was among them. "We cannot expect to succeed if we allow ourselves to waste valuable time in envious fault-finding or jealous bickering and strife," she instructed in June 1888. "Suppose we do harbor 'some like snakes within our walls'? . . . What does it matter? Shall we degrade ourselves in answering in kind? . . . When we have our meeting, if there be differences of opinion on any subject of importance, let us have full and free discussion. . . . Let us harmonize to the fullest extent possible in our business workings. If we vote cooperation, we must cooperate."[213]

A "True Sister" from Gillespie County agreed: "It is our duty to attend every meeting and give strict attention to every subject that may be presented . . . and study both sides of the question thoroughly that we may be able to vote intelligently. . . . The majority of Alliance members fail to express their own opinions even if they have one. . . . If we would only speak our true sentiments either for or against anything while in convention, there is a chance, if we are holding to a wrong idea, to be corrected."[214]

The Alliance Begins to Decline

The number of women's letters peaked during the fall of 1888 and declined swiftly thereafter. Several issues during the following few months of that year contained no letters at all from women, although a woman's page still existed.[215] At the end of October 1888, the *Mercury* made its "Ladies' Department" into a section called "The Family," soliciting letters from the "good mothers and wives, the boys and girls—in short, the families of the country." However, the section was small and over the next months offered little of substance—letters from children; a cure for corns (apply *liquor potassae*); recipes for pickled pork, apple butter, and hasty pudding; a historical account of a war hero in revolutionary Vermont; an article from *American Magazine* concerning the proper clothes for November; a reprint from *Farmer's Home* teaching boys to pick up their clothes. There was nothing from women, nothing political, nothing concerning suffrage.

The women whose words were published remarked again and again upon the absence of letters. It is an indication of the extent to which they had come to anticipate reading each others' contributions in the paper. The writers' voices are silent, and the readers feel the loss acutely. The letters had become more than information and descriptive discourse. They had become reflections of the women themselves, evidence of their emerging strengths and abilities, their heightened self-esteem. "Attention, sisters! What is the matter with you all?" wrote "Country Girl" from Concord Alliance, McLennon County, in September 1888. "So many of the good contributors have ceased to send in their spicy letters and we miss them so much. Come to the rescue, some of you gifted talented farmers' daughters; our page is almost half full of advertisements which will never do. What has become of Ann Other? I am afraid that she is asleep and will have one of those fearful dreams of hers. Oh, Charitie, how we miss you, Rosa Lee, and many others. Our Alliance is on a standstill, but we hope that when the weather gets more pleasant and sickness subsides it will do better."[216]

The next month, Sallie Pangle from Fanbion, Burnet County, wrote:

> Looking over the *Mercury* of September 18, I see only three very short letters from the sisters. Why is this, dear sisters? Is it our fault that our page is being filled more and more, each week, with advertisements? Are

we getting negligent or tired of writing and reading the interesting letters written by the sisters? Indeed I am not. The Ladies Department is the dearest page of all the *Mercury*. I read it first and then I am ready for the letters full of good advice and teeming with knowledge which our farmers have never had any credit for having. . . . Some of our young ladies write letters full of merriment, romance, and poetry, and others write words full of wisdom showing how deep into the fountain of thought the feminine mind can penetrate.[217]

Ann Other also commented that the paper was no longer "spread out in the social manner it used to have when it came with so many neighbors." She missed the mental "feast" supplied by Charitie, "Western Reader," and Sister Rebecca: "I am real hungry and want each of the sisters to send me something for my mental table."[218] Ellen D. wrote: "I have watched the woman's department with much pride and interest, until, alas! it completely failed to make its appearance at all. Our talented writers have deserted us."[219]

Some students of the agrarian movement have suggested that, as the Alliance became politicized, its social function declined in importance. However, according to McMath, in the years following 1890, local Alliance leaders placed increased emphasis upon recreational activities. They made their meetings more socially attractive, first to counteract the decline of the cooperatives, and later in an attempt to revive the order after the divisive campaign of 1892.[220] As things got tougher, the resilience and dedication of Alliance women became even more necessary to the order, if not to the *Mercury*. This suggests that the women's contribution had assumed an importance far beyond the social arena: the women had become a vital nexus of the organization, an essential segment of its spiritual backbone, a component, possibly, of its very survival. Wrote Mrs. P. H. Hall of Guadalupe County: "I have not seen many letters from the ladies in the *Mercury*. I think they have lost all interest in the Alliance and that causes the men not to take the interest they would. I am sorry to say ours is not doing much now; we have our regular meetings twice a month but they are very poorly attended. . . . When the ladies attended our meetings regularly there was a very good turnout, but they have nearly quit going and so have the men."[221]

The *Mercury*, as well as the Alliance, was in crisis over the Exchange. A cryptic paragraph from the editors in an October issue said, "A great many of our readers are holding back the money they have saved to renew their subscription to the *Mercury* until everything was clear to them, or until the executive committee secured control of the paper. As the latter has been accomplished, all should renew at once."[222] The reference is to the charge that Macune and other Exchange directors were incompetent, an accusation that had replaced the original explanation—merchant-banker opposition—for the failure of the Exchange. Alliance members had been warned not to put their hard-earned money into the doomed venture. The *Southern Mercury*, which was under private management and not under the editorial control of the state Alliance, took up this idea and, by the late summer of 1888, was taking a definite anti-Exchange stance, lambasting Macune and other Alliance leaders. The paper argued that the fortunes of the Exchange and the Alliance were not inextricably linked, but this was wishful thinking.

An investigatory committee fully vindicated Macune and the Exchange of any wrongdoing, and Macune in turn accused the *Mercury* of betraying the Alliance to avoid losing advertising patronage. The reaction of the rank-and-file Alliance members to the controversy was bitter, however, and the consequences devastating. Local alliances began reporting immediate declines in membership. Although control of the *Mercury* passed into the hands of the state Alliance, the new editors never reversed the editorial position of the ousted editors. They simply located the failure of the Exchange in the refusal of Alliance members to capitalize it adequately.[223]

The absence of women's letters may have been caused by genuine reader disaffection or by the *Mercury* editors' reluctance to entertain and print further dissonant, argumentative correspondence during this conflictual period. MaryJo Wagner's work supports the second analysis and suggests that family involvement dwindled as the Populists became less radical, less concerned with farm grievances, more willing to compromise with the Democrats in the hope of winning the 1896 presidential election, and more concerned with the single issue of free silver. Fewer newspapers carried women's columns. Women's issues no longer appeared on the front pages of the *Nonconformist*, for example, and the remaining women's columns devoted themselves to fashions and cooking, rather than women's rights and politics.[224]

This certainly seems to have been the pattern for the *Mercury*, which at this time—not coincidentally, I suggest—happened to offer the following advice in its "To Wives" column: "Remember that you are married to a man not a god; be prepared for imperfections. Once in a while let your husband have the last word; it will gratify him and be no particular loss to you. . . . Be a companion to your husband if he is a wise man, and if he is not, try to make him become your standard. Raise your standard; do not let his lower yours. . . . Don't always be teasing him for money. . . . Respect your husband's relatives."[225]

To this, Mary Ussery of Lavaca County replied crossly:

> I picked up my paper which is always so welcome. . . . The first thing my eye encountered was two columns and a half of "Advice to Ladies." That was quite enough for one evening, but then I found "A Little Advice to Wives" and threw it down in disgust and wished the person who was so very thoughtful of our comfort as to bother his ingenious brains with writing no less than eight or ten pages of foolscap of advice for the benefit of poor women is—well, no matter where. . . . Now, Mr. Editor, what would you incorrigible men think if in every book, paper and magazine you took up you would find at least half the contents were articles of advice addressed to the gentlemen? . . . But I am more fortunate than some of my fair sisters, as the advice does not apply to me, for I am not a wife, nor am I likely to be until next year, or until, confidently speaking, when women have their rights.[226]

Is this the voice of the timid rural woman of even a year ago? Hardly.

The failure of the Exchange led Macune to develop the most significant proposal in Alliance history: the subtreasury plan. The plan called for the establishment of locally situated federal subtreasuries, along with warehouses and elevators in which farmers could store certain nonperishable commodities. The government would provide short-term credit at low interest, giving the farmer more independence in marketing his crop. As projected, the system would end the deflationary glut of commodities on the market at harvest time and create an expanded, flexible currency that would reverse the decline of farm prices.

The proposal was a watershed for the Alliance. It brought the order directly into party politics, a move that, as many had predicted and feared, generated friction and divided the Texas Alliance.[227] It precipitated the final protest strategy of the Alliance movement—the Populist party. The party siphoned off Alliance energy and led to the movement's demise. Then the party itself fused with the Democrats in the 1896 presidential election, lost the support of Texas Populists who refused to fuse, and eventually died out.

In 1891, the Alliance lobbied both major parties for subtreasury support, to no avail. The parties refused to endorse its reform demands. In early 1892, a general conference of reformers convened in St. Louis to form the People's Party and to organize for the presidential nominating convention, scheduled to take place in Omaha, Nebraska, later that summer. Approximately eight hundred delegates representing twenty-two organizations—Greenbackers, Bellamy's Nationalists, Henry George's Single-Taxers, the Knights of Labor, the Women's Christian Temperance Union, and the Alliance—gathered in St. Louis to debate diverse priorities of the movement. Bettie Gay and Dr. Ellen Lawson Dabbs, of Sulphur Springs, came as Alliance delegates.[228] Also present was the National Women's Alliance (NWA), an organization of farmers' wives and women of trade unions and wage workers who hoped to use the national Alliance movement to increase women's political impact.[229]

Before the Populist conventions in St. Louis and Omaha, women had been excited about the potential of a new party—a party which included them, which might give them suffrage, which recognized the importance of home and family and woman's central role, which might support prohibition, and which would solve the economic problems of the farmers. Bettie Gay, in an essay in the *National Economist,* spoke about a party which "would give us food and raiment, and pay us for honest toil."[230] Suffrage and temperance resolutions had been adopted at previous conferences of Alliance and Labor.

However, in an opening speech in St. Louis, Ben Terrell of Texas urged delegates to consider only questions of "economic" reforms. "Moral reforms" should be put off until a later date, while other differences between Northern and Southern elements in the movement were bridged. Leaders hoped to avoid antagonizing the Southern delegates, who were less united behind the Populist party. Many Democrats whom the Populists were wooing opposed women's suffrage; it was considered a fatally divisive issue that should be sacrificed for the Populist cause.[231] The other major moral reform, prohibition, also was lost. Despite widespread support in Texas for prohibition, there were Republicans, blacks, Catholics, and Lutherans who opposed it.[232] To build a consensus and win elections, Populists needed support from the wets and the antisuffrage thinkers.

The official platform was drawn up later that summer, on the Fourth of July, at the national nominating convention in Omaha, Nebraska. It restated the Cleburne Demands, including unlimited coinage of gold and silver, prohibition of alien landownership, government regulation of transportation, and the later subtreasury plan. It did not include women's suffrage or temperance. Gen. James G. Field of Virginia was chosen as the vice-presidential candidate to run with James B. Weaver of Iowa, who was nominated as the presidential candidate.[233]

The Populists did not fare well in the 1892 presidential election against Republican Benjamin Harrison and Democrat Grover Cleveland. In only five Southern states did the total Populist vote amount to more than one half of the Alliance's potential voting strength at its peak.[234] In Texas, the order was split, as many moderate Alliancemen remained loyal to the Democratic party and looked to the popular young governor, James S. Hogg, for leadership.[235]

The third party fared better in Kansas and Colorado, however. Both states elected Populist governors and substantial numbers of state Populist officials and legislators. Colorado passed an Equal Suffrage Bill, which was strongly supported by the newly elected Populist governor, Davis Waite. When Waite failed to gain a second term in office, he became convinced, despite his original support of suffrage, that if women had not voted, he would have won reelection.[236] Angry letters and editorials ensued among the women, the *Mercury,* and Waite concerning his election defeat.

These letters comprise many of the newspaper's dwindling letters from women. They also provide insight into the era's attitudes about suffrage and electoral practices. *Mercury* editors viewed voting not as a right but as a privilege given, or rescinded, depending upon how one voted. Central to the discussion emerging from the Populist struggle, however, was a new woman—one with a voice full of outrage and determination, one whose focus now was suffrage. This woman had tasted participation in the public arena. She no longer would be discounted.

In the January 1895 *Mercury,* former Governor Waite spoke disparagingly about the Republican tactics that had defeated him. "Every vote in the state—negro, Mexican, Italian—had been bought up like cattle for $5 apiece," he said bitterly. "We know this, for the Italians, hundreds of whom we had paid the expense of naturalization, frankly told us so, and offered to stay with us if we would raise the republican bid, which we declined to do. . . . Then 20,000 servant girls in the state, whom the Populist policy of equal rights of the sexes elevated to the dignity of full American citizenship, were led to the polls by Populist enemies like sheep to the slaughter only to cast their votes against their best friends."[237]

Again in December, the *Mercury* weighed in, maintaining that while some readers had taken exception to the November article, "Woman suffrage had became a reality in Colorado" mainly because "the populist party of Colorado . . . championed the suffrage question. . . . Despite this the women not only voted against reform and in favor of the party or parties that had brought ruin upon the country but also against the party that had championed their cause." This, the *Mercury* stated, was "incontrovertible evidence that women were not sufficiently educated in the duties of citizenship to exercise the functions conferred on them by the ballot." Hereafter the party would favor a "gradual advancement of women to the position of voting citizens," letting them "vote on minor officers such as school commissioners and other non political offices first [until] they gradually grow into a knowledge of the [voters'] responsibilities. If the populists of Texas should, at one stroke, confer the right of suffrage upon 250,000 or 300,000 women in Texas, there is little doubt that they would repeat the mistakes made by the sisters in Colorado."[238]

In December 1894, both Bettie Gay and Alliancewoman Dr. Grace Danforth of Granger, Texas, responded fiercely. Said Gay, "I listen to men talk sometimes til I think they ought to be disfranchised til they learn self-protection, to vote for self-protection and the protection of oppressed humanity. Talk about woman suffrage! Many of the women are better posted on political economy than many of the men. We have a nation of cowards, because our women have been slaves."[239] Reacting as well to a gambling house referendum, Danforth exclaimed, "What an unjust and an unfair thing it is to expect women in one election to right all the wrongs masculine rule has fostered upon society! The women of Colorado had no angels to vote for. . . . They had only men and they are largely whisky-loving animals, no matter what political party they chance to belong to." The *Mercury* stuck hard to its position, replying, "The 'whisky-loving animals' did not expect the women to convert earth into a paradise at one election, doctor. But they did expect them to exercise the right of suffrage in the interests of morality and temperance which it appears they did not do."[240]

The following month, a *Mercury* editorial repeated this theme: "Texas women who are crying like John the Baptist in the wilderness . . . for equal rights should define the measures they propose to champion when they secure equal rights. . . . This vote would have the balance of power, and might be wielded for good or evil. In Colorado it was wielded for evil. The populists at least desire to know whether the women of Texas are going to vote for reform or not before that party helps lift the yoke of bondage from the necks of down-trodden female humanity."[241] Bettie Gay's answer was one of the last of the women's letters to appear in the *Mercury*. Her equanimity and patience had deserted her completely. "The women have been in the wilderness for one hundred years," she wrote. "It is time for them to come out. . . . The wise women of Texas will yet lead the men out of darkness, as they (the men) have been a failure in the management of governmental affairs. We propose to have a say in the laws that govern us, as intelligent beings, and not as idiots and criminals. We propose to elect representatives, not debauchees. . . . No party will give women her rights till she demands them. The time is not distant when she will demand, and not ask. . . . Light is dawning and humanity will soon assert its rights."[242]

These rights were not to be delivered by either the Alliance or the Populist Party. In 1896, the Democrats co-opted the free-silver issue and nominated Nebraska's William Jennings Bryan for president. The national party fused with the Democrats; the Texas Populists preferred to stay in "the middle of the road" between the major parties. Neither strategy worked. Bryan lost the election to William McKinley, although he received more popular votes than Grover Cleveland had garnered in 1892.[243] It was essentially the end of the party. The Alliance already had died.

Strong urban agitation for suffrage had begun in Texas in 1893, when the Texas Equal Rights Association (TERA), an auxiliary of the National American Woman Suffrage Association, was formed. It is not surprising that Bettie Gay was among the rural women who moved from the Alliance into TERA. Joining her were Alliance sisters Grace Danforth, Ellen Dabbs, and Margaret Watson.[244] Nor is it surprising that the rhetoric of TERA tended to be more radical on the redefinition of sex roles than that put forth two decades later by the suffrage organizations that resuscitated the movement after TERA had died.[245] TERA probably was "too far in advance of public opinion," said Jane Y. McCallam, a leader of the later, gentler, and ultimately successful Texas suffrage effort.[246]

Lawrence Goodwyn has suggested that the most important contribution of the agrarian revolt was to create "the visible evidence of community that gave meaning and substance to all lesser individuals."[247] Politically, women were among those lesser individuals. But the Populist movement challenged the status quo; with the help of the *Southern Mercury,* it provided many women with community, meaning, and a stronger sense of self. It also introduced them to what Hannah Arendt later would define as ideal public life—an arena of freedom and equality, a space where citizens become visible to each other as speakers of words and doers of deeds, engaged in debate and decision on matters of common concern. Rural women's participation in the Alliance and the Populist party undoubtedly helped break the ground for later social legislation, including that for women's suffrage.

By the time of Bettie Gay's death on June 7, 1921, when she was eighty-four years old, the Nineteenth Amendment had been adopted. Time also was required for the acceptance of other Populist goals, but within forty years of the party's demise, most of the platform of 1892—the subtreasury, direct election of senators, income tax, effective control of railroads, and expansion of currency—had been enacted, although without fundamentally altering the direction in which corporate America was developing.[248]

Notes

1. Samuel P. Hays, *The Response to Industrialism, 1885–1914* (Chicago: Univ. of Chicago Press, 1957), 24.
2. MaryJo Wagner, "Farms, Families, and Reform: Women in the Farmers' Alliance and Populist Party" (Ph.D. diss., Univ. of Oregon, 1986), iv, 1; Lawrence Goodwyn, *The Populist Moment: A Short History of the Agrarian Revolt in America* (New York: Oxford Univ. Press, 1978), vii.
3. Robert C. McMath, *Populist Vanguard: A History of the Southern Farmers' Alliance* (New York: Norton, 1977), xi, 21; Michael Schwartz, *Radical Protest and Social Structure: The Southern Farmers' Alliance and Cotton Tenancy, 1880–1890* (New York: Academic Press, 1976), 14; Donna Ann Barnes, *Farmers in Rebellion: The Rise and Fall of the Southern Farmers Alliance and the People's Party in Texas* (Austin: Univ. of Texas Press, 1984), 3; John D. Hicks, *The Populist Revolt* (Minneapolis: Univ. of Minnesota Press, 1931), 112–13; Roscoe C. Martin, *The People's Party in Texas: A Study in Third Party Politics* (Austin: Univ. of Texas Bulletin, 1933), 231; *Southern Mercury*, Jan. 1, 1889.
4. Wagner, "Farms, Families, and Reform," iv.
5. McMath, *Populist Vanguard*, 141.
6. Keith Lynn King, "Religious Dimensions of the Agrarian Protest in Texas, 1870–1908" (Ph.D. diss., Univ. of Illinois at Champaign-Urbana, 1985), 265.
7. Julie Roy Jeffrey, "Women in the Southern Farmers' Alliance: Reconsideration of the Role and Status of Women in the Late Nineteenth-Century South," *Feminist Studies* 3 (Fall 1975); Martin, *People's Party*, 1933, 46; King, "Religious Dimensions," 118–19.
8. Theodore R. Mitchell, *Political Education in the Southern Farmers' Alliance, 1887–1900* (Madison: Univ. of Wisconsin Press, 1987), 14.
9. Melissa Gilbert Wiedenfeld, "Women in the Texas Farmers' Alliance" (M.A. thesis, Texas Tech Univ., 1983), 7, 16; *Southern Mercury*, Sept. 13, 1894.
10. McMath, *Populist Vanguard*, 67
11. Schwartz, *Radical Protest*, 120; Mitchell, *Political Education*, 96–100.
12. According to Schwartz, *Radical Protest*, 120, businessmen chose not to advertise in what they considered radical journals. As a result, the reform editor was almost totally dependent on subscribers for support of the paper and frequently went broke. According to Mitchell, *Political Education*, 99, Tracy continued as *Southern Mercury* publisher during Alliance and Populist periods. He, Jones, or possibly Bennett may have first invited women to correspond.

13. Schwartz, 121; Martin, *People's Party,* 190; Wiedenfeld, "Women in the Texas Farmers' Alliance," 30; King, "Religious Dimensions," 133.

14. Wiedenfeld, "Women in the Texas Farmers' Alliance," 33–34.

15. Wagner, "Farms, Families, and Reform," 3, 11–12.

16. Nancy A. Hewitt and Suzanne Lebsock, "Introduction," in *Visible Women: New Essays on American Activism,* ed. Nancy A. Hewitt and Suzanne Lebsock (Urbana: Univ. of Illinois Press, 1993), 6; Joanne V. Hawks and Sheila L. Skemp, eds., *Sex, Race, and the Role of Women in the South* (Jackson: Univ. Press of Mississippi, 1983), xi; Anne Firor Scott, *Making the Invisible Woman Visible* (Urbana: Univ. of Illinois Press, 1984), 249.

17. Wagner, "Farms, Families, and Reform," 3–5; Robert P. Swierenga, "Towards the 'New Rural History': A Review Essay," *Historical Methods Newsletter* 6 (1973): 111.

18. Anne Firor Scott, ed., *Unheard Voices: The First Historians of Southern Women* (Charlottesville: Univ. Press of Virginia, 1993), 1; Anne Firor Scott, "Historians Construct the Southern Woman," in *Sex, Race, and the Role of Women in the South,* ed. Joanne V. Hawks and Sheila L. Skemp (Jackson: Univ. Press of Mississippi, 1983), 97. Biographical studies include Richard Stiller, *Queen of Populists: The Story of Mary Elizabeth Lease* (New York: Dell, 1970); O. Gene Clanton, "Intolerant Populist: The Disaffection of Mary Elizabeth Lease," *Kansas Historical Quarterly* 34 (Spring 1968): 189–200; Dorothy Rose Blumberg, "Populist Orator: A Profile," *Kansas History* 1 (Spring 1978): 3–15; Connie Weddel, "Annie Diggs" (M.A. thesis, Wichita State Univ., 1980); Rhoda R. Gilman, "Eva McDonald Valesh: Minnesota Populist," in *Women of Minnesota,* ed. Barbara Stuhler and Gretchen Kreuter, 55–56, 348–51 (St. Paul: Minnesota Historical Society Press, 1977); Pauline Adams and Emma S. Thornton, *A Populist Assault: Sarah E. Van De Vort Emery on American Democracy, 1862–1895* (Bowling Green, Ohio: Popular Press of Bowling Green State Univ., 1982); and John E. Talmadge, *Rebecca Latimer Felton: Nine Stormy Decades* (Athens: Univ. of Georgia Press, 1960); Wagner, "Farms, Families, and Reform," 4, 11–12.

19. Joan M. Jensen, *With These Hands* (Old Westbury, N.Y.: Feminist Press, 1981), 142–60.

20. Jeffrey, "Women," 72–91.

21. Wagner, "Farms, Families, and Reform."

22. Sandra L. Myres, *Westering Women and the Frontier Experience, 1800–1915* (Albuquerque: Univ. of New Mexico Press, 1982), 142, 172, 228–29, 233, 237, 267; Wiedenfeld, "Women in the Texas Farmers' Alliance."

23. McMath, *Populist Vanguard,* 68–69; Wagner, "Farms, Families, and Reform," 42–43.

24. McMath, *Populist Vanguard,* 65, 66. Merchants, bankers, lawyers, and other undesirable sorts were barred, as were townsmen; Schwartz, *Radical Protest,* 15; Lawrence Goodwyn, *Democratic Promise: The Populist Movement in America* (New York: Oxford Univ. Press, 1976), vii, 3.

25. Jensen, *With These Hands,* xviii. Literacy rates generally were low all over the South, and particularly among farmers. While they were comparatively higher in Texas—74.4% in 1890—this was partly because Texas had fewer newly emancipated black farmers than other southern states. Mitchell, *Political Education,* 53–55.

26. Hawks and Skemp, *Sex, Race, and the Role of Women,* xii; Scott, "Historians Construct the Southern Woman," 98.

27. Jeffrey, "Women," 75.

28. Shirley Abbott, *Womenfolks: Growing Up Down South* (New York: Ticknor and Fields, 1983), 18.

29. Patricia B. Nieuwenhuizen, "Minnie Fisher Cunningham and Jane Y. McCallum: Leaders of Texas Women for Suffrage and Beyond" (Senior thesis, Univ. of Texas at Austin, 1982), 54.

30. Elizabeth Hayes Turner, "'White-Gloved Ladies' and 'New Women' in the Texas Woman Suffrage Movement," in *Southern Women: Histories and Identities,* ed. Virginia Bernhard, Betty Brandon, Elizabeth Fox-Genovese, and Theda Perdue (Columbia: Univ. of Missouri Press, 1992), 130.

31. Sarah Evans, "Women's History and Political Theory: Toward a Feminist Approach to Public Life," in *Visible Women: New Essays on American Activism,* ed. Nancy A. Hewitt and Suzanne Lebsock (Urbana: Univ. of Illinois Press, 1993), 119, 127, 132; Hannah Arendt, *The Human Condition* (Chicago: Univ. of Chicago Press, 1958), 178–79; Mary P. Ryan, *Women in Public: Between Banners and Ballots, 1825–1880* (Baltimore, Md.: Johns Hopkins Univ. Press, 1990), 11, 17–18. These are only a few of the many theorists and feminists who have deliberated, theorized, and broadened the definition of the public sphere.

32. King, "Religious Dimensions," 109.

33. Stanley Howard Scott, "Angry Agrarian: The Texas Farmer, 1875–1896" (Ph.D. diss., Texas Christian Univ., 1973), 5; Goodwyn, *Populist Movement,* 22.

34. During the Civil War, the Union legislature passed the National Banking Act. Because of timing and the vindictiveness of Republican legislators, the act almost completely ignored the South in allocating startup money for national banks. As late as 1895, the former Confederate states lagged behind all other regions in the number of national banks in operation. Notes from state banks had a 10% surcharge, imposed by the Banking Act, which effectively prevented their use as circulating currency. Few private banks existed. Mitchell, *Political Education,* 28.

35. Barnes, *Farmers in Rebellion,* 2–3; Goodwyn, *Populist Movement,* viii, 22; Stanley Howard Scott, "Angry Agrarian," 20; King, "Religious Dimensions," 37.

36. King, "Religious Dimensions," 36–37.

37. Barnes, *Farmers in Rebellion,* 3; Goodwyn, *Populist Movement,* 27, 46.

38. King, "Religious Dimensions," 39; McMath, *Populist Vanguard,* 3–4, 9; Wiedenfeld, "Women in the Texas Farmers' Alliance," 26.

39. Hicks, *Populist Revolt*, 112–13; Martin, *People's Party*, 24. Four northern states (usually designated the Northern Alliance) cooperated with, but refused to join, the new association, disdaining the secret ritual and segregated membership. King, "Religious Dimensions," 39.

40. Barnes, *Farmers in Rebellion*, 4; Martin, *People's Party*, 30, 47; Goodwyn, *Populist Movement*, 44–51; Ernest William Winkler, *Platforms of Political Parties in Texas* (Austin: Univ. of Texas, 1916), 293–97.

41. Carl Degler, *At Odds: Women and the Family in America from the Revolution to the Present* (New York: Oxford Univ. Press, 1980), 338.

42. King, "Religious Dimensions," 118–19; Jeffrey, "Women," 75.

43. Wagner, "Farms, Families, and Reform," 19.

44. Mitchell, *Political Education*, 61.

45. Wagner, "Farms, Families, and Reform," 9.

46. *Southern Mercury*, May 10, 1888 (reprinted here as letter 17).

47. *Southern Mercury*, Apr. 19, 1888 (letter 6).

48. Schwartz, *Radical Protest*, 111.

49. *Southern Mercury*, May 3, 1888 (letter 12).

50. Jeffrey, "Women," 76.

51. *Southern Mercury*, May 17, 1888 (letter 24).

52. *Southern Mercury*, June 6, 1889 (letter 130).

53. Myres, *Westering Women*, 7.

54. Ibid.; Jeffrey, "Women," 84–85.

55. *Southern Mercury*, May 3, 1888 (letter 12).

56. *Southern Mercury*, Apr. 19, 1888 (letter 6).

57. *Southern Mercury*, May 17, 1888 (letter 22).

58. *Southern Mercury*, Aug. 14, 1888 (letter 70).

59. *Southern Mercury*, May 10, 1888 (letter 14).

60. *Southern Mercury*, May 17, 1888 (letter 24).

61. *Southern Mercury*, May 17, 1888 (letter 26).

62. *Southern Mercury*, Apr. 19, 1888 (letter 3).

63. *Southern Mercury*, June 27, 1889 (letter 138).

64. *Southern Mercury*, May 10, 1888 (letter 30).

65. Charles Cannon, "The Ideology of Texas Populism, 1886–1894" (M.A. thesis, Rice Univ., 1968), 43, 84, 92.

66. Goodwyn, *Populist Movement*, vii–viii, 33.

67. *Southern Mercury*, Sept. 11, 1888 (letter 82).

68. Richard Hofstadter, *The Age of Reform: From Bryan to FDR* (New York: Vintage Books, 1955); 34–35, 40, 71; King, "Religious Dimensions," 283.

69. *Southern Mercury*, Dec. 12, 1889 (letter 157).

70. King, "Religious Dimensions," 175.

71. *Southern Mercury*, May 3, 1888 (letter 11).

72. Goodwyn, *Populist Movement*, xix, 33.

73. *Southern Mercury*, Sept. 11, 1888 (letter 83).

74. *Southern Mercury*, July 12, 1888 (letter 58).

75. *Southern Mercury,* Sept. 4, 1888 (letter 79).
76. *Southern Mercury,* Aug. 14, 1888 (letter 69).
77. Wagner, "Farms, Families, and Reform," 20, 118, 208.
78. Eight anarchists were tried for bombing the labor rally.
79. *Southern Mercury,* May 3, 1888 (letter 12).
80. *Southern Mercury,* July 31, 1888 (letter 65).
81. McMath, *Populist Vanguard,* 28; King, "Religious Dimensions," 42.
82. Barnes, *Farmers in Rebellion,* 4; Schwartz, *Radical Protest,* 15.
83. Goodwyn, *Populist Movement,* 73.
84. *Southern Mercury,* Aug. 28, 1888 (letter 73).
85. *Southern Mercury,* July 5, 1888 (letter 50).
86. *Southern Mercury,* May 10, 1888 (letter 19).
87. *Southern Mercury,* May 10, 1888 (letter 20).
88. *Southern Mercury,* May 17, 1888 (letter 22).
89. *Southern Mercury,* May 10, 1888 (letter 17).
90. *Southern Mercury,* Apr. 19, 1888 (letter 3).
91. *Southern Mercury,* July 12, 1888 (letter 61).
92. Wagner, "Farms, Families, and Reform," 2; Alwyn Barr, *Reconstruction to Reform: Texas Politics, 1876–1906* (Austin: Univ. of Texas Press, 1971), 151; Goodwyn, *Populist Movement,* 181.
93. Geographical and climatic conditions greatly determined Texas farmers' prosperity and their consequent advocacy of Populism. Counties in the post-oak belt received inadequate rainfall and suffered severe drought in 1885–87. Soils there ranged from blowing sand to black clay. East Texas counties received more than sufficient precipitation, but the red sandy loam lacked the fertility of the blackland or coastal prairies of regions bordering East Texas. Between 1892 and 1898, Populist electoral strength was concentrated in the less endowed western post-oak belt and eastern pine forests of Texas. Isolated pockets of Populism existed outside these two areas. Titus, Rains, and Van Zandt counties in the northeast post-oak region, and Delta and Navarro counties in the blackland prairie voted Populist. Between the critical shortage of rain in the post-oak strip and the marginal soils of the pine forests lay eleven million acres of prime blackland prairie, where successful Democrat farmers resided. Martin, *People's Party,* 58–70; King, "Religious Dimensions," 60–61.
94. *Southern Mercury,* Sept. 4, 1888 (letter 77).
95. *Southern Mercury,* Sept. 25, 1888 (letter 84).
96. *Southern Mercury,* Apr. 18, 1889 (letter 118). Local option meant that a community could choose for or against prohibition. It was an Alliance measure that avoided alienating Germans and other "wets."
97. *Southern Mercury,* May 30, 1889 (letter 125).
98. *Southern Mercury,* Feb. 28, 1889 (letter 108).
99. King, "Religious Dimensions," 61.
100. *Southern Mercury,* May 10, 1888 (letter 19).

101. *Southern Mercury,* May 17, 1888 (letter 23).

102. *Southern Mercury,* Aug. 28, 1888 (letter 75).

103. Mitchell, *Political Education,* 5, 80, 82.

104. Wagner, "Farms, Families, and Reform," 158–59; Winkler, *Platforms of Political Parties,* 282, 296, 333.

105. King, "Religious Dimensions," 64.

106. Martin, *People's Party,* 17.

107. *Southern Mercury,* Apr. 19, 1888 (letter 3).

108. *Southern Mercury,* May 30, 1889 (letter 127).

109. *Southern Mercury,* June 6, 1889 (letter 128).

110. *Southern Mercury,* July 12, 1888 (letter 58).

111. *Southern Mercury,* Apr. 25, 1889 (letter 119).

112. *Southern Mercury,* Oct. 23, 1890 (letter 168).

113. *Southern Mercury,* Sept. 11, 1888 (letter 81).

114. *Southern Mercury,* Oct. 23, 1890 (letter 167).

115. *Southern Mercury,* Dec. 12, 1889 (letter 158).

116. *Southern Mercury,* Feb. 6, 1890 (letter 159).

117. *Southern Mercury,* Apr. 4, 1889 (letter 117).

118. Wiedenfeld, "Women in the Texas Farmers' Alliance," 50.

119. King, "Religious Dimensions," 133.

120. *Southern Mercury,* Oct. 30, 1890 (letter 169).

121. *Southern Mercury,* Oct. 30, 1890 (letter 170).

122. *Southern Mercury,* Sept. 25, 1890 (letter 163).

123. *Southern Mercury,* Sept. 25, 1890 (letter 164).

124. *Southern Mercury,* Oct. 9, 1888 (letter 90).

125. *Southern Mercury,* May 16, 1889 (letter 123).

126. Martin, *People's Party,* 24–25.

127. Goodwyn, *Populist Movement,* vii.

128. *Southern Mercury,* May 17, 1888 (letter 26).

129. *Southern Mercury,* May 17, 1888 (letter 25).

130. *Southern Mercury,* June 14, 1888 (letter 34).

131. *Southern Mercury,* June 21, 1888 (letter 39).

132. *Southern Mercury,* May, 9, 1889 (letter 122).

133. *Southern Mercury,* July 5, 1888 (letter 48).

134. *Southern Mercury,* Sept. 11, 1888 (letter 82).

135. *Southern Mercury,* July 5, 1888 (letter 55).

136. King, "Religious Dimensions," iv, 109–10.

137. McMath, *Populist Vanguard,* 62–63; Barr, *Reconstruction to Reform,* 243–44.

138. Mitchell, *Political Education,* 50, 53; Goodwyn, *Populist Movement,* 34, 44.

139. *Southern Mercury,* July 31, 1888 (letter 64).

140. *Southern Mercury,* July 24, 1888 (letter 62).

141. Mitchell, *Political Education,* 94–98; Wagner, "Farms, Families, and Reform," 76–77.

142. Wagner, "Farms, Families, and Reform," 72.

143. Ibid., 65.

144. Ibid., 23.

145. *Southern Mercury,* May 3, 1888 (letter 9).

146. *Southern Mercury,* June 7, 1888 (letter 29).

147. *Southern Mercury,* July 5, 1888 (letter 50).

148. *Southern Mercury,* Aug. 22, 1889 (letter 151).

149. *Southern Mercury,* June 14, 1888 (letter 35).

150. *Southern Mercury,* June 21, 1888 (letter 38).

151. *Southern Mercury,* July 24, 1888 (letter 62).

152. *Southern Mercury,* July 12, 1888 (letter 59).

153. Barr, *Reconstruction to Reform,* 95.

154. *Southern Mercury,* Mar. 7, 1889 (letter 109).

155. Wagner, "Farms, Families, and Reform," 101.

156. *Southern Mercury,* May 10, 1888 (letter 17).

157. Wagner, "Farms, Families, and Reform," 122.

158. *Southern Mercury,* May 10, 1888 (letter 19).

159. *Southern Mercury,* Feb. 28, 1889 (letter 106).

160. Schwartz, *Radical Protest,* 218.

161. *Southern Mercury,* Aug. 28, 1888 (letter 75).

162. Charles W. Macune, "The Farmers Alliance" (typescript, 1920; Eugene C. Barker Texas History Center, Univ. of Texas), 35; Schwartz, *Radical Protest,* 218.

163. Goodwyn, *Populist Movement,* 79.

164. *Southern Mercury,* Mar. 14, 1889 (letter 112).

165. *Southern Mercury,* June 6, 1889 (letter 129).

166. *Southern Mercury,* June 20, 1889 (letters 132 and 133).

167. *Southern Mercury,* June 27, 1889 (letter 135).

168. *Southern Mercury,* July 4 and 11, 1889 (letters 139 and 140); *Southern Mercury,* Sept. 5, 1889 (letter 153).

169. Schwartz, *Radical Protest,* 219.

170. Annie L. Diggs, "The Women in the Alliance Movement," *Arena* (Boston) 6 (July 1892): 170. Betty Becker (Bettie Gay's great-granddaughter), Columbus, Texas, interview by Marion K. Barthelme, Mar. 1992.

171. Wagner, "Farms, Families, and Reform," 42.

172. McMath, *Populist Vanguard,* 69.

173. Nelson A. Dunning, *The Farmers' Alliance and Agricultural Digest* (New York: Arno Press, 1975), 308–12.

174. Bettie Gay's obituary, *Colorado Citizen* (Columbus, Tex.), June 10, 1921.

175. Jeffrey, "Women," 74, 84–85, and Wiedenfeld, "Women in the Texas Farmers' Alliance," 8, find this to be true for North Carolina and Texas Alliance women. Wagner, "Farms, Families, and Reform," 5, 361, says this is the case for Kansas, Nebraska, and Colorado Populists.

176. Wagner, "Farms, Families, and Reform," 10.

177. Ellen Carol DuBois, *Feminism and Suffrage: The Emergence of an Indepen-*

dent Women's Movement in America, 1848–1869 (Ithaca, N.Y.: Cornell Univ. Press, 1978), 18.

178. *Southern Mercury,* June 28, 1888 (letter 43).

179. Wiedenfeld, "Women in the Texas Farmers' Alliance," 37.

180. Wagner, "Farms, Families, and Reform," 143; *Southern Mercury,* July 5, 1988 (letter 53).

181. Nancy F. Cott, *The Bonds of Womanhood* (New Haven: Yale Univ. Press, 1977), 9, 194, 197.

182. A. Elizabeth Taylor, *Citizens at Last: The Woman Suffrage Movement in Texas* (Austin, Tex.: Ellen C. Temple, 1987), 13, 14.

183. *Southern Mercury,* May 10, 1888 (letter 14).

184. *Southern Mercury,* May 10, 1888 (letter 15).

185. *Southern Mercury,* June 7, 1888 (letter 29).

186. Donald B. Marti, *Women of the Grange: Mutuality and Sisterhood in Rural America, 1866–1920* (New York: Greenwood Press, 1991), 9; Karen J. Blair, *The Clubwoman as Feminist: True Womenhood Refined, 1868–1914* (New York: Holmes & Meier, 1980), 1–4.

187. *Southern Mercury,* May 10, 1888 (letter 13).

188. See letter 27 for note on Frances Willard and her address to the Senate.

189. *Southern Mercury,* May 31, 1888 (letter 27).

190. *Southern Mercury,* June 14, 1888 (letter 33).

191. *Southern Mercury,* June 21, 1888 (letter 41).

192. *Southern Mercury,* June 28, 1888 (letter 43).

193. McMath, *Populist Vanguard,* 133.

194. King, "Religious Dimensions," 173.

195. Marti, *Women of the Grange,* 8.

196. *Southern Mercury,* June 28, 1888 (letter 43).

197. King, "Religious Dimensions," 232.

198. *Southern Mercury,* June 28, 1888 (letter 44).

199. *Southern Mercury,* July 5, 1888 (letter 51).

200. *Southern Mercury,* June 28, 1888 (letter 45).

201. *Southern Mercury,* June 28, 1888 (letter 46).

202. *Southern Mercury,* Sept. 5, 1889 (letter 154).

203. *Southern Mercury,* July 5, 1888 (letter 53).

204. *Southern Mercury,* Aug. 28, 1888 (letter 73).

205. Wagner, "Farms, Families, and Reform," 122.

206. *Southern Mercury,* Aug. 28, 1888 (letter 74).

207. Myres, *Westering Women,* 8.

208. *Southern Mercury,* July 31, 1888 (letter 66).

209. *Southern Mercury,* Aug. 21, 1888 (letter 71).

210. *Southern Mercury,* Sept. 4, 1888 (letter 69).

211. *Southern Mercury,* May 3, 1888 (letter 9)

212. Harry C. Boyte, "The Pragmatic Ends of Popular Politics," in *Habermas*

and the Public Sphere, ed. Craig Calhoun, 346–49 (Cambridge, Mass.: MIT Press, 1992); Evans, "Women's History," 130.

213. *Southern Mercury,* June 7, 1888 (letter 32).
214. *Southern Mercury,* Feb. 28, 1889 (letter 107).
215. Wiedenfeld, "Women in the Texas Farmers' Alliance," 33, 34.
216. *Southern Mercury,* Sept. 4, 1888 (letter 80).
217. *Southern Mercury,* Oct. 9, 1888 (letter 89).
218. *Southern Mercury,* Mar. 7, 1889 (letter 109).
219. *Southern Mercury,* Oct. 23, 1890 (letter 169).
220. McMath, *Populist Vanguard,* 74.
221. *Southern Mercury,* Jan. 24, 1889 (letter 102).
222. *Southern Mercury,* Oct. 16, 1888.
223. Barnes, *Farmers in Rebellion,* 94–95.
224. Wagner, "Farms, Families, and Reform," 188.
225. *Southern Mercury,* Dec. 6, 1889.
226. *Southern Mercury,* Dec. 13, 1888 (letter 101).
227. King, "Religious Dimensions," 44–45.
228. Marilyn Dell Brady, "Populism and Feminism in a Newspaper by and for Women of the Kansas Farmers' Alliance, 1891–1894," *Kansas History* 7 (Winter 1984–85): 285; Wagner, "Farms, Families, and Reform," 318.
229. Brady, "Populism and Feminism," 284.
230. Wagner, "Farms, Families, and Reform," 294.
231. Ibid., 259–60, 264–65, 285.
232. King, "Religious Dimensions," 226.
233. Wagner, "Farms, Families, and Reform," 265; Martin, *People's Party,* 47–54; Norman Pollack, *The Populist Mind* (Indianapolis, Ind.: Bobbs-Merrill, 1967), ii.
234. McMath, *Populist Vanguard,* 142.
235. Barnes, *Farmers in Rebellion,* 144. This division already had shaken the *Mercury* badly. In 1890, when its editor Sam Dixon stood behind Gov. James Hogg and the other Democrats who refused to endorse the subtreasury concept or a third party, the Alliance discharged Dixon. He was replaced by Milton Park, a Baptist activist and college president (Southern Alabama College and Kyle Baptist Seminary). As *Mercury* editor, Park became a pillar of agrarian politics and a Populist party loyalist who obstinately refused to accept fusion with the Democrats. King, "Religious Dimensions," 134–37.
236. Wagner, "Farms, Families, and Reform," 290.
237. *Southern Mercury,* Jan. 31, 1895. According to Wagner, "Farms, Families, and Reform," 291, there is no evidence that women voted in larger numbers than men against Waite.
238. *Southern Mercury,* Dec. 6, 1894.
239. *Southern Mercury,* Dec. 27, 1894 (letter 172).
240. *Southern Mercury,* Dec. 27, 1894 (letter 173).

241. *Southern Mercury,* Jan. 3, 1895.

242. *Southern Mercury,* Jan. 17, 1895 (letter 175).

243. King, "Religious Dimensions," 50.

244. Taylor, *Citizens at Last,* 87.

245. Anastatia Sims, "The Woman Suffrage Movement in Texas" (Senior thesis, Univ. of Texas at Austin, 1974), 35–36.

246. Nieuwenhuizen, "Cunningham and McCallum," 5.

247. Goodwyn, *Populist Movement,* 311.

248. Arendt, *Human Condition,* 178–79; Wiedenfeld, "Women in the Texas Farmers' Alliance," 57.

Part II

Letters to the
Southern Mercury

Letters to the *Southern Mercury*

✻ Microfilm of the *Southern Mercury*—four reels of incomplete runs, dated from January 22, 1886, to March 7, 1907—exists in libraries at the University of Texas, Austin, and the Kansas State Historical Society, among other repositories. The "Ladies' Correspondence" section, which first featured the women's letters, initially appeared in the *Southern Mercury* on April 19, 1888. As anyone who has ever researched old newspapers will understand, I was thankful for any issues and pages of the minuscule print that were not missing, torn, permanently creased in celluloid, or otherwise illegible.

Since the formal academic training of the writers of these letters is not documented, the letters remain the best evidence of their individual eloquence and educational accomplishments, their pedagogical sensibilities and concerns. Thus I have included a majority of the letters I found, preserving their format, syntax, punctuation, and spelling. I have abridged only those that seemed excessively redundant and rhetorical—epistles which came, I imagine, from inspired new writers who found themselves in a long moment of unaccustomed quiet and told all to the distant *Mercury*. As the letters poured into the *Mercury* from both brethren and sisters, *Mercury* editors edited where necessary but, as the paper claimed in its October 30, 1888, issue, basically treated the correspondence as "visitor" reported—"as the pulse which tells the condition of the people" and the Alliance.

The *Mercury* also reprinted in its women's column or on its front page essays and public addresses given by women at suballiance meetings. These are included in the collection, as well as a few letters from writers from outside of Texas—Louisiana, specifically—because they are particularly descriptive of rural life or indicative of the women's concerns, or because the authors' voices are integral to the dialogue or the "mesh," as one writer put it, which became established. As fewer and fewer women's letters appeared in the "Family" section toward the end of the *Mercury's* life, from this period I reprinted letters I found in other parts of the paper. I also have included comments from the *Mercury* editors about these later letters, because the occasionally angry but respectful interplay tells the story of women's struggle for suffrage and equal rights better than I ever could.

The *Southern Mercury* "Ladies' Correspondence"

Alliance-building; the farmers' plight

1.   April 19, 1888. Woodstock. LaBelle.

EDITOR MERCURY: Papa has been taking your paper ever since it was first published, and I have been a constant reader all the time. I have never seen any letters of anything from this portion of the country and I thought I would write something about Hickery Grove Alliance, No. 2042, to let other Alliances know there is such a place.

This Alliance is not entirely in the background and it is not dead, either. The members are working on patiently and faithfully. This order is not very large yet, only about forty members, but it is rapidly increasing in membership and work. Petitions are put in at every meeting and it bids fair to be an able Alliance if the members will work on patiently and wait long enough, success will crown their efforts . . . what they have so long waited and watched for. I think the Alliance is a good and noble cause for if anybody needs help and protection it is the poor, hard working farmers. I am a farmer's daughter, it is true, but I am young and inexperienced and really don't know what hard times are and of course can't sympathize with the poor hard-run farmer who, from one year to another, goes in debt deeper and deeper and who never knows what rest is from morning till night, who toils and works to keep the wolf from the door.

I read in letters written by intelligent men and women, vivid descriptions of the would-be success and advantages of the Alliance business if the members would take hold and help move the great undertaking forward.

This order is trying to, and will by-and-by, successfully oppose monopoly, but if they work with the same spirit as monopolies what will monopoly be? Is the order for the benefit of the poor and needy or not? If it is, let those who are able go ahead and do what they can for the order and not stand and blow about those not being willing to help. Pa is an Alliance man and he thinks the *Mercury* is the best and cheapest paper in the world and, Mr. Editor, I agree with him. I do not belong to the Alliance but I am an Alliance girl from head to foot. I am going to join as soon as I am old enough.

I will close for this time; think I have written a very lengthly *[sic]* letter. Yours respectfully,

First mention of publishing anxiety

2.   April 19, 1888. Fannin County. Mrs. D. E. Guess.

EDITOR MERCURY: As I have to write you to send up some renewals, I cannot desist from penning a few thoughts which you can use as you see proper.

I am a constant reader of the *Mercury* and am well pleased with it, but I think it would be more interesting if different correspondents who are

Members attending the first formal meeting of the Alliance in Pleasant Valley, Lampasas County, Texas, 1877. Courtesy Wooten Studios

advising us to stick together would also tell us how to stick. [Obliterated] . . . and I would like to see change in the representation of our country.

Now brothers and sisters, let us do our duty in every respect. Let us read the *Mercury*, attend our meetings and keep that Alliance ball moving until we have accomplished the aims of the Alliance and then we can enjoy ourselves as none but free people can do.

My letter is getting long, and as it is my first I fear it will find the waste basket if I don't watch, however I expect it will look better there than any where else, but I have an anxiety to see it in print.

Success to the *Mercury*. Yours fraternally,

Rural pride; the importance of education

3.   April 19, 1888. Belton. A Country Girl.

EDITOR MERCURY: As the hours are passing slowly by this Sunday morning, I entertain myself by writing a short letter to our swift-winged messenger of truth and peace.

I am a young girl and a strong believer in the Alliance cause. I believe the farmer should be the most independent of mankind. I do not believe it will be long before we will accomplish our object. What can be more pleasant than a nice country home? There is nothing mean and debasing in farming. It leads a man forth among scenes of natural grandeur and beauty; it leaves him to the workings of purest and most elevating of external influences. City gentlemen are glad to lay down their city enjoyments and wander out into the country where vegetation puts forth all its magnificence and the merry songs of the birds inspire within him an admiration and love for nature and the honest, heart-felt enjoyment of country life.

I heartily agree with some of our sisters and brothers, in regard to living within our means. Those merchants who seem to be so obliging by selling to us on time, are charging three times the cost of the articles bought, and by trying, we may do without a great many things we think we are compelled to have. But there is one thing I think we could go into debt for if we cannot obtain it otherwise, that is an education. "Knowledge is power"; farmers, if you have children growing up in ignorance, send them to school and teach them the value of an education, teach them to love and crave knowledge. They can never be swindled out of that. Teach them the principles of the Alliance. Teach them civil government. Educate your girls that they may be independent. Educate your boys that they may perform the work assigned them through life with intelligence and then our country homes will be a paradise surrounded by the beauties of natural scenery and occupied by enlightened sons and daughters of toil and prosperity.

Success to the *Mercury*.

Advice about the work ethic

4.   April 19, 1888. [Name and location of author obliterated.]

BEAUTIFUL HANDS

Are those that do the work that is honest, brave and true. In starting life no one should ever forget there are few things beyond the attainment of real merit; if his or her ambition be of that kind which springs from talent and good common sense they will triumph. True merit is always modest. There is a time to sow and a time to reap. It is in the morning of life that the seeds are sown, the fruit of which we reap as the evening draws near.

The Omnipotent Creator of all things has given us, to a large extent, the control of the greatest of all earthly blessings, health, and it is our duty to try and preserve it. It is as culpable to slight the physical welfare as to neglect the mental[,] for the mental and physical are very closely connected in this work-a-day world of ours. The happiest are they who wisely mingle work and recreation. Men and women, the rich and poor, all have something to do; but there is no need for anyone to over-work, for it is wrong.

How many of our sex are to-day suffering from bad health which could have been avoided if they had only been content to accomplish less labor in a specified time. They rise early and toil carefully and rush through the day after the fashion of a train of cars. Meditation is out of the question; books are a crime, and the newspaper a snare and a delusion. Little things worry and fret, for the mind contracts to their measure. Overwork sours dispositions otherwise tolerably sweet, and the air grows full of innuendoes, fault-finding and all manner of bitterness that fall quite as often on the heads of the just as well as the unjust.

Judicious work hurts no one. Industry, economy and prudence are the sure forerunners of success. They create that admirable combination of powers in one which always conduces to eventual prosperity. If constancy in endeavor is good in anything it should be in work and economy. True economy does not consist in denying ourselves the necessaries of life nor does it consist in stinting the table or wearing our clothing threadbare.

A judicious man who studies the interest of his family is sure of plenty;

but labor without judgement is time spent in vain. Of all good qualities, that of energy is of most value; work at the thing we are compelled to do with a will. All snatch work is sure to end bad and things done only at intervals and laid aside for idle pleasure are never worth even the small amount of pains bestowed on them. This is more than half the reason why woman's work is not, as a rule, equal to man's. And until woman learns to stick to her work she will always be the dependent woman. "Everything runs more smoothly the less its flow is broken," and to make work a pleasure, whether of head or hand, depends upon the way in which it is done. Whoever goes to work reluctantly will have. . . . [Remainder of letter torn]

Publishing anxieties

5.   April 19, 1888. Gates Valley, Texas. Fannie D. Petty.

[Front of letter torn] . . . teaching in the Lucas neighborhood, about fifteen miles east of this. I do hope we will get her back to teach for us next fall.

I am always so proud to read the *Mercury*. The first thing I do is read Mr. John Goode Hope's letter and to look for Uncle Snort's letter [*Mercury* editors and contributors], but have failed to find it several times. But I see he has spliced his rope and I hope it will never break again.

I expect that this will find its way to the waste basket, but I am so anxious to surprise my papa by seeing a letter from me unexpected to him.

Mamma says for me not to sign my own name though I can never think of disowning it for I was named for such good people (the Rev. W. D. Johnson and his loving wife Fannie). Now, Mr. Editor, if this makes the way through without being cornered I will try to do better the next time. My best wishes for our paper and all the little cousins.

Very Respectfully,

Female modesty

6.   April 19, 1888. Lavaca County. [Name missing.]

EDITOR MERCURY—As you have so kindly offered us space in your valuable paper I will try and write a few words, hoping to be pardoned for the errors that I may make, as this is my first attempt to write for a newspaper. As some of our sisters have said, I have been waiting and wishing that some of our "big-brained" brothers would write who are better able to write something that would be more instructive and interesting to the readers of the *Mercury* than I can.

Our Alliance met at Halletsville on the third and fourth inst. The new Alliance and co-operative store house, is very near completed, and will . . . soon be ready for business.

My husband was sent as a delegate to the county Alliance and says it is fast gaining members and interest all over the country. He says it has twice as many members as it had at this time last year. I am glad that the farmers have awoke from their slumbers and see that it is high time that they were up and doing something that will break the yoke of bondage which they have so patiently carried for so many years. If they would take a dose of the *Mercury* once a week, they would soon get all right and be ready to work for the interest of the order. If the farmers will only be steadfast in this enterprise, victory is theirs and at no distant time.

We get the *Mercury* regularly and think it one of the grandest papers to read. It does my heart good to read many good and instructive letters by many of our noble men and women. . . . [Rest of letter torn]

Trying to understand the system

7.   April 19, 1888. [No location.] A front-page essay by Mrs. Anna Grey.

BROTHERS AND SISTERS: The time has arrived when we must have perfect harmony and unity of action throughout our entire order. If we hope for success in the demands of our just rights we must be true to our motto, "United we stand, divided we fall," for in unity lies great strength. Why are the farmers getting poorer every year? We work harder, are more economical than we have ever been.

A few years since[,] money was plentiful, the demands for labor were great; now there is very little in circulation, laborers are more numerous, begging employment but the farmers are not able to hire them. What was once the common necessities of life are now high priced luxuries. Why is it that our produce when carried to market is priced by others? Why is taxation more burdensome than during the civil war? Have we less energy? Are we more effeminate? Are we less capable of managing our affairs? Are we truly the empty-headed class we are represented to be? Why have we not been respected as a class, as a great power in the land? Is it because we failed to organize at the proper time as all other classes and occupations and organizations have done? Or is it because we failed to pledge our means and sacred honor for the advancement of our just right? Is it not because we have placed all confidence in our representatives, thinking they had the interest of the whole country at heart? Have they not sold us to the bankers, the monopolies, the trusts, the rings, to all for filthy lucre's sake? A few years since it was considered an honor to be an American citizen but we as a people have fallen into corruption and there is none so poor as to honor us.

Our country is as productive as ever. There is more money in the treasury vaults in Washington than at any previous time, but 'tis not for the laboring class to handle. 'Tis for the benefit of railroad monopolies, national banks to loan to the people at usurious interest; 'tis also for public buildings which is of very little benefit to the people, 'tis squandered by congress in appropriations but none of it goes to lighten the burdens of those who live by the sweat of their brow. There was an appeal for aid sent to congress last year for the drought stricken sufferers. Did they receive aid? Some seed in the agricultural department was bestowed upon them; congress turned a deaf ear to the cries of suffering humanity and don't forget, it is the same democratic president and congress that wants your votes next November.

I here copy a few words from the *New York Sun* of date February fifteen of the proceedings of the senate on February ninth. On that day several senators, republicans and democrats, raised their voices in holy horror at the awful waste and expenditure of money in the erections of public buildings. . . . Mr. Edmunds said the abuse was one of long standing, and had gone far enough. . . .

Morale boosting

8.   April 19, 1888. Stonewall Alliance, No. 2414, Rusk County. Lizzie Dunklin.

EDITOR MERCURY: With your permission and space in your widely spread paper, and our friend, which we feel we could not get along without, I will endeavor to write a few lines, though I have never written anything for publication. I see so many of the sisters writing words of encouragement, I thought I would try and see if I could say anything.

We all think we have a hard time because some do not speak in favor of the Alliance. Think a moment what the members of Wise, Parker, Jack and other counties had to undergo when the Alliance first started there. They were accused of being thieves, robbers, murders, and a lawless set of people.

If we will think of this we will be revived and will go to work in earnest and attend our meetings. Take the *Mercury* and read it and then we can see what the Alliance is doing.

I say honor to such men and J. N. Montgomery, Dr. O. G. Peterson, S. O. Daws [early Alliance leaders] and others too numerous to mention. Christian gentlemen who looked to a higher power than ours where we all should look if we expect to be benefited. How true it is that there is no excellence without great labor. The Alliance is a living illustration of that fact. It has bravely battled with the public sentiment before which so many good measures have failed to stand the test, so work, brothers and sisters, attend your meetings regularly, and keep the grand order moving on and on until the victory is won.

I am glad that we have such leaders as C. W. Macune and Evan Jones. They were left orphans and had to work to make useful men of themselves. If I had a good education I would write and write, but I have not the education to express my thoughts. Many poor people are deprived on an education and therefore are kept from being useful men and women.

I will close by wishing that kind Heaven may help us to be guided in the future as in the past by patriotic principles, may the purity of our order and our interest in a common cause unite us heart and hand to secure the love and allegiance of every member to the principles of our grand institution.

First mention of women's suffrage; first mention of a third party; trying to understand the system

9.   May 3, 1888. [No location.] Western Reader.

EDITOR MERCURY: An issue of the *Mercury*, April 3, contains an editorial commenting on the urgent necessity of purifying the ballot. As with many of your correspondents, the necessity of this reform and that reform is often discussed, but as to the manner of effecting such reforms, none of you seem very explicit. However, enough is gathered from all that is said to infer that you regard suffrage, the untrammelled vote of every male citizen, as the true remedy. A purified ballot can never exist while ignorance and poverty enslave the voter. Would the poor man sell his vote if he did not need the price of it? While concentrated capital controls legislation and the "staff of life," will it not drive its employees as it listeth? It is in the interest of our masters to keep all labor so busily employed getting a bare subsistence that none shall have time to inform themselves as to the cause of our degradation, nor study a proper method of remedies.

An editorial in the *Atlanta Constitution,* April 5th, argues in favor of conferring real benefits, genuine bread crumbs, to the laborer by giving more continual work. This ancient chestnut of an argument has been used by the heartless tyrannies of all ages, notably during the monstrous reign of the Louis's of France. Ceaseless, incessant labor brutalizes, as the *Atlanta Constitution* well knows. How John Claiborne (who is a graduate, an A.M. in the school of pseudo-politics) would slyly teach us, saying "rise a little earlier, work a little harder, economize and try to make the *Mercury* more interesting by writing recipes for whitewash and preserves. (A few more Sugar Trusts will make it impossible for farmers to have preserves by any receipt.) Work hard, farmers, and don't meddle in questions concerning your political existence."

Farmers, ignorance and poverty are effects, effects of preventable causes!! If you continue to bind yourself to such leaders or to either one of the present two parties, to cringe when its astute leaders crack their whips, to ignore the study of politics, to try to make a cookbook out of your present organ, then you deserve to have your suffrage bought and yourselves the slaves of big-salaried law-makers who are faithful guardians of their own interests. Don't fear a third party no matter how the grand straps of the other parties croak. If you gain nothing, you surely have nothing to lose by a third party.

Every intelligent effort you make to understand your wrongs and apply remedies is an advanced step. Study politics. Study socialism, which Webster defines to be "a better and more just system of government." Fear not the cries of those who are wedded to the present system, yet pretend to ardently espouse the cause of the horny-handed, honest farmer. They tell you that they honor you for those horny hands but really they score you for this badge of servitude and they know that only because you are on your knees, do they appear great and superior.

Universal suffrage, guided by intelligence will be a powerful weapon, not withstanding [the fact that] some blushing, stay-in-our-own-sphere sisters, shiver with apprehension of the degrading results. I fail to understand why casting a vote would deprive womanhood of the bloom of modesty [any] more than mingling in social entertainments, attending colleges, church or other gatherings with their fathers, sons and brothers. It seems a rather gauzy, St. Paul, effete kind of a fear, quite natural to hear from egotistical trouser-clad fogies who always interpose their beefy corpora in the battle of progress, but if I were free, I would fear no contamination from walking with my husband to the ballot box any more than going with him to a store to do a little shopping. The *Dallas News* lately gave us a rich nut to crack in a terse, concise statement of the difference in the wages and condition of the farmer and laboring classes now and a hundred years ago. Don't be sidetracked, Alliancemen, by such statements which remind one of the man, Edward Atkinson of Boston, whom John Swinton used to dub "the mumble-pated idiot" because he was often trying to prove by figurative nonsense how easily a laboring man could comfortably live, raise a family, and accumulate a fortune on one hundred cents a day. The question is, not are you as well off as the ancients, not are you better off than the peasants of Europe, who many times are glad to get the same coarse bread as they feed their horses, but are you as well off as you ought to be? Every farmer, every adult citizen of this country should take the same interest in politics that you would in any other business or cooperative enterprise. No matter what Democratic governors or any other party leaders may advise, meet and study the science of government and cast your vote for only your own representative. How can you expect the aristocrats of the senate, the bankers, the lawyers and peacock tricksters of the house of representatives to efface their own selfworship and be mindful of interests which you foolishly pay them to trammel and neglect?

Windy orators assure you that this is the golden age of civilization but it is civilization that feeds on slavery and with all its boasted progress, its countless inventions of labor saving machinery, the toil and grinding of the labor of the working masses has not been lightened. The wealth of the world has increased, the cost of living [has] increased, the laboring class has grown poorer. This vaunted civilization has given birth to some monstrosities, which, as a recent writer declares, are a "disgrace to man and a libel on God," viz.: the railroad king, the cattle king, and their children, an army of drones. Farmers, this is no longer a democratic government. A purified ballot no longer exists, and never can, while starvation threatens the voter. An oligarchy of wealth holds the reins. The "primaries" meet and tell you how your masters wish you to vote. Your courage is gone. Liberty is sweet but the laborer can only dream of it. To him it is a mirage. Slowly but surely the spirit of democracy, the exalted, ennobling idea of equality and fraternity, which animated the hearts of those immortals, who framed the declaration of July 4th, '76, is being annihilated. Our press and vanity-laden orators . . . stultify themselves with hollow declamation about "our liberty" while . . . heartless avarice and gaunt poverty proclaim them hypocrites.

An out-of-state letter; on mother love

10.　May 3, 1888. Ruston, Louisiana. Charitie.

MOTHER CHILDHOOD

I am on the sick list to-day, or blue one whatever one may choose to call it so I will try and write for your paper. I don't know anything about politics. I will leave that for our brothers to make peace over. So, to my subject. It has been said that "Mother, Home and Heaven" are surely the most beautiful words in the English language. Mother is the first word that we learn to lisp, and the last one that is thought of when we leave this world. One of the sweetest memories of my early life is that of coming home from school, with a feeling that I had been away a long while, and seeing the house at a distance. Just the house and there standing in the door, my mother waiting for me. At that sight my heart would leap until I could reach her and kiss and hold her in my arms. Oh, how well I love that home of my childhood. Never shall I forget those days; the simple pleasures of our life, the sitting room, where we gathered in the evening, and my mother's old chair. Yet before all, comes that picture in the door—my mother waiting for me. It has been many years since then, but blessed memory, it will be fresh— seeing her looking, or at least waiting for me. Today as I write, my heart breaks over the thought that she is dead. I was quite a child when my mother was taken from me. And it has been many years but be they few or many, it will seem long until I shall see her. For no love is so true and tender as that of a mother. Never until we are parents ourselves, do we quite comprehend a mother's love. I was not left alone, altogether, for I had a dear, good papa, left me—but he is no more. I can see him now, with his much worn bible, his spectacles pushed up on his forehead, his toil-hardened hands clasped upon the book which had pointed him all along life's journey to the ever present help in trouble. How many a gentle mother and kind father are leading those that would otherwise be wayward and unruly sons in the ways of right and truth. Even when they are sullied with crime, it is the mother who will say, bring him to me. I will love him still. So few ever think of a mother's love until it is too late. How many then will look back through lapse of years, viewing his childhood, the thoughts of his dear old mother will come rushing upon his memory, he can hear her voice, gently pleading for him to change his course, he sees the loved face becoming prematurely old, the raven locks turn to snowy whiteness, and the once graceful form bent beneath the load of toil, sorrow and disgrace that is her recompense—for long years of toil and trouble and ungrateful children.

Sweet asylum of my childhood, content and innocent—there careless as the birds that sung upon the trees, I laughed the hours away; nor knew of evil. . . . Yesterday, in arranging my book case, my hands chanced to alight upon a dusty and worn volume, on looking at it, I found it to be one of my old school books, and written on one of its leaves was this: "Never forget your true friend—Mattie Duncan." [Mattie Duncan became an Alliance member and contributed egg-and-milk-money toward the Exchange.] Immediately my mind turned back in its flight to my school and college days. Those days which have now gone glimmering through the things that were. While I gazed on the faded lines written by my friend and classmate, I felt as if I were a school girl again . . . when life was all sunshine and care with its indelible pen had not as yet begun to write our troubles on our brow in wrinkles deep and long. And as I mused o'er those happy scenes and thought how many hours I had wasted in idle folly and useless pleasure, which had I employed rightly, I might have been what I once dreamed. As I replaced the old school book, I thought how many of our young men and girls are wasting their best days in idle pleasure. Time, thou mighty change worker; and who can stay the ravages of thy onward march? And who is free from the impress of thy hand? Before thy coming all things fade and sink into the nothingness of the past. Yet, we would also praise as well as fear thee, for although thou art a despoiler, thou also are a builder up. Ah! surely I shall yet see my mother as I saw her in my old school days, the sunlight on her forehead, her hands out-stretched, watching and waiting for me at the door. Yours truly,

Class consciousness; use of allegorical name, Parson Smallsoul; allusion to Pilgrim's Progress

11.   May 3, 1888. [No location.] Sally Beck.

THE FASHIONABLE WIDOW'S MAID

EDITOR MERCURY: I have been too busy since my last letter, describing the Christmas visit to a friend, to notice the shafts hurled at a forlorn old maid by such keenly perceptive critics as Maria Labouchere and others equally as comfortable and fortunate.

It may possibly increase their happiness to state that Sally Beck has been for a long time, and is yet, cooking, washing, ironing and playing maid for Widow Skinner and her three fashionable daughters (of course I have lily-white hands).

I note one result of my letter; it elicited a chorus of indignation from farmers' wives and children (some folks cannot read between the lines, Mr. Editor), quite disputing the story we hear of the stringency of times among the monopoly-ridden farming class. As a general thing, to read the *Mercury,* which I do every Saturday night, one would suppose that our vast army of farmers are fast drifting into slavery, enchained by poverty and mortgage. But a rift appears in this somber, threatening cloud, happily furnished by Maria's description of her pleasurable life and abundance of leisure; a leisure that will enable one to revel in a weekly *Atlanta Constitution* is a luxury I covet.* Once I attempted that enjoyment; it was the issue containing the royal reception of President Cleveland and the first lady of the land, extended by the city of Atlanta. I reached the exciting part where two gallant military companies guarded the president, his valet, the first lady and her maid Lena (so English) all night when Mrs. Skinner called me to finish dusting the parlor.

I guess Marie Labouchere and her class of farmer folks were not in attendance at the circus last fall. I heard Parson Smallsoul say at the supper table (I fried two chickens for "tea" that evening), that he attended the circus with a long string of school children and while they were gazing at the animals in the menagerie, he found interest in studying the faces and appearance of the country people who clustered around the different cages. Mrs. Skinner loftily said, "Humph! Country people have so little style, I don't see anything interesting about them." Parson Smallsoul said he didn't doubt that it was unavoidable for her to feel that way, it being the opinion of Alexander Hamilton and great men of our own times that people are naturally divided into two classes, the one, the well born, the rich, the other the laboring people and the laboring people are most numerous and necessarily the foundation or broad base of the pyramid of society and being one of God's shepherds he felt interest in all his flock and with that the melancholy man helped himself to a third big spoonful of peach jam which I worked so hard to make last summer.

Sometimes my blood boils at sentiments I hear expressed by these dead souls, these butterfly, frivolous society folks who come and go, chattering like magpies. I often wonder as I vibrate between my kitchen work and the front door, admitting the stylish callers to the parlor, do "hired girls" belong even to the less considered lower class or to one even lower, too insignificant for consideration. My wages is all I ever get; never any sympathy for a tired body after a long hot day's work, never any recognition that I am a social creature with a love for companionship, a craving for pleasure outside of menial labor.

The complaints arising from the farmers of this land strike a responsive chord in my heart so that I find pleasure in reading of their high resolves to kick; for to hear that they will kick is sure evidence that their legs are not yet tied. Farmers' wives, farmers' sons, I am glad some of you are yet comfortable and feel the thrill of aspiration. It is my humble old maid's opinion that all true pleasures, all the graces should attend on and dwell with the farmer and may the education they are now seeking enable them to bring a wise and peaceful solution to the difficulties now seeking to overwhelm them.

This letter does not survive, although others by Marie Labouchere follow.

Morale boosting

12.   May 3, 1888. Mansfield, Texas. Ida Jones.

EDITOR MERCURY: I have waited to see if anyone of our Union would write to the *Mercury*. Some members could write a much better letter than I but I will see if I can inspire them to write.

My father takes the *Mercury* and insists on everybody to take it. Antioch Union No. 316 has a membership of forty-two. Two more will enter next meeting day. I am glad to say all the members are in good standing.

Antioch Union was organized last August. My father is president. Now, as our aims are high and noble, let us press forward. I hope the day is not far distant when the downtrodden farmer can look back and say, we have gained the victory at last; for if any class of people have been slaves it is the farmers. We all have something to do, then let's be up and doing. We all know that "time and tide waits for no man." Let us improve the golden moments that pass so swiftly by. If ever there was a time when the farming and labor elements should stick together it is now.

The sisters are attending and seem more interested than at first. I hope they will become more interested in the future than in the past. Let us strive to use all our influence to persuade all good farmers, their wives and daughters to join the alliance. Some say, well, I don't believe I will join yet; I will wait awhile and see what it is going to do. If they would all go ahead and join they will soon find out what it would do. We have slept on our rights till they are nearly gone beyond our reach; yet it is not quite so late that all hope is lost. There is in the distance a ray of hope that we may yet regain our rights and rejoice in freedom. I know that if the brothers and the sisters work faithfully together we will come out on the right side.

May the Alliance grow and prosper til like the small oak, it forms a great tree with wide spreading branches under whose shade the weary and oppressed may find peace, profit and pleasure. I hope all the members of the Alliance may stand by their colors. A faint heart never won a battle, it is the brave only who win the prize. I hope they will soon lay off the yoke of bondage under which they have striven for so long and come forth a free and independent people. Let everyone keep his or her obligation for truth is mighty and will prevail. Let every heart and hand be in the work for there is good in it and something for everyone to do. I would not give a copper cent for a man who will object to ladies joining the Alliance. May the Lord bless John Goode Hope for praising women and when he comes to die, take him to rest where joys immortal follow and sorrow is known no more. Very respectfully,

Alliance rhetoric; the woman's sphere

13. May 10, 1888. Excerpt from an essay originally read by the author before the Bell County Alliance and later reprinted on the front page of the *Mercury*. Mrs. J. Morton Smith.

Honored by the unexpected call to meet you on this occasion, I come happily and grateful for the surroundings that greet me today, and in be-half of Midway Alliance, we welcome you, as typical representatives of the agricultural interest of our Lone Star State. We have assembled here as a united brotherhood to perpetuate the principles of an organization whose laws are "reason and equity." For more than one hundred years, the grand march of American intellect has been projected from southern brains and the fire of America's patriotism has germinated around the hearthstone of the rural home.

It is owing to the unparalleled nerves and ceaseless industry and un-heard-of energy that our farmers have struggled against adversity, while they "cleared the brown path to meet their coulter's glean" and dug from the fertile soil of our rich fields and broad prairies the prosperity we now enjoy. Is it not this united southern civilization that has supplied the courage, indomitable perseverance and Teutonic pluck which have wrought from the ashes of ruin and desolation the grand prosperity of which the South boasts to-day? No people on earth have ever accomplished so much in an equal length of time. I ask how long can this prosperity continue, when all articles needed for home consumption are to be purchased from protracted industries, controlled by capitalists who, guided by self interest in the accomplishment of sordid, selfish gain, are defrauding so many efforts at reform demanded by the people of our state and national government, so much so that your principal articles of export have become in reality a golden argosy on the currents of speculation, enriching the few and sapping the very life blood from an occupation that should be fostered as the nucleus from which radiates the wealth of the nation. This combined with the great trust companies which are getting control of the leading articles of consumption. If this system continues, the struggle for existence must inevitably become fierce and heartless, all consideration for the common good be strangled in the bitter struggle, and the finer sensibilities . . . destroyed. Even friendship will become a myth and patriotism an absurdity. Is it strange that under such a system dishonesty is fast becoming the rule and that trickery, bad faith, betrayal of trust, and treachery in positions of honor, are becoming common? Of course all of this must unavoidably create cruel demands and unjust discriminating taxation, equal to the yoke of English tyranny which burdened our ancestry.

It is the products of your labor that give ballast to the barque which plows the crested waves of Old Ocean, without which the wheel of commerce would be blocked. We have only to be guided by the principles of the Alliance, to labor for the education of the agricultural classes. It is through organized effort alone that we can hope to do this successfully. . . . I cannot too strongly urge you to direct your attention to this question as will guarantee to the youth of your land the advantage of a thorough education. Secure, if possible, persons of high intellectual ability, combined with purity of character and morals, to take charge of your schools, for 'tis here their youthful hearts are brought to bow at the shrine of science and treasure up unfading jewels from the balmy fields of thought. . . .

And now in conclusion, a word to the weaker sex (of which I am one). The true history of the world is the record of the home life and the characteristics of its people. It is to woman we owe the little niceties of social intercourse and to her we look as the "star of Bethlehem to light the way to a higher and better life" and we must remember that her presence in a home, however humble, is a subtle influence permeating everywhere. We are thankful that the vigorously demanded woman's rights have been denied us. If it were not for the restraining influences of conventionalism, it is possible woman would never have acquired the genius shown in all ages, all climes and under all circumstances but never so marked as now for adorning and refining home. The cultivation of flowers, the lavish use of the painter's brush, sculptor's chisel and artist's pencil as well as the various exquisite embroideries transform the rude hut into a vine-wreathed cottage, making it a "thing of beauty and a joy forever." Every dainty piece of fancy work speaks of aspirations for higher and nobler things. When Queen Margaret wrought with her maidens that wonderful history of Harrold now read in the Bayeux tapestry, she did far more toward ennobling her race than if her vote had been polled at the ballot box or her voice heard in the political arena.* Our homes are said to be crystalizations of our ideas; then let us keep them so cleanly and so pure that the gleam of the fireside, the flowers at the door, the very birds in the trees may waft a welcome to loved ones and say to the stranger that old-fashioned southern hospitality is not a thing of the past but the latch string still hangs without the portal. Mungo Park** tells us that to the native African no water is sweet but that drawn from his own well and no shade is refreshing but that of the Tabba tree besides his native dwelling. . . .

*Actually, an embroidery attributed to Queen Matilde, wife of William the Conqueror, chronicling the Norman conquest of Harold, King of England at Hastings in 1066. It is a valuable document on the history and costumes of the time.

**A British explorer (1771–1806) who explored the Niger River

Female modesty

14.   May 10, 1888. DeWitt County. Addie McCaskill.

EDITOR MERCURY: Modesty is decidedly the most beautiful characteristic of a real lady but there is a false modesty or boastfulness that should not be mistaken for the genuine. By reading the *Mercury,* I see that many of our ablest men are urging the ladies to take a more decided stand in the great cause we have espoused. If by doing so we can wield a greater influence, it is our duty to do so, and modesty never required anyone to neglect a duty. So keenly do I realize my inability to write an article to be read by so many people that nothing but a true devotion to the cause could prevail upon me to attempt it.

I notice that some who write for the *Mercury* seem to be in favor of woman's suffrage. I do not presume to be a criterion upon any subject, but if I am not entirely wrong we, as a sex, have no desire whatever to extend our privileges beyond what they are now. I believe in ladies attending public gatherings, and going abroad and lightening, in every manner possible, the burdensome cares of life; but I do not wish to be misunderstood when I say that home is the field in which we can wield the greatest power of influence.

Bro. Harry Tracy says it takes more good sense and management to make a forty acre farm profitable than it does to run a national bank. And the same rule will apply to the lady whose whole study is to make those in her home happy, and the one whose every thought is occupied in planning some scheme to out-rival some lady acquaintance in point of fashion requires a great deal of study and daily application. We encounter many perplexing vexations which one without experience would never think of, and to dispose of them as should be done requires great generalship; and our possibilities to do so depend greatly upon the assistance rendered by our husbands. If our husbands are kind and helpful we have everything for which to be thankful, and our attentions upon our duties at home become a pleasure in place of a burden. But the woman whose misfortune it is to be married to an overbearing, cold-hearted man who regards his wife as his servant is indeed in a pitiable condition.

But whatever may be our lot in that respect, let us remember that kindness is our scepter, and the human heart that cannot be reached by loving kindness is out of the reach of all power of woman's. Let us look to the up-building of our homes; to properly rearing our children; in short to the realities of life and leave the giddy, gaudy, fickle fancies of fashion to those who have time to devote to such frail frivolities. . . .

First mention of pride in fellow letter writers; first reference to Adam and Eve

15.   May 10, 1888. Travis County. Homespun Dress.

EDITOR MERCURY: I am not a member but I am very much in love with the Alliance. My husband joined last year and like every good and pure institution, the more he knows of it the better he likes it, and when he takes an active interest in a thing I know it is good because he always looks before he leaps. I also have one son belonging and several others who will join and swell the ranks of its grand army as soon as they are of age.

I will call myself a step-sister as I only lack the initiative step to make me a member. As I understand the Alliance, it allows the ladies equal rights with the men. This, I think, is a great inducement to them to join, as we don't have it anywhere else, some not even at home.

I like [contributors] Mr. John Goode Hope and Mr. Jas. A. Sowell because they seem to have such an exalted opinion and high appreciation of my sex, and especially that they think so much of their wives, which proves two things, that they have lovable wives and are appreciative husbands.

I don't know that Mr. Sowell is exactly right as to Mother Eve's part in the garden but if she was like most of us she did little else but talk. However, one thing is certain; Adam obeyed Eve, whether she was put there to rule or not. Let us not, like Eve, influence our husbands to eat forbidden fruit but climb up with them, hand in hand, step by step, to a higher, nobler plane of existence.

Miss Lula Wade's essay on "Usury and Mortgages" is the best and most logical I have ever had the pleasure of reading from the pen of a lady. She is certainly a deep thinker. I see other interesting letters from ladies too numerous to mention. I am proud to see so much intellect among farmers' wives and daughters. I believe, according to our opportunities, we do equally as well as the men.

Let all farmers everywhere both individually and collectively do everything they can to improve their condition, both temporal and spiritual; let us improve our hearts and minds as well as our farms and the blessings of heaven will surely attend us.

I'm afraid you will find this letter . . . has not much Alliance in it but if ever I get into the Alliance I may do better. Success to the *Mercury* and Alliance. Your step-sister till promoted,

16.   May 10, 1888. Essay read before Cedar Gap Alliance and reprinted in the Mercury. Mrs. J. R. Cope.

> *The following essay was read to the Cedar Gap Alliance and ordered sent, if the majority approved, to Taylor County Alliance and to the* Mercury *for publication.*

DEAR SISTERS: We have enrolled in this noble work and yet have not done all we could do. I will make a move that the Sisters of every Alliance organize a class.

1st. For the purpose of educating ourselves in the manufacture of household goods as there are so many of us who have had such poor chance of learning to make our own clothes that we are forced to hire them made by monopolies at their own price and they charge twice the worth of their work; and it is breaking down the poor working man to pay such extortionate prices for so little value.

2d. For the purpose of adapting some mode of dressing and that we form something suitable for farmers and their families as there are many of us patronizing such an extortionate way of dressing. I think we can get up something among ourselves that would suit us much better and make us feel more like one band of free sisters than we ever have felt.

3rd. That we have us a guide published at our own printing house. We could have it published cheaper.

4th. That we send delegates from subordinate Alliances for the purpose of selecting and electing some suitable lady to write a delineator of forms to be guided by.

5th. We want ladies who will do away with so much style of dress and adopt something only neat and nice; why not have our hats in a comfortable style made by some firm, and let our Exchange purchase them and our cooperative stores keep them; then we will not have to buy from other stores and cause disturbance among us—a band of free and independent people. Let us have a right to our own idea in which we should dress. Then let us have our own magazine published quarterly by our Publishing house, and each Alliance family take it for a guide.

Alliance building; growth of political consciousness

17.   May 10, 1888. Limestone County. Mary.

EDITOR MERCURY: I am so pleased with the good, kind letters from the brothers and sisters from all over the state that I must write to our paper and tell them to keep the ball rolling. Don't stop writing. Your words of encouragement will assist the weary toiler to bear the burdens and crosses of life. He will feel that he stands not alone, but that other brave hearts and perhaps more fertile brains are tying to pave the way for the emancipation of the toiling men and women from slavery. This is why I write. I feel encouraged to bear the burden and go on uncomplainingly yet awhile longer. There are clouds, and it is yet dark, but surely the day will come soon. I know we may trust our leaders and know they would not bid us hope in vain. If we only trust and sustain them they will pilot us through. Let us take heed every order and soon we may see prosperity again smiling on our now poverty stricken people. . . . Let us make a firm resolution to attend our meetings regularly, not to go through routine business, but to discuss questions of vital importance to us. . . . In our Alliance meeting is a good place to discuss the why's and wherefore's of the exceeding scarcity of money but there is another question, it seems to me, of great magnitude. Why is it that there are so many homeless men and women, men who would till the soil for a living, and yet there are thousands of acres of land lying idle. Why did our state officials give the railroads so much of the people's land, and compel the poor to rent? Why did they give so much land to build a state house? Would it have not been better policy to have given that 3,000,000 acres of land to the poor renting farmer and built a less palatial house by direct taxation? These and other questions should not be ignored, let us keep ourselves posted, and when the time comes to send our men to legislative halls, let us be sure to have our former law-makers retired to private life, and there to stay. About the best legislating we could have now would be a wholesale repeal of a lot of nonsensical laws, and the enactment of a few, plain, wholesome laws that it will not take a Philadelphia lawyer to understand.

I would say something about cultivating the social features of the Alliance, but somebody's toes might get pinched. But, brethren and sisters, I will say this: Don't neglect your poor, don't neglect the sick even though they may be strangers. . . .

Then there are two other "patches," the mental and the moral and here, sisters, is our work laid out. In the Alliance, our moralizing influence is such that no good Alliance man ever wants to meet unless the sisters are there. That is what I have heard many other brethren say. Then there is the training of our children at home. Endeavor to store their minds with all the knowledge you can give. It is the duty of the parents of children who are unable to send them to school to strain every point to teach those boys and girls not only to work but to read, read and think. If we are to go on in progress, we must make men of our boys, men who think while they work.

A true friend to the Alliance and *Mercury,*

Moral and religious rhetoric

18.   May 10, 1888. Gonzales County. Mrs. C. H. Swann.

EDITOR MERCURY: I concluded to write you a few thoughts. I am a member of the noble order. You will do as you see proper with this. I hope it will not be lost. God prosper the Alliance; may we yet see a grand rally to victory and be independent. In God's dealing with men, his first purpose is to prepare them for happiness in the world to come. But we are likewise assured that he desires his children to enjoy the present world. The life we now live is so short and insignificant when compared with the great eternity before us that if it were necessary to forego the happiness of either, it would be far better to suffer now and rejoice hereafter. It is not necessary, however, that either should be one of torment. . . . The same renewal of nature that prepares us to die prepares us to live. . . . It is the privilege of every Christian to enjoy a state of perfect contentment while on Earth and it is likewise his duty. We sometimes feel that it is impossible to be fully reconciled to our surroundings and that contentment should not be expected nor required. . . . Contentment is the inevitable result of an equity of demand and supply. Whatever the desire of the heart perfectly corresponds with the available sources of gratification, we are satisfied. Hence it may be said that contentment is complete harmony existing between man and his surroundings. It is possible for every man to attain that harmony. This may be done in two ways, by increasing the supply or decreasing the demand—by supplying our wants or removing our wants, though it cannot always be accomplished without a severe struggle. . . . It is wonderful to what extent our personal feelings influence judgement. The lazy farmer is very apt to think that too much hoeing is not good for corn or cotton. The lazy preacher is very apt to think too much study ruins his sermons, and the lazy church member will generally tell you that it is not conducive to spiritual growth to attend preaching twice of Sunday. This is not true. . . . Success to the *Mercury* and the Alliance.

    Yours fraternally,

Growing political consciousness

19.   May 10, 1888. McKinney Alliance, Luling, Texas. Aunt Slow and Easy.

EDITOR MERCURY: Will you please admit another one of the frailer sex into your chosen circle, since you admit ladies. Now, Mr. Editor, I am not going to discuss the things of state like our noble leaders. It is raining today, part of us are gone, myself and smaller ones are alone. I have not got a fresh *Mercury* to read. Now my sister, let's have a little talk. I just like Aunt Huldey's letter splendid. It is very elevating to read such letters. Come again in the near future, H. We who have a house full of little ones and an empty purse know how hard it is to get off and when I tell you I have been in the Alliance but once this year, you will not rebuke me but sympathize. I am very much opposed to Congress allowing pensions to Mrs. Logan or Mrs. anybody else just because their husband figured largely in public. Our big men in congress and senate have done enough to rob the poor farmer and congress would tax our poor, half-fed and thinly-clad farmers to pay these pensions while our farmers' wives [who] are left helpless with large families to support and perhaps no home, are passed completely by with silent contempt; only the tax assessor and collector gives them notice if they have anything they can tax. Now sisters when we go to the store, let's get that which will go the farthest and wear better. I pray God to strengthen them, give them courage and enable them to stick together and take turns and pull for shore—that bright, shining shore; have the Bible for their way-bill, the Savior for their guide and they will anchor by and by.

And let's have singing in our Alliance meetings, and have the ladies and gentlemen read essays and perhaps that will encourage all to read more and perhaps as they become better posted there will be greater strength in our order. Let's gain all the information we can, strengthen our order, stand by our leader, beat down every obstacle, put confidence in our chosen ones so when victory is won it will be ours as well. Let's have truth, honor, justice, and charity for our leader, and join in the cry, "hallelujah." May God speed the day when this war cry will be over and done with the immigration plank, and let us all get homes in our sunny South and not be crowded out by the vast tide of immigration, a good many of whom are like the very worst class, and some are worthy people and will help to build up.

Well, Mr. Editor, this is enough to put in the basket for this time but if it should escape it perhaps it will induce someone to write who is better posted on what our Alliance is doing. Come out from the corners, brothers and sisters, those of you who can wield the pen, do all you can, and it might be more than we are aware of. I am not a subscriber but will be one just as soon as I get the money. At present a good brother furnishes us the paper regularly every week and I do assure you it is a rare treat for which we are truly thankful.

I will close by wishing all success to the *Mercury* and long may it wave to carry the glad tidings to the masses. Adieu,

Morale boosting

20.   May 10, 1888. Morris County. [Name obliterated.]

EDITOR MERCURY: I have been solicited by several brethren of the Alliance at County Line to write something for the *Mercury*. As no one as yet has written, I will say something in regard to our lodge. We number between sixty and seventy members. All bear a countenance of content-ment and are willing to work as we see the good that has already been done by our efforts. The plundered plowmen are now feeling the strength of this great restorer. I call them plundered because we have been plundered of all that we have made for many years by the monopolizing merchants.

Monopoly has had a long turn at the grab game but many will soon be at the plow handles, or make up a club of tramps. Some are selling now at cost. We regret that any Alliance member will trade with them no matter how low they settle. Such as do we call two-bit members.

But we have some of the right material and we hope ere long they will learn cooperation, and trade only through the Alliance. The most of our sisters are slow to turn out at our meetings but I think County Line is as near up as any of the sub-Alliances around here.

I hope some one will be stimulated to write a better letter than I am able to write.

Yours fraternally,

Morale boosting

21.   May 10, 1888. White House, Texas. Beula M.

EDITOR MERCURY: Seeing no letters from this portion of the coun-try, I will write a few lines to let the world know we are not dead, not expecting to say anything that will be of any interest or benefit to the public.

We have a well organized Alliance at this place of something over one hundred members, of which I am a member. Everything is moving along smoothly with us. Now, my sister friends, what do we belong to the Alli-ance for? To go and be in the fashion because we hear others talk about being in the Alliance? No, it should be the good intention of every member to work for the interest of the farming class of people, who have been and will be so greatly oppressed. And unless we, each and every one, put our shoulder to the wheel—which will be hard to turn—we can not accomplish anything, but will turn back and say we are a poor, no-account class of people, and can do nothing. Now; we must not expect to do it all at one time. We will have to go slow. Now, kind sisters, we must not be idle and say there is nothing in the work for us to do. We must be active and do well our part by industry and economy around our homes, and not run our fathers and brothers in debt for things we can make at home or do without; for you all fully realize the great need of something being done for this cause. I am young and have not had much experience but I can see a great deal for us to do to fulfill our duty; but I am afraid if some of our members don't take more interest in this high and noble aim, that small will be our profit. Sometimes it looks like they want to keep themselves and their lodge a secret from the world. They must be ashamed to own they are farmers. But if you are farmers, be true to yourselves and friends and use all the pluck and energy you possess to gain the victory. I do feel a great interest in this cause but will admit we have not done our duty through the past. . . . Well, I had better stop, this time, for fear somebody will think I am saying too much for my ability and trust some of the more intelligent brothers or sisters will be ashamed of this weak letter and write something that will . . . [letter obliterated].

Alliance building

22.   May 17, 1888. Waco, McLennan County. Farmer's Daughter.

EDITOR MERCURY: As we have not received but two copies of the *Mercury*, and I did not see an article from any of the sisters and brethren of Concord Alliance, No. 912, I have concluded to write a few lines and let you know that we are not quite dead. I am glad to say that our lodge is getting along splendidly. Our Alliance is on a boom.

Brother Reed gave us a splendid lecture last Wednesday night and there was a very good congregation out to hear him. The brethren also formed a Union Labor Club of about thirty members.*

Our lodge has voted the two dollar assessment and I think it is a very good thing. We have some as good Alliance men in our lodge as I know of and I can't see why some of the brethren don't write to the *Mercury* and tell how our lodge is progressing for the weather has been so bad, the

---

ladies couldn't attend as regularly as the brethren therefore cannot tell much about our lodge as some of the brethren who attend regularly. I think the reason they have not written is for want of confidence in themselves. I have never seen the brethren more wide-awake to their interests, for we have been slaves long enough for the rich, and I hope to see the day when we will be free; and now we see a way out, let us all pull together and we will succeed after awhile . . . but we must not be in too big a hurry, for we all know that haste makes waste.

I have been a member of the Alliance for over a year, also my father and two of my brothers. As this is my first attempt for the press, I will close, for fear of the waste basket which I expect would be the best place for it but if I see this in print I may write again. Success to the *Mercury*. Fraternally yours,

*Another early third-party effort, which collapsed in 1888.

Alliance building; love of education

23.   May 17, 1888. Grandview, Johnson County. Lula Thompson.

EDITOR MERCURY: Here comes another farmer's daughter to join the innumerable caravan, called the "Sisters of the Alliance." Though quite young and inexperienced in the art of letter writing (especially of this nature), I am resolved to do the best I can, which is all anyone can do. We all have an influence either for good or evil, and I sincerely hope what little influence I may have in this noble cause will be for the better. And believing it is the duty of every woman to develop the power God has given her, and to fulfill her destiny as best she can, I will try to get my pen in action and distribute what little news there may be from this part of the Alliance world. I, myself, am not a member, but expect to be at an early date. My father is a member and the secretary of Peville Alliance, No. 351, being secretary of the same. There are but few of us as yet, only 25 in number, I believe, but growing some yet, and I hope it will continue until this glorious new cause shall be victorious.

I am only sixteen and the eldest of six children. I have been attending school at Hope Institute, Italy, Texas, for the past three years, but circumstances prevented me from attending this year. I love my books, never tire of devouring their contents. I often while away the weary hours by reading and rereading the pages of some favorite study which brings back to me the dear familiar faces of old—I speak of my classmates; these that seem dearer to me than all others. How I would enjoy another bright season with them! I know the hours I spent in study there, were and are still the most pleasant I have ever known. I love dear old Italy for the sweet recollections thereof. I will ever point to her as the model school of intelligence and learning.

Perhaps when we have gained the victory over our many oppressors, I will be able to go back to the dear old spot. If it be too late for me, I have brothers and sisters whom I want to be noble, intelligent young men and women; and I am satisfied that more hearts than mine would be made glad at the thought.

I expect I have already trespassed on your patience long enough for the first time so I will close and write again if I see this in print.

Success to the *Mercury* and its readers.

Publishing anxieties; Alliance building

24.   May 17, 1888. Henderson, Rusk County. Mrs. S. E. Redwise.

EDITOR MERCURY: At the last meeting of our Alliance I was appointed to write a letter for the Ladies' Department of our paper. It is with a great deal of embarrassment that I attempt to write this letter, for I feel my incompetency in trying to entertain the many readers of our valuable paper; but however I will do the best I can. It is not my disposition to say I can't. When I go into anything it is with my whole heart and soul, and I intend to perform every duty the Alliance sees fit to put upon me to the best of my ability. I think the Alliance the grandest institution on earth, except the church. It has done more for the laboring people than any other organization in existence, or that has ever existed.

The Alliance is a power in the land and if we will but be true to our noble order we can remove all oppression and then we will be a free, prosperous and independent people.

Mt. Vernon Alliance has a membership of about sixty. Some have fallen by the wayside, but their places are being filled by truer men and women who I think will stand up for the Alliance to the end. Newer members are coming all the time; there were five initiated at our last meeting. Perfect peace and harmony prevails throughout our Alliance and the members all seem to be more interested than ever before.

Our county Alliance met on the 5th of April at Antioch with full attendance. The ladies were all there and had dinner on the ground. It was a nice one, too. We have a cooperative store in Henderson, and it is just booming, doing more business than two or three stores put together, although the merchants have put their goods down to almost nothing. I understand there is one firm who say they don't intend to make anything on their goods this year; that they are going to break down the Alliance. I expect they would like to break it down but [I] think it will take them a long time to do it; by that time they will have starved to death and it wouldn't profit them much if they were to accomplish what they so much desire. But I tell you, there is no danger; the people are sticking right square up to their store with a few exceptions.

Now, in conclusion, I will say to the sisters, attend every meeting of your Alliance. If you become disinterested you need not expect your brothers, fathers and husband to be very much interested.

Success to the *Mercury* and to its many readers.

The "emigration boom"; the need to economize

25.   May 17, 1888. Limestone County. Fannie Kerley.

EDITOR MERCURY: I have been for some time desirous to join the sisters in asking a small space in the columns of your most excellent and highly esteemed paper but seeing that you were crowded, have deferred until the present.

My husband, myself and six children, three sons and three daughters, all belong to the grand and ennobling Alliance and each owns a stock of from three to five dollars in the cotton yard. We are opposed to the "emigration boom."* The Shiloh Alliance to which we belong has grown rapidly. It now numbers over one hundred with accessions at every meeting. We all read the *Mercury* and are highly delighted with it. I have seen but two letters in your paper from the Shiloh sisters at which I am somewhat surprised as we have some among us who are eminently qualified.

I have just returned from Galveston Bay. While in Chambers County, I met a number of good Alliance people; and by the way, I learned a good lesson in economy which I think is worth trying. It is how to make four pounds of coffee go as far as eight: Take four pounds of potatoes chopped fine and dried, mix with an equal quantity of coffee, parch together, and the oldest Texan cannot detect the difference. And now, sisters, let us all lend a hand and see if we can't help our husbands and sons out of the fearful bondage in which we have suffered ourselves to be placed, as slaves to the mercantile class. May God help us unite and stand steadfast while time endures. Your sincere friend and well-wisher.

We tried potatoes alone from '61 to '64.—ED.

Presumably a reference to southern and eastern European immigrants arriving during the 1880s. Organized labor and the Know-Nothing movement opposed these "foreign" influences.

Economizing

26.   May 17, 1888. Round Pound Alliance, Rusk County. Eddie.

EDITOR MERCURY: The ladies in this section of Rusk County are very timid in regard to the Farmers' Alliance. I have never written anything for publication but other sisters writing in the *Mercury* from different places, induces me to write too.

I have been living in this community for about four months during which time I have not attended the Alliance but once. My mother and myself are members of the Alliance, which numbers about forty or fifty members in good standing and I think we are blessed with a reasonable portion of intelligence.

We can be the most independent people in the world if we will only try. First, we must economize. If we want to accomplish anything, raise everything that we can at home, wear old clothes and keep out of debt. I like the principles of the Alliance and hope it may continue its onward march until the farmers all over the land can shout "Victory." Yours in truth.

First mention of Frances Willard, advocate of temperance and suffrage; first letter from Ann Other

27.   May 31, 1888. Ennis, Texas. Ann Other.

WHERE SHALL WE LOOK FOR HELP?

EDITOR MERCURY: As we are searching for facts on this subject, and I sincerely believe that none of us are writing for argument's sake, let us look candidly on the matter and sift each point, and try to give fair and unprejudiced opinion on the arguments. . . . Now, Sister Rebeca *[sic]*, you say, "The whiskey ring in the territories may have been broken by the absence of so large a per cent of negro voters." Now, we well know the negro population in our northern territories is a very small per cent, and has but very little effect upon politics, and even if not, would not have been the same before the women voted that it was since, or vice versa. Again you say, "If all women were good women, and would vote, then the new element injected into the life of our nation would have a salutary effect."

Now, must we conclude from this that the majority of women are bad, or is anywhere near the majority bad? Is there even one tenth part of the women in America bad? If not, how will the element of bad women hurt our ballot as long as the majority rules? Or are we to conclude, we who have come to the conclusion that ourselves and children could be better protected by our having a voice in the laws that govern us, as a majority are bad women? The conclusion must be one or the other. And which ever you cling to, please give me your authority for the conclusion, for I have studied deeply on this question from impartial writers before I adopted my present standpoint, and if I have been misinformed, I am anxious to know it.

Yes. "Well did Byron understand it," for if you had looked the world over, you could not have found a poet whose history gives a more intimate knowledge of that class of woman.

You class the decline of patriotism with the rise of the popularity of universal suffrage and "woman neglecting her duty in her proper sphere." Now will someone kindly tell me what is her proper sphere? I have always heard the expression, but have failed to locate it by any series of studies I have taken up. I am obliged to conclude it is whatever the state of society dictates to her.

Men have intruded and wrestled from her what were formerly her legitimate occupations. And her present effort is only to recover a useful sphere in life by those who have become weary for others to do that which God intended she should do for herself.

Women used to be our bakers, brewers, dry-salters, butter-makers, cooks, dressmakers, cheese-makers, confectioners, jam and jelly makers, pickle makers, soap makers, spinners, weavers, sock makers, lace makers, embroiders, and midwives. Thus crowded out of her old fields of labor by men's intrusion and invention, she must either accept a life of idleness, and be satisfied with such as her brothers see proper to give her, or she must demand a more useful and energetic life. The woman in idleness naturally loses the bright vigor of her mind, and a "scheming mama" must look for an "eligible partie" for her daughters, for society in its present state has so limited her sphere of usefulness in life that there is nothing left for her to do but marry, and the mother knowing there is no comfort or happiness in the married life without an eligible partie, naturally aspires to that.

But when society becomes enough advanced in marking the bounds of woman's sphere to give her the untrammeled right to write her name as high on the book of fame in any sphere her tastes dictate, as her brothers, then we will see mothers having higher aspirations for their daughters than marriage only as it may come by the dictates of their own lofty sentiments.

Yes, I am aware that the W.C.T.U. has the suffrage plank a movable plank, but when our leaders are boldly advocating it, what effect will those who cling to their shirts* [sic] and cry against it have but to slightly impede its progress in that one direction?

Have you not seen Frances E. Willard's address before the senate committee?** For fear you have not, I will quote a little from it: "I suppose these honorable gentlemen think that we women want the earth, when we only want one half of it. Our brethren have encroached upon the sphere of women. They have very definitely marked out that sphere and then they have proceeded with their incursions by the power of invention, so that we women, full of vigor and full of desire to be active and useful and to react upon the world around us, finding our industries largely gone, have been obliged to seek out new territory and to preempt from the sphere of our brothers, as it was popularly supposed to be, some of the territory that they have hitherto considered their own. So we think it will be very desirable indeed that you should let us lend a hand in their affairs of government." It is said that if women are given the right to vote, it will prevent their being womanly; how it is a sentiment of chivalry in some good men that hinders them from giving us the ballot. They think we should not be lacking in womanliness of character, which we most certainly wish to preserve but we believe that history proves they have retained that womanliness, and if we can only make men believe that, the ballot will just come along sailing like a ship with the wind beating every sail.

Again see her [Willard's] letter in *Union Signal* to the Kansas women urging them to let no false modesty keep them from registering and voting, as now the eyes of the world were upon them, to see if women would exercise the right of franchise if they had it.

"It is inconceivable to me why some women, simply because they do not wish to vote, should clamor so loud against giving the right to those who do, as there would be nothing compelling any to vote who did not think they could benefit the laws by doing so."

You "fear that men will lose their respect for women who assemble with them at the ballot box." Now I think those men who could think less of a woman because she took a judicious interest in the laws of her country would not be worth the while to mourn over; whether they respected her or not they would be obliged to respect her laws. When you hear men talking of women losing men's esteem by using the highest and most sacred right of an American citizen, you can rest assured that his esteem is not worth having. . . . If you are obliged to associate with all whom you meet at the polls, do not go there, for your soul is just as liable to be contaminated as mine.

I have written these few thoughts from a sick-bed. I do not think anyone can do justice to their subject when the physical machinery is out of repair but I do hope you will candidly consider the few thoughts I have tried to sketch out for you. Your loving friend,

*This typographical error embarrassed Ann Other, and she comments on it in letter #43.

**On April 2, 1888, members of the National Woman Suffrage Association spoke before the Senate Committee on Woman Suffrage. Among them were Susan B. Anthony, Julia Ward Howe, and Frances E. Willard.

An out-of-state letter; A separate sphere; early antisuffrage sentiment; the beginnings of mutuality; the importance of education

28.   May 31, 1888. Ruston, Louisiana. Charitie.

A HELPMEET WE SHOULD BE

Perfect contentment, as far as it is possible for mankind to attain, is only found in those pursuits which by nature and circumstances, we are best suited. If it is true man will find contentment in his home where he is surrounded by happy hearts and smiling faces, when he would fail to find it in the whirl and excitement of public life, where personal integrity and self-respect are so often forfeited in the fierce struggle for place, how much truer is it when applied to woman?

Man, in his hardy, rugged nature and strong physical frame is better fitted to meet the opposition and overcome the difficulties that all must, to a greater or less degree, encounter than is woman. It is a question if the muddy stream of immorality, that at present pollutes and tarnishes our social, and especially our political structure, will be purified by the admission of women to the right of the ballot box. I have given the subject very little thought until recently; our laws need to be refined, but how?

In this day of political corruption even pure-minded and high-toned men distain *[sic]* to approach those by-ways that lead to disputes, dissensions and sometimes to dishonor, feeling themselves above mingling with a class of persons that they would blush to number among their acquaintances. Can a woman be brought in close and constant contact with so much evil and not be defiled? If men shun politics because they are an abomination, how much more would necessarily the good, the true, the noble and unselfish woman shun them as they would a dangerous and loathsome disease? We all know there are corrupt women as well as men and these would flock into politics by the thousands, and this would promote the evil, inasmuch as it is a peculiar quality of human nature that it can be more easily influenced for evil than for good. It is not a question simply of intelligent, thinking women, but implies the whole female element with its joint influence for good and evil. The opinions, which some hold, that only certain classes will avail themselves of their franchise, seems to be not well considered. Has not woman already duties, cares and responsibilities sufficient, that she should voluntarily bend her back to another burden? Already they crowd upon us too thick and fast for us to waste our time. There are homes we must make happy; our own erring husbands and sons to redeem; want, misery, despair and crime are calling upon us everywhere. The question is, can we help by going to the ballot box?

Woman has been the dependent one for centuries; why has it been so? Civilization and custom have shown that she can compete with man in the highest branches of science and art, and [it] is but justice to say that her power is acknowledged. I think every woman should have the right to maintain herself, and the right to be independent.

It is to the Alliance and Farmers Unions we should look for help; let us beseech them to help us equip ourselves against the real hardships of adversity. Business education and instruction in some occupation or mechanical art, our girls could be instructed in, by which, should there come a reverse of fortune, they could maintain their own independence. There, then would be fewer spiritless, subdued, snubbed female hangers-on, and fewer still of the unhappy hapless sort.

To teach our girls printing, telegraphy, shorthand writing and other light arts should be considered the parents' actual duty to their daughters, more binding upon them than such training for their sons. Let us be a helpmeet; together make a home, each bearing their portions of toil and pain and sorrow; but let us not usurp the duties of the sterner sex without their consent. Just laws can be enacted by good men for dependent and helpless women, without necessitating them to step forth from their own sphere to enact them.

My better half is more in favor of woman suffrage than I am. This world may grow better by our farmers' organizations. "The mills of the gods grind slowly but exceeding true," and perhaps they are on the grist now and if the time ever came when our brothers can with pride offer us the right of voting, then we can accept it with honor. Until then, let us improve ourselves mentally and morally, and we shall do our duty, and our brothers then will be proud to have us help them.

Sister Rebecca, your ideas and mine are the same. Let us give the hours devoted to politics to the moral training of our children. How foolish in any of us to exchange this crown of gold—our influence over man—for the questionable honors of sharing with them political rights and privileges.

Birdie, I imagine how you look, bright and saucy; am I right? I never have met any of you, only through the magic of pen pictures. How much I would prize an album with each one of your pictures in it. Can you all not send me one? How nice it would be, and how much I would prize it you would never know. I will ever remain,

An alliance between farmers and organized labor; mention of the Know-Nothings

29. June 7, 1888. Essay reprinted in the Mercury's "General Correspondence" section after being read at the Wood County Alliance, Winsboro, Texas. Annie Mims.

Dear brothers of this grand and noble order, the Alliance: I feel that I must send you greetings and wish you grow and strengthen each day in this great and good work.

I am but a woman yet women have an influence, as you all well know, as in that little affair about the apple and as women of all ages and conditions of life contributed to man's happiness, so man might assist in all enterprises for good and reform. I need not tell you I am Alliance, prohibitionist, greenbacker and know-nothing.* I also believe in woman's rights as far as suffrage, and as woman has the credit of leading to the fall, when she is granted the right of suffrage, she will assist in uplifting and reinstating you; and women who constitute the best and purest part of this government, should have the right to make the laws under which we live. I think it is time for woman to assert her rights, as I fear nothing short of the ballot box with woman suffrage will lift us from the oppression of class legislation, monopolies, and trust combinations. Look at the condition of our government. What has become of our glorious old bird of liberty whose notes of welcome could be heard from the coast of Maine to the golden sands of California, inviting the oppressed of every clime to take shelter under her outstretched wings in this free land of ours? Alas, free no longer. Uncle Sam is throttled, and, like Prometheus, chained to the barren rock, the shylocks, vulture-like, eating the beast daily, and the old eagle dead drunk can only croak monopoly; and the whisky traffic has put us in the fix. What Herculean power can or will cut the chains that thus bind this government and place the proud eagle on its perch again? Let me answer, the Farmers' Alliance can do it, with, if need be, the assistance of other labor organizations. . . . There remains little of the original timber in the old ship of state. It now behooves the Alliance in behalf of the suffering, starving crew to board and man the once proud old vessel and with a long pull, a strong pull and a pull all together, drag her from the dirty stagnant waters and launch her on the smooth, silvery waves of tranquillity, where she can harbor in peace and prosperity beneath the banner of a free and united brotherhood and a free American republic. . . . Jeffersonian democracy cannot exist in this age of pooling and combined swindling. I have taken my last democrat quietus and say, down with monopolies, trust companies, and bank associations. . . .

An anti-immigration movement which sought to elect only native Americans to office and to require twenty-five years of residence for citizenship.

Morale boosting

30.   June 7, 1888. Lavaca County. Ida H.

EDITOR MERCURY: If you will allow me space in your valuable paper, I will write a few words. I am a member of Seclusion Alliance. We are getting along very well but would like to do better. I am a regular reader of the *Mercury* (my father being a subscriber), and I see a great many nice letters from the sisters but very few from the sisters of our Alliance. It makes my heart glad to see the wives and daughters of the oppressed farmers cheering them even with their presence in their struggle for relief from the burden to which we have hitherto been slaves. I feel myself too weak for anything more than to offer words of encouragement. I think the farmers have been in bondage to monopoly long enough and if they will only stick together and ask the Great One to aid them in this grand cause then success will be ours before long. I believe the farmers should be the most independent of mankind. What can be more pleasant than a nice country home? I agree with some of our sisters and brothers in regard to living within our means. I believe we should all try to make ourselves as comfortable as our means will admit but to be comfortable does not mean for us to be extravagant in our wishes. As an old adage has it, contentment is the secret of success. Let us try to be contented. Farmers, if you have children growing up in ignorance, send them to school and teach them the value of an education and how to appropriate it. Teach them to have and to crave knowledge. They can never be cheated out of that. Teach them the principles of the Alliance. Educate young girls that they may be independent. Educate young boys that they may do the work assigned to them through life, intelligently.

I wish some of the sisters and brothers of the order would write to the *Mercury* who are more competent than I am. Respectfully,

Prohibition

31.   June 7, 1888. County Line Alliance. Mrs. Frank Sloan.

AN OLD WOMAN'S WORDS

EDITOR MERCURY: I thought my little might, perhaps, would encourage some of the sisters of this Alliance to write, as I have not seen one letter from any of them.

I am a member of the County Line Alliance but not having an opportunity of attending regularly I cannot say much about it. Being a farmer's daughter I feel a deep interest in the grand cause which is now being agitated by the farmers. . . . The ruling principle in the character of our Savior was going about doing good. I think if the brothers and sisters continue working faithfully, we shall yet come out on the right side. I feel that the hand of God is in this noble work; that the cries of the poor and the oppressed have reached the ear of the Lord of hosts.

Oh, sisters, there is work for us to do. I am going to work for prohibition, the Alliance, and for Jesus as long as I live, and I will try and stay out of debt. We could do without some things if we would think so.

We have prospects for a good crop this year; let us try not and owe it all to the merchants. I have seen the time when women worked and made what they wore and we had more leisure and pleasure and better health than we have now. . . .

Moralizing and advice

32.   June 7, 1888. Marion County. Rebecca.

PEACE, HARMONY AND UNITY OF ACTION

EDITOR MERCURY: The subject of this feeble attempt has in it the essential elements of our success. We certainly cannot expect to succeed if we allow ourselves to waste valuable time in envious fault-finding or jealous bickering and strife, the source of which is individual spite. Suppose we do harbor "some like snakes within our walls that the black slime of slander betray them as they crawl," what does it matter? Shall we degrade ourselves in answering in kind? No, we will pass it by in peace and wait for "time, which at last, sets all things even," and make them in their "leprosy of mind" "as loathsome to themselves as to mankind." We will in kindness pass by it for, "Is it worth while to jostle a brother/ bearing his load on the rough road of life?/Is it worth while that we jeer at each other/ in blackness of heart, that we war to the knife?" When we have our meeting, if there be differences of opinion on any subject of importance, let us have full and free discussion giving each who wish it the opportunity to ventilate his views, thus helping each other to more clearly understand the subject before us. Let us harmonize to the fullest extent possible in our business workings. If we vote co-operation, we must cooperate. Or if we trade by the contract system, let us stick to our contract until the other party breaks it. We should not promise our trade to one man under certain conditions and when so far as we know, those conditions are being complied with, huff ourselves up and sail off under the wing of some little two-bit merchant who may offer us some special types of goods at a lower rate than our house offers. Be assured that when they have caught you, you will pay for the whistle. I know what I'm talking about. It is part of the merchant's scheme to get us disorganized for they well know if they can sow dissension in our ranks and destroy our unity, it is only a matter of time when we will be the slaves we once were. . . . [she gives examples of a merchant overcharging farmers] . . . I know one who kept a store in a little town near here and has been known to swear to the purchaser of certain articles that he was only making ten per cent on articles sold and no sooner did the customer leave, remarked in the presence of bystanders, "There went an article for fourteen dollars that cost me just seven." So we see it's not for love or philanthropy that the merchants are sore troubling themselves; but to get us dissatisfied with the Alliance. . . . Yours, till we get there.

Morale boosting; trying to understand the system; racial sentiments

33.   June 14, 1888. Belton, Bell County. Annea Yarbrough.

EDITOR MERCURY: I am only a girl in my teens. I have belonged to the Alliance about eighteen months and am a constant reader of the *Mercury*. I see from the different writers that we have not attained to that proficiency in education that is necessary for a unity of action, which to my mind, is the only road to success. I believe the Farmers' Alliance has pluck, energy and liberality enough to succeed in a reformation of our laws and let all laws protect alike our fellowman, and we will proceed as soon as competent to relieve the people of unjust burdens.

I see some of the correspondents think that our political parties are all corrupt. I hope they don't mean by that that Mr. Mills, Coke and Reagan are not good men.* It is true that I did wish to could choke Mr. Mills on a cold potato or stop his mouth some other way when he was round here making big anti-prohibition speeches, but when I read about how hard he has tried to reduce taxes I feel rather proud of him. Don't you suppose that if our government was run by such men as Mills, Coke and Reagan, they would take the tariff off the necessaries of life and also change our national banking system?* I heard Mr. Mills say several years ago that he was opposed to national banks. Would not they regulate railroad charges? It seems to me that some of our officers did try to get a bill through congress some years ago to that effect. Now these are some of the evils that we have been complaining of. Let us not abuse those who have labored for our interest.

Perhaps I am getting into politics too much for one of my age and sex, but I see woman's rights are being discussed so if I had to vote I would want to know what I was voting for. My opinion is there are a great many men as well as women who should not vote.

When we the youth of our country [are] educated, we have a board of examiners to test the competency of the teachers and should have; but when we have officers to elect, to whom the safety of our whole nation depends, the most ignorant Negro, whose vote could be bought for a glass of beer, is perfectly acceptable.

Mr. Editor, I will close for fear I render myself odious on so short an acquaintancy. I am respectfully yours,

Roger Q. Mills, U.S. congressman from Texas; Richard Coke and John H. Reagan, U.S. senators from Texas.

The first letter from Bettie Gay; economizing; morale boosting; the Exchange

34.   June 14, 1888. Columbus. B. G. [Bettie Gay].

EDITOR MERCURY: This is the third time I have written to the *Mercury,* and if this goes the way of Uncle Snort's wagon load of letters, all right.

I see in the *Houston Post* of May 24 inst., that speculation in cotton, sugar and coffee, is checked on account of indifference of buyers. So far as sugar and coffee are concerned, it would cause a greater indifference if all the laboring people were to resolve to do without it till it could be bought at living prices. Several of the counties have passed resolutions to do without coffee till they can buy at twelve and a half cents per pound, but that will not do any good unless the whole Alliance gets into it. We tried to get our county to adopt resolutions to the same effect, but there were many who thought they couldn't live without. How did they do during the war without it? Did anyone die from want of it? I am an old Texian, have been here since '39, am able to buy coffee, but for the benefit of the millions of slaves, I am willing to do without until it can be bought by everyone. When you send your delegate to the state convention in August, try and get them to get the whole state to adopt such resolutions. If we go as a unit, we can accomplish anything.

I see a letter from a sister M. A. Crier of Kingsbury, advising the sisters to return to the spinning wheel and loom.* I am in sympathy with every economical move, but I differ from the sister, widely. In the first place, it is killing on any one to card and weave. I speak from experience, for we had to do it during the war. It will take three days to weave one yard of cloth; at twenty-five cents per day, it would cost seventy-five cents per yard to spin and weave a yard, besides the expense of the machinery, so you see there is no economy. It would be more healthful to raise a cotton patch, work in the open air and buy calico or muslin for five cents per yard. You would have more and play half the time; besides one pound of cotton will make five yards or more of goods and you might drudge your life out and not accomplish anything unless the men will unite and vote in a solid body of men who will represent our interests. You might spin, weave and work until you would faint by the roadside and the evil would be the same.

I saw some sister writing about dress making. Anyone can make a full skirt, with body or redingot, and we as farmers do not care to put on style till our independence is declared. What should we care for style? If we are not able to buy fashionable bonnets or hats, get a nice piece of gingham and make a neat bonnet. They are very becoming.

Our Exchange and manufactories are our salvation; let us work to save them and go without styles and luxuries except what we can raise at home.

I have a splendid garden, I believe I can beat Janie without any help. We are going to have a picnic on the 7th of July; everyone who has an interest in the Alliance, come and let us have good speakers and have a good lesson learned us, not all fun but business too. It is good for young

Bettie Gay at her home in Columbus, Texas. Courtesy Beth B. Nolen

people to talk of fun, but older ones have things more serious to think of. Too much rain, crops are not so good; hope to make good cotton crops so we can help in every enterprise.

Letter not found.

Alliance and religious rhetoric

35.   June 14, 1888. Armstrong, Erath County. Mrs. Louisa Crowder.

WORDS OF ENCOURAGEMENT

EDITOR MERCURY: The Alliance movement is not a mere local affair. Its interest strikes through all the working nation. There are some who say the Alliance movement will not go on; that it is a sentimental affair. The Alliance movement will go on. Point me a reform that ever stopped. Why reform is a motion ceaselessly acted upon by the impulse of acceleration. So it is with the Alliance movement. From whatever standpoint you look at it, it is seen to be in exact harmony with the age. Nay, it is a part of the age itself. The great civil revolution is to be supplemented with a great social revolution. God has so written it down; he has blessed the efforts of its friends until it has already taken a hold on the popular heart. Its champions are no sentimentalists, only terribly earnest. Back of them are memories which will not let them pause—impoverished circles and mortgaged homes. The cold sodden ashes of the once genial fires urge them on. . . . No man or combination of men can stop this labor move. Its cause lies deep as human feelings itself. It draws its current from sources embedded in the very fastnesses of man's nature.

The Alliance movement will go on because its principles are correct and its progress beneficent. The wave which has been gathering force and volume for many years will continue because the hand of the Lord is under and back of it. And the denunciations of its opponents and the bribed eloquence of the unprincipled can't check nor retard its onward movement. Upon the white crest of it thousands will be lifted to virtue and honor, and thousands more who are before it will be submerged and swept away. The crisis through which this movement is passing will do good. It will make known its friends and unmask its foes. The concussions above and around us will purify the atmosphere; and when the clouds have parted and melted away we shall breathe purer air and behold sunnier skies. We know not what is ahead; what desertions of apparent friends may occur; what temporary defeat we may have to bear nor against what intrigues we may be called upon to guard. I count on the opposition of parties; I antici-pate the double dealing of political leaders. We more than once may be betrayed into the hands of our foes; more than once be deserted by those who owe it . . . But no good cause can ever be lost by the faithlessness of the unfaithful; no true principles of government overthrown by the op-position of its enemies, nor the progress of any reform, sanctioned by God and prompted by human want. . . . Over hundreds of proud empires the Gospel of Christ has marched, treading banners and emblems of ri-valry proudly under its feet. . . . On this rock I plant my feet and from this elevation contemplate the future as a traveler gazes upon a landscape waving in golden-headed fruitfulness underneath the azure of a cloud-less sky. Our cause is right; our principles are good. God is ever with the right.

Brothers and sisters, stand firm to your post of duty and fear nothing. It is only a question of time when victory will crown our efforts. Yours fraternally.

A response to Sally Beck's letter of May 3, 1888.
36.   June 14, 1888. Grayson County. Marie Labouchere.

A CHATTY, READABLE LETTER

EDITOR MERCURY: This is the first time I have attempted to enter these columns since my zeal was dampened and my sensitive pen nearly paralyzed by the resignation of our former patient and obliging editor. The valedictory, February 9, was the most unexpected of all the unexpected surprises to me. I have summoned courage to come now in response to sister Lena's kind inquiries, May 3, concerning my insignificant self and I wish her to know that I appreciate the very encouraging compliment she was good enough to bestow upon my previous humble but faithful efforts to entertain the readers of this wonderful paper.

Miss Sally's [Beck's] pleasant little sallies on poor me caused a little amusement in La'chere family. Her allusions, whether sincere or ironical, to my "pleasurable life with abundance of leisure," must seem very absurd to those who are familiar with farm life and its innumerable responsibilities. We who are the workers know it to be one ceaseless enervating race with time, which favors none, but outrides the indolent and improvident.

True to Miss Beck's guess, we did not attend the circus last fall; nor have I been inside such canvas since I was a modest and extremely bashful young girl and then I fainted "dead away" on seeing the clown divesting himself of his garments. I was so afraid the fellow had gone crazy and would not know just when to desist. I am really ashamed of this silly reminiscence and wish Miss Sally Beck had not reminded me of a circus.

The reading of "Mother Childhood" suggested to one of the members of our family the singing of that once popular and still favorite melody "Rock Me to Sleep, Mother." So one evening last week, daughter Maria placed the singing book on the table as we sat in our unpretentious sitting room and in less than a minute we all had our parts. Mr. La'chere gave us the pitch and then lowered his voice to bass and off we went. The youngsters all chimed in most harmoniously and even little Tot hummed himself to sleep in the cradle. There was pathos in all their voices and a spiritual expression settled on the features of all which told of the happy impression being made on each memory, to be pleasantly recalled, perhaps, years from now. There was a foolish and trifling incident occurred in connection with this family concern which brings a blush to my face as I recall it, for it lowered me so in my own estimation as I always had a horror of being considered superstitious. The facts are as follows. During the rendering of the concluding chorus I became so weak that I could have been tipped over with a straw while I remained silent to listen to a ghostly accompaniment which I felt could only have been performed on my dear old dead grandfather's Scotch bagpipes. Mr. La'chere heard it too and noticed with apprehension the extreme pallor of my countenance; he opened the door immediately and outside stood, not the ghost of my grandfather with his musical instrument, but old lady and gentlemen Spry, our next neighbors, whose broken voices were the supposed bagpipes as the dear old souls tried to echo the song we were singing, Mr. Spry's cracked tones being an exact imitation of the "drone" and his wife's shrill squeak furnished the "chanter" of the old-fashioned instrument to perfection.

I was in a cold perspiration and La'chere placed the cap on the climax by whispering in my ear, "you dear old superstitious somebody."

I will say in conclusion that wherever this paper is taken and appreciated, there is no grumbling over work done in that home for the young folks have always something pleasant to think and to chat about. Thus it is, without a doubt, that the mental appetites of our children are prevented from becoming morbid by the wholesome and truly invigorating tonic abundantly supplied by the farmer's true friend, the distinguished *Mercury*. Yours,

Alliance rhetoric; morale boosting

37.   June 14, 1888. Southland Springs. Eunice Whitby.

EDITOR MERCURY: I have just finished reading the *Mercury* of the 24th inst. and feel thoroughly aroused in the interest of our noble order. And I believe that the hardest battle of the whole campaign is just ahead, and that we, as Alliance women, must constitute the power behind the throne, and arm our brethren for the battle by strengthening their breast-plate of faith in the order by our encouragement, and keep our motto ever before them, for in union there is strength.

The grand crisis of success or failure has been hastened by the convulsions of the desperate monster, monopoly, and if he is defeated now the victory is ours forever, but if we succumb we may expect to be enthralled in chains more galling than those which bind the galley slave. Since literal chains are not to be compared to the fettered pinions of an aspiring mind, and if this battle is lost, every standard will be gauged by the scale of dollars, and merit, virtue, truth and justice must all bow down before the "golden eagle"; then, liberty, veil thy pitying face and weep, that thy children's unavailing cries are raised in supplication to thee and thou art thyself powerless to help them. But I will not believe that we can fail! Let the world say what it will, but there is a moral strength among our Alliance leaders which has been fostered by the hardships and privations, and matured by the necessities of these troubled times, which all monopolies of the world cannot entirely overthrow, and although they may thwart their designs for a time, they will rise from the fiery ordeal with tenfold the strength of former times and lead their followers on to victory and peace. . . .

Humor; allusion to *Pilgrim's Progress;* domestic arts

38.   June 21, 1888. [No location.] Sallie Beck.

EFFECT OF SAVORY DISHES

EDITOR MERCURY: Being an "old maid," perhaps I have no right to criticize but I generally do a little of it when I have a chance.

What puzzles me is that Western Reader should object to Farmer Claiborne [another *Mercury* writer] making a cookbook out of the *Southern Mercury*. It is evident that Farmer Claiborne is a very wise man and he must understand, judging by the way he writes, that a man's soul is in his stomach and human misery will be apt to disappear with good cooking. To cook well, to compound savory and toothsome dishes with French economy and French skill, is a useful art and it is my humble opinion that Farmer Claiborne understands the idea. How can farmers or any other people study politics, or anything indeed, while suffering and wrestling with the gloomy horrors of dyspepsia. If the prohibitionists would open cooking schools at every cross road, neighborhood, post office and meeting house, they might find them less costly and more comforting than butting heads against heart-of-oak planks, and finally see the saloons gradually close for want of patronage. The preachers too would . . . quit their dismal croaking about the "bad place," chiefly painting the joys and delights of Heaven. I have already called Widow Skinner's attention to that, for whenever Parson Smallsoul eats Sunday dinner here which he does quite often, though he only eats from a sense of duty, yet he loves to do his duty, then his night sermon is all about the blessings of life and the joys of Heaven. I really believe if Parson Smallsoul boarded here and were kept chock full of good soup, roast and fried chicken, apple dumplings, chocolate cake, jams and jellies, cream and home-made pickles, he would never preach any more about the fires of hell nor the glories of Heaven. The other night Widow Skinner's married daughter (who is visiting here) was playing "Last Hope" on the piano for some friends. I went in to hand some refreshments and overheard the son-in-law in a growling tone say to Parson Smallsoul: "I wish her mother had spent some money in teaching her to perform on the cookstove instead of confining her accomplishments to the piano."

And so it is, girls, you may be beautiful as Cleopatra, learned in Greek and Latin, poetry, German, metaphysics and French philosophy, dance like a sylph, sing like a Patti, radiant with grace and amiability, understand how to sew on buttons so they can't come off, and to embroider holes in well-worn socks, yet, if you know not the mysteries of making English plum pudding and French puff paste, you are counted as utterly insignificant, unworthy to share the high destinies of the lordly voter. It is highly probable that men fed on sodden bread and watery turnips are capable of wife-beating and conspiracies against even the democratic government of the present day. Doubtless Farmer Claiborne is the author of that pithy maxim, "No people can be better educated than fed," and he proves himself a genuine reformer when he insists that the farmers learn how to make good preserves and good bread and cakes before they try to digest such stuff as politics, having learned from experience that the latter, no matter how ethical and fresh, is innutritious and not near so soul-inspiring as light puffy fritters, temptingly helpless in a sea of amber honey. A savory dinner will make the most saturnine counterpart of our Creator smile graciously. Flattery may capture the weaker vessel but an apple pie is sure to entrap the lords of creation.

A nation's civilization, it is said, can be judged by the bread it eats. Liberty bread is light, spongy, untaxed and nutritious and the songs of the cooks while making it are cheerful, inspiriting as if flowing from plucky hearts. This bread always rises and is always a brown success. The heavy, black bread of the protected Russian peasant, mixed in tears and weariness, kneaded in hopeless sadness and despondency, suggests the cruel, despairing bondage of those who subsist on it. Tortillas engender monthly revolutions as our child-loving neighbors, the Mexicans, will testify. The French, who are pioneers in every sense of the word, are the true disciples of Lucullus and it is these artists, great as scientists, as soldiers, as statesmen, as social reformers, that Farmer Claiborne desires you farmers to become like, the first effort toward attainment being a practical study of good receipts.

Anger; economizing

39.   June 21, 1888. Eagle Cove, Callahan County. A True Friend.

EDITOR MERCURY: I have put off writing to the *Mercury* for a long time but when I read so many letters from the sisters crying economy to the farmer's wife, I am bound to say something.

Sisters, why don't you preach economy to one who has the power to economize? One sisters says, let us help our husbands by patching old clothes and make them last another year. We have been in the habit of patching as long as we could make things respectable. Another sister says, let us make over our old clothes. We have been in the habit of doing this also. And by the way, we have sold butter and eggs to buy the dye to color them and for a while in the spring, we got fifteen and twenty cents per pound for butter, but very soon they began to say, "We can't give but ten or twelve cents." Now that is poor encouragement for we are at the cow-pen late at night, and work our butter every morning to have it nice.

Now a farmer's wife has a heart and wants to see her family look nice at least once a week to go to church, and if one has a flopped hat and another a patch on the knee and a third has his toes out, must we still economize and work so hard all week that we can't enjoy the sermon on Sunday?

I think the Alliance is to help the oppressed as who is more oppressed than the farmer's wife? Now, if some good sister can tell us how to keep our house neat and clean without so much hard work, so when our husbands come in we will not be too tired to talk and can have more patience to teach our children, I think most of them would appreciate this, much more.

Dear Sisters, let us try to help one another. My husband takes the *Mercury* and we all enjoy reading it very much. We both belong to the Alliance and think it is a grand and noble order. I will close for fear some one will condemn the farmer's wife for putting things in their true light.

Second letter from Ann Other; allegorical writing

40.   June 21, 1888. Ennis. Ann Other.

FEVER FANCIES

'Tis strange what one's brain takes on in a fevered condition of the system, and sometimes I think then the mind looks deeper and strikes truths closer

Milking time. Courtesy Library of Congress

than when in a healthy condition and surrounded by the natural work of life which diverts the mind and divides it among many trifles. . . .

As I lay a few days back in this condition, I all at once became impressed that I must join a long caravan that was filing past, for I thought they had some great objective for good in view. All were traveling in a straight line, one team directly behind another as far as the eye could reach like one steady stream. The wagon in which I was seated was going along with the others, and after what seemed like years to me, I began to see the road was terribly rutty, so much so that it seemed to require all our united strength to pull out of one rut only to drop into another, and while some were blaming the road, most were employed in making those following believe it was the best road ever conceived, and the only safe road, for say they, pointing to the millions who have travelled the same road ahead of them, "They all travel this road and look at the multitude in the rear who are following directly in our footsteps. . . . "

And thus we worked and toiled, never daring to dream there was any other way, till finally someone stopped and drew straight out of the line and took a side track, as it were, where there was no marked track at all, but still pointing in the same direction, working for the same goal. This solitary driver had the audacity to break from the old line and do his own pioneering. We of the old road shook our heads and croaked all sorts of warnings, but he only cracked his whip and trotted on, leaving us way in the rear. . . . But finally we are dismayed to see others pulling out of the old ruts we had travelled so long in spite of all our warning; their road is so much smoother than ours we cannot help but acknowledge they get along better, and attain the goal for which they started much sooner than we, but still we cannot help believing some great calamity will surely overtake them; "progress cannot be made in such rapid strides. . . . "

Our side track is becoming so much more populous that we do not know what will become of the old road if we abandon it, so we remain, giving fair warning to others to not leave the old beaten ruts of thought and work.

But finally there comes a halt in our line, and we do not know what is the matter; we work harder than ever before, but we are making no progress, and word is sent backward and forward with the swift command and entreaty of anxiety to keep moving, the goal will be reached if you only keep steadily praying and talking; but someone says, "There is no progress being made, there must be something wrong in the front," when here comes back one of our sidetrackers who says, "I told you that old road was worn out long years ago and ought to be abandoned, it is full of ruts that expend all your strength to pull from one only to fall more deeply into another without perceptibly advancing. The teams of your leaders are in ruts to the hub. Why don't you try some other route and move forward?" At which I and thousands of others cry: "What! Get on that dreadful side track? No, oh no; I will trust to my good influence to reach the goal without soiling my hands with the work, it is too vile for us, you must do it for us."

And then noble men come forward from the sidetrackers and say: "We need you, there is a certain class who 'influence' will not touch but wholesome laws only can reach; we need your help, get out of the ruts and help the others out." While many accepted the invitation, I, with many many others, dare not the risk and still cling to the old train with all its drawbacks of ruts and slow progress, or no progress, and as we look dubiously ahead to see if there is a ray of hope, we see the front teams so deep down in the ruts that we can only see the mule cars of the leaders as they wag their warning to the clamoring crowd of sidetrackers and as my fever passed away, I wondered if it was to illustrate reform. Yours Very Truly,

Strong antisuffrage rhetoric

41.   June 21, 1888. Harmony Ridge. Rural Widow.

EDITOR MERCURY: Sisters Ann Other and Charitie have sounded the alarm and I will add my mite. To vote or not to vote, that is the question for our womanly consideration, eh, Ann Other? The air is full of prophecy that is voiced by the spirit of the times. Sisters, I profess no skill in exegesis, but is this not what the spirit saith, "Woman will vote?" Hasten slowly to the dawning, of, faithful *dies irae,* black with woman's doom! But when, oh, prophetic time spirit, when will women be degraded to political factorship? Hark, yo! my sisters, and rejoice with Rural Widow that the evil day is not yet. When? Not until patriotism is a blear-eyed, palsied dodard; not until the republic is sick unto death with party strife as internecine in mutual hatred as that which cursed Dante's Florence in Guelph and Ghibeline days; when the freemen of equal strength—the giants democrat and republican—have exhausted the ballot armory of its weapons, the strongest ever made for weal or woe, preparatory for the last desperate struggle for the supremacy, the one over the other, then will women be thought of seriously as a weight, the last expedient, to throw into the scales politic, to counter the equipoise of factional strength; then will woman, alas!, poor woman! be in demand as a voting machine; as an engine of political warfare, a missile thrower to be employed by Sir Cavalier or any Lord Puritan in the emergency, requiring more votes than the men can vote, for the annihilation of one party with the aggrandizement of the other; and then, with flourish of trumpets shall woman, the woman of the discontented, strong-minded masses, wearing the mock crown and robe of purple, be escorted in triumph to the polls by one or the other of the cyclopean factions to cast her vote in favor of the one which, as a coup d'etat, will have procured for her the right (?) of franchise. "And is this the only meaning the ages past have taught," that pseudo-American progress, grown mightier than Jehovah, can make woman man's equal in the state? Is this the end, the bitter, bitter end to be attained before the perfection of statecraft be reached? Faugh! O, Juggernaut progress! Turn backwards the ever-whirling blazing wheel. Take us back! Take us back to the childish pagan days when woman was a pretty plaything; soulless, it is true, but harmless, rather than lead to the very Christian era when woman shall be man's equal.

But I forgot. Progress does not retrograde, so they say, but continues to move onward and upward, flying as the wings of morning to the full and perfect day. Then swift and ever-gracious progress, as a specimen of thy wondrous handicraft, first make man woman's equal in the state. Ha! I snap my womanly fingers in thy face with exultation, thou striped, so distant progress, and say what is known without the telling, that you cannot do it. Neither can woman ever be man's equal; for the Creator intended them to remain unequal, incomparable. What shall be the reward of the faction of the future? . . . Will the hydra-headed monstrosity, the would-be men reformatory sisterhood, who are now growing hoarse with demanding it as a natural right, bless him and hail him as a deliverer from bondage? Yes, and he will have another exceeding great reward. The consciousness that, for self-aggrandizement, he will have bartered manhood, degraded womanhood, destroyed the home sanctuary and set at defiance God's laws.

. . . I cannot bear to think of the national shame with the iconoclasm of all that is pure and beautiful, that will befall our republic when women become a political factor? Better an oligarchy; better no government at all than that of a republic without homes and home-keepers. Say I, better, far better for the woman of the "solid South" to preserve silence than vote after men at the ballot-box. Women without the right of franchise cast the mightiest vote for good is a truism we all know full well.

We the keepers of our beloved Southland, sheltered by the strong walls of God-blessed homes, do we realize the evil that will come with the downfall of woman's so-called emancipation day? Already the taxation of humanity aggregates the income of surplus resources, and when the dollar policrats are heaped upon the head of overstocked feminine poverty, [indiscernible] . . . will be worn destitute of red borders, and empty-stomached children will become the advertisers' medium of domestic economy.

Suballiance report; publishing anxiety

42.   June 21, 1888. Anderson County. Dailie Brown.

EDITOR MERCURY: I have been reading the *Mercury*, and not having seen anything from Oldham Alliance, I thought I would write a few lines. I am by no means a good writer, so you will see, but "where there is a will there is always a way."

We have an Alliance here of about thirty members, and more coming in. I hope it is doing good work. . . . The farmers here have a big smile on their faces over the beautiful prospects of a good crop; and if they continue, many an orison will go above thanking our Heavenly Father for what He has done for us. We have not the richest food but we are thankful that we have plenty to eat and good health to enjoy it. Our valley, known as Beaver Valley, is supplied with neat church houses; we have good meetings and a public school well attended. Our Alliance meetings are well attended and are, indeed, very interesting. We meet once each month, Saturday before the first Sunday. We have voted the Exchange assessment, but all have not paid yet, but will as soon as possible.

I must not close without stating that Bro. Helcher, lecturer, was with us on the 9th inst., and gave us some good advice. He is delivering a series of lectures to the various sub-Alliances in our county, and it is to be hoped his efforts will beget much interest in our order.

Now, Mr. Editor, I beg you and the brothers and sisters not to criticize this too closely.

Prosuffrage; religious hypocrisy

43.   June 28, 1888. Ennis. Ann Other.

CHANGES

EDITOR MERCURY: Alas! alas! What small things create a great change. Now, dear *Mercury*, you know the sisters have already classed me outside

---

of the "good," "the true," and "unselfish," and with the "bold and clammoring," and now, alas! I fear you have caused them to also put immodesty with my category of sins; and in imagination I see sister Rebecca laying down the paper with a firm resolve to never again read one of sister Ann's letters until she's convinced her "leprosy of mind" is cured; and sister Charitie and others are blushing behind their handerkchiefs and sisters who have been kind enough to come to my help, are wishing they had remained silent: And all because your type-setter substituted an 'h' in the word skirt in my article of May 31st. But 'tis said mistakes occur in the best of families, and I suppose printers are no exception to the general rule. 'Tis said that the Prince of Wales, when being banqueted in the city of New York, made sixteen breaches of etiquette (I wonder how much the one ate who kept tallie). One of his mistakes is said to have been his thanking a servant for passing him some article. I suppose he thought he would introduce a change and we, as laborers, and the "sovereign" would be very thankful if our "servants" would do something for us that we could be thankful for. We would like to try to change.

Sister Charitie speaks of some men who disdain the priviledge of ballot, because of corruption in politics. I confess she has found a specie of the human family I have never seen, so let's have their portrait in the *Mercury* for a change; although I will acknowledge I have my fears for the vigor of their minds. From the *Oak Cliff Weekly* I take the following: "Twenty years ago women could not vote anywhere, today they have full suffrage in Washington and Wyoming territory; municipal suffrage in Kansas (single women and widows), England, Scotland, Ontario and Nova Scotia; and school suffrage in these fourteen of the United States: New Hampshire, Vermont, Massachusetts, Colorado, Nebraska, Minnesota, Kentucky, Indiana, Michigan, Oregon, and Wisconsin."

I addressed, a short time ago, a letter to Mrs. M. S. Salter, of Argonia City, Kansas, who I suppose the sisters all know was the first woman mayor ever known. She is the daughter of a lawyer and a man of much prominence in his time, I have heard. I asked her several questions in regard to woman suffrage in Kansas, and for the benefit of the sisters I will give a portion of her letter. To the question, do a majority of the women vote, she says: "Yes, a majority vote and they are the very best of society; true some of the disreputable also vote—don't the men do the same? Men are more careful in the selection of the officers for they know we vote in such affairs for the best men who will help us protect our homes. Woman as a voter is the same as ever. We feel we have more freedom, we feel we have a few rights but boldness is not ours only to ask for full and equal suffrage. Our polls are respectable places with no loitering or peddling of tickets within fifty feet of the polls. Our women come with their husbands, fathers, lovers or other friends, each casts her little slip, gives her name and passes out. Insults have been rare, if any. I myself presided over a council composed of men bitterly opposed to woman's suffrage. The meetings were public but seldom any one came in, and often my husband was absent; the meetings would sometimes last two hours or more. They have been very courteous, kind, true, noble and whole-hearted."

Are our southern men less courteous or noble-hearted? I think not. As to some objecting to suffrage because they think it incapacitates her for returning to her household duties, I would say the day Mrs. Salter wrote me, she had been washing, and says she has seven boarders and four children, and says she does all her own work with the assistance of a little girl twelve years old. Now I would ask if the burden of office at six hundred per year is any greater than keeping boarders and doing all your own work. If politics are corrupt, what is the matter with our churches that our great Methodist conference refused to seat the lady delegates sent? Is it, too, too corrupt for women? How think you all noble womanhood ought to feel to know that Miss Francis Willard and other ladies like her, had the door shut in their face while they saw admitted sixty colored brethren, one Chinaman, several Germans and Scandinavians and other European delegates? While our noble American women were refused admittance and then to add insult to injury, one minister took up his text, "Behold the enemy cometh in like a flood, but I will raise up a standard against him," meaning her. When church debts are to be paid or minister's salaries to be raised, then the ministers think there is no harm in woman's counsel and woman's energetic work but when it comes to admitting women delegates they fear this may prove a stepping stone to the pulpit and thus the salaries of men and they are frowned down. It looks to me that this is a direct violation of the "Golden Rule" and the teachings of Christ.

Sister Charitie says she thinks the theory of only a certain class of woman voting not well founded. I know it has no foundation and no one claims it but those opposed to suffrage. I challenge anyone to bring up statistics to show that more bad or ignorant women vote than the intelligent and I would suggest that until you can substantiate that theory it be laid on the table. I would say to Sister Charitie you are in advance of where I was when I first began to study suffrage for I am free to confess that then I thought women's only ambition should be to read the latest novels, work green dogs with pink eyes on cardboard and other ornamental (?) work, keep her house and children clean and healthy and "always meet your husband with a smile" but now I am satisfied that with suffrage, she can benefit her country, keep her own womanly traits and have more just laws for herself and better protection for her children.

You say, "there are homes we must make happy, our own erring husbands and sons to reclaim." I know of no better way than to make laws to put temptation out of the reach of erring sons; and alas! dear sister, you seem to think that every sister in the union has a home, a husband and son. 'Tis strange to me that some women never seem to realize that all are not as pleasantly situated as themselves.

Now, according to our statistics we have 888,208 more females than males in the United States, so how is it possible for all to have homes to make happy or husbands wither to reclaim or not? And if you will cast your eyes around you, I dare say you will find bachelors, old maids and widows, thus proving there must be even more single women than these figures show. Who are the most likely to work for their interests, themselves or the husbands, and sons of their neighbors? As an instance I saw in a Chicago paper last year that on one street there had been voted a tax of $14,000 to put in waterworks on that street and on investigation it was found two-thirds of the property belonged to women, consequently not voters. Where were your good men in acting just laws for women then? You speak of our educating our girls; how many of our colleges in the Union are supported or aided by direct tax, think you, will admit our daughters within their walls if they knock for admittance, remembering woman's property is taxed just the same as man's for this purpose? . . . I could quote enough instances of these "just laws" to fill two columns of the *Mercury* and not be half done. Don't worry about our "usurping the duties of the sterner sex without their consent." They have the power and there is no danger of taking it without their consent. Yours very truly,

Prohibition; prosuffrage; suballiance report

44. June 28, 1888. Greer County. Mary M.

EDITOR MERCURY: As I have never seen a letter from this part of the country, I thought I would give you a few hints from Fair View Alliance of which I am a member, and I hope a good one.

The Alliance met in a mass meeting on the first day of June for the purpose of making resolutions that they will do all in their power to uphold the Exchange against monopoly. Several took shares in the Exchange and some were against it; of course there must be some drones among so many working bees. We had a nice lecture from Professor Nie, a worthy member of the Alliance, and also from Brother Simpson, our lecturer in Fair View Alliance.

I have been reading sister Ann Other's letters and I think they're splendid. I can't understand why some are so opposed to us ladies voting. One good sister thinks it would be a downfall to the female sex to go there among so many grades of people. Well, have we not got all kinds of people in our country and do we have to stop and shake hands with them and tell them we are on their side? No Sir, God forbid all such. If a true-hearted man, or woman, goes to the ballot box with a thousand bad persons, I don't see that will hurt them for I know a good heart will have no dealings with them. Where would whiskey have gone if women had been allowed to vote? There would not have been a drop of whisky now in existence. I have got a house full of children who will be left sometime, in this troublesome world, to work for themselves and I know that [if] by me casting a vote that would make the laws of this country better, I would surely vote.

Alliance building; prosuffrage

45.   June 28, 1888. Gribble Spring Alliance, Denton County. Ann Too.

EDITOR MERCURY: As I've seen nothing from our lodge, I thought I would write and see if it would not stir up some more able members. We have got one of the best lodges in the country. It is said to number somewhere between seventy-five and eighty with petitions coming in all the time. We've got some of as good material as can be found anywhere, and some, I am sorry to say, that are afraid of everything and everybody; they seem to think just to have their names on the roll and to pay their quarterly dues is all that is needed. It seems that they had rather see the Alliance with all her enterprises sink than invest five cents that they thought they might not get full virtue for. I have often heard it said that a man that suspects everyone else of being stingy was far too stingy himself; but while I admit this to be true in some cases, I don't take any of it myself, for if I was as well able to take stock in our county Exchange as some of them, I would not let the women come up with me; but some don't care for being behind.

I have just been reading the lady correspondence of April 26.* Sister

Rosa Lee talks to suit me: I think it is a bad thing to say that the ladies have not got as much sense as the negroes, when one half of them can't read or write, and it seems absurd to me that voting would make a woman rough or forgetful of her duty at home. I don't believe I would forget to wash the children on election day, or forget that I was a woman either, and as for going to the bar and taking a drink, I know I would not do that for I don't love the stuff and if I had any say I would do away with it. It seems that Rebecca would have us think there are more bad women than good ones. She says there are corrupt women as well as men; then the vote would not be materially changed, leaving the impression that she thinks good women are in the minority. Speaking for my neighborhood, I don't think we have many women who could be bought for a drink of whiskey but can't say about the men. I am going to defend my sex the best I can. I say like what Mary Ussery says, we have a hard time anyhow; don't throw any obstacles in each others way. I have said enough for the first time. With good wishes to all, I subscribe myself,

A missing issue.

Antisuffrage; the corruption of public places; the black vote

46.   June 28, 1888. Jefferson, Texas. Rebecca.

EDITOR MERCURY: As a rule women are not such logical reasoners, or their arguments so conspicuously convincing, that they would wish to parade them forth merely for argument's sake. In trying to meet Sister Ann Other's able essay, I have no object but to arrive at the truth of the matter, "whether women should or should not vote." At present, I of course, firmly believe in, and steadily uphold the negative side of the question; but as all persons of truth and right should be, I am still open for conviction. So far I have endeavored to weigh both sides carefully, and not launch forth an assertion which could not be substantiated. Yet, my sister, you seem to insinuate that, according to the natural laws of gravity, my positions maintained in a former letter have, one by one, sought a common center; your overwhelming arguments, the agency, of course, by which my false (?) propositions were removed. But hold, I am not quite ready to yield the position I have assumed. I still contend that the whisky ring in the territories may have been broken by the fact that there was perhaps a majority of intelligent upright voters and not having to contend with the negro voters as we did here in our late defeat. I believe the results in those territories would, taking into consideration the popularity of the temperance movement there, have been the same, leaving out the women's votes, and the results here, unchanged had women's votes been counted in. The negro voters, hugging to their bosoms the personal liberty dodge, the vile hangers-on of saloons, with their attendant train of evils (and their women no doubt followed in their wake), was what defeated the measure with us, and not the absence of female suffrage. As I have before stated, whether or not women be allowed to vote, our laws would presumably remain unchanged. I still affirm if all women were good women, and would vote, we of course could have reason to expect a better political state. . . .

Now please withhold your vials of wrath while I reassert that there are corrupt women as well as men and will further affirm that women are neither mentally nor morally stronger than men . . . if they are exposed to the same corrupting influences of political vice and intrigue, might we not reasonably conclude that there would be as large a percent of corrupt women as of men? Corrupt, politically, to the extent that their votes could be bought and sold; and in voting for men or measures, their own selfish aims a consideration rather than the good of the masses or the welfare of the country. Reasoning from the above standpoints led me to assert, that the popular vote would not be materially changed, were we to be allowed a voice in the affairs of state. . . .

Female suffragists harp upon the string, that we need not become intimately associated with the "low and vulgar herd," at the polls. Admit that, but would our ladylike deportment and modest refinement which you say we could preserve through it all intact—protect us from the low and scheming aspirant for office, who sets forth upon his electioneering tour reeking with the fumes of bad whisky and vile cigars? Would he not, as he was wont to do among the people whose votes he meant to secure, introduce himself familiarly into our very presence, and talking by the hour, force us to listen to perhaps blasphemous vituperations of the opposing candidate, and perhaps wind up by offering a cigar or a drink of the "very best"—revolting thought. The idea has gone abroad that should we vote, our womanliness would be destroyed; and too many who had not an overpowering burden of respect for womankind before would be but too ready to take advantage of our position and treat us with a disrespect that under our present social system is disallowed, by all chivalrous gentlemen. But you no doubt suppose that when I read your cutting criticism of Byron, that I would refrain from mentioning him again, but not so. Byron was a bad man and was, I suppose, intimately associated with the vices of his day. But the grave faults by which he was characterized were largely due to the influence of early training by a mother who was incapacitated, as a true mother, because of her own ungovernable temper and want of firmness. A knowledge of the fact that his own mother was weak and also vicious may have warped his judgement a little; and then that vile creature to which I referred before, who, with her malicious schemes, succeeded in driving his wife from him. Is it a small wonder that he gave vent to his feelings with a bitterness that has rarely been excelled? But if you are acquainted with his writings, you are bound to admit he knew something of woman in her better aspects. Read but his Marino Faliero and see therein his grand conceptions of true womanly devotion and chastity, as well as the character of the young wife of the Doge of Venice. In the tragedy of Sardanapalus, note the exalted character with which he endows "Marsha," the Roman slave, who chose rather to die with her lord and master, weak and effeminate though he was, than to survive his disgraceful death. . . .

Take Shakespeare, if you wish, among whose heroines we find some of the most exalted conceptions of female character; yet he could create a Lady Macbeth whose unholy ambition (I think she wanted female suffrage) caused her to suggest and help execute the murder of her king, and which ambition finally resulted in the ruin of herself and the overthrow of her family. Thus it is often the case when a woman obtrudes herself beyond her legitimate sphere. It often results in ignominious shame.

But you ask, where is woman's sphere? Is it possible to have let the golden grain of small opportunities slip through your fingers and still sit with empty heart and hands, waiting for universal suffrage before you deign to consider life as worth the living? You profess to have a longing for higher and more exalted attainments, that your sphere be widened. But have a care my sister; Mother Eve conceived the idea that by enlarging her sphere she would be wiser and happier. You know the result; now make the application.

From your position we are led to conclude that we are under more obligations to follow out the dictates of society than we are to carry out the noble aspirations that are planted within us by an allwise Creator. Very well; such things are getting to be old-fashioned and to keep ourselves fully abreast of the times we must allow old things to pass away. But aren't you getting things a little tangled, when further on you assert that it is an evidence of irrationality on the part of mankind to accept custom as dictate of nature? You say men have intruded and wrestled from women her lawful occupations. What an assertion! Never before in this world's history has there been such a field open to women as at the present.

To begin, we find women in the factories and sewing rooms earning as much, perhaps, as she did in lacemaking; we see her attending industrial schools, perfecting herself in the several pursuits that she may successfully compete with her brother in the different channels of trade and industry. In the sales room we find women commanding good salaries; we have women farmers; also our queens of the ranch. I am told that there are plenty of women who are successful real estate brokers. Telegraph operators and bank cashiers of the sex are met with every day. The old groove of midwifery, being the only department for women, has been extended and widened until she may now take a thorough course in any or all of the branches belonging to the medical profession. She may plead law or preach the gospel as she may be induced to teach school or write books quite as successfully as any man; but in spite of all these avenues we are told she is forced to remain in idleness. Oh, woman, thou art indeed "coy, uncertain, hard to please," if with all the inestimable rights there is still a longing for the unattainable and a wasting of time in inexcusable idleness.

I cannot imagine a Mrs. Southworth, a Mrs. Augusta Evans Wilson, a Grace Greenwood, or a Louisa M. Alcott sitting with folded hands, waiting for something to turn up. I do not suppose that Susanna Wesley as she sat rocking her nineteenth baby while teaching her older ones anathematized her life as a failure because the right of franchise had been denied her. No; she knew that in training up her little flock she had the privilege of training immortal souls for a happy eternity and in giving to the world a John Wesley. She accomplished a result for good, no clamor for equal rights, so called, could have ever reached. I hold that, as a rule, intelligent thinking women have higher aspirations for their daughters than to just simply have them married. As a matter of course, should the time come when her daughter is sought in marriage by an honest, intelligent, noble-minded man, it is well; but she is not dependent in such contingency to realize her high hope of her daughter's success in life.

I have not seen Miss Willard's address before the Senate committee but I have no doubt as to its being masterly; yet the greatest of us sometimes make grave mistakes as to what our aim in life should be. As a temperance advocate, I aim every other woman should honor her, but in struggling to obtain female suffrage she is wearing her life away in a struggle for that which, if attained, the wisdom and propriety of same will forever be questioned.

You refer to her letter in the *Union Signal* urging women to vote. The necessity for her urgency is another proof of my position, that women will not all vote. But you say you do not see why we who do not wish to vote should clamor so loudly against it. Well, in a few words, here is the reason. We know some good women. . . . [print obscured] But there are thousands of corrupt women who will always flock to the polls to defeat any measure for good that may be put forth. Thus you see, although unwilling we may be forced to vote no matter how nature abhors it.

Truly yours in all things except suffrage, I am yet,

Morale boosting

47.   July 5, 1888. Shelby County. Lucy Hatcher.

EDITOR MERCURY: At the last meeting of our Alliance I was appointed to write a letter for the Ladies' Department. In trying to write to the many readers of our valuable paper I will do the best I can. It is not my disposition to say I can't, for if a person will never try of course they do not know what they can do. I intend to perform every duty the Alliance sees fit to put upon me to the best of my ability.

I think the Alliance and Exchange the grandest thing the poor people can start if they will just hold out. My father, mother, eldest sister and myself are members of the Pleasant Hill Alliance which has a membership of about thirty-five most all of whom are working members. We are moving along slowly but surely. We have a smart president who always attends to his duties.

We all read the *Mercury* and are highly delighted with it. I have not seen a single letter from our Alliance. I hope this will be published.

May God help us to unite and stand steadfast while time endures. Success to the *Mercury* and Exchange.

Class consciousness; farmer's plight; education

48.   July 5, 1888. Albany, Shackelford County. Justice.

EDITOR MERCURY: I am not a sister in the Alliance but a "looker-on in Venice," and a farmer's daughter. I feel a deep interest in the cause of the "bone and sinew" of our land and hope the day is not far distant when the classes will be compelled to loosen their hold upon the masses. I am glad to see the progress the working man is making. He is no longer content to do all the work and let others do his thinking. He is asking, "Why is it I toil early and late, live on the poorest food, wear the cheapest clothing, only give my children the advantage of the free school, model my house for the least cost and shelter my stock with the heavens; yet after all this close economy, when I have lived my three score years, and am called to join the 'great majority,' I shall perhaps be laid in the potter's field, my children doomed to be hewers of wood and drawers of water and meet the same fate."

Yes, he is turning these and similar questions over, studying nature and the productive capacity of this grand and glorious country. He is now a philosopher and will no longer submit to all oppressions and console himself with the old idea of ill luck, or the decree of Providence. He knows "though he may take the language of prayer it is blasphemy." May he go on in the good work of educating himself and family to think and act for themselves, and thus avoid that undesirable state of affairs that other nations have known when lords and peasants are the only classes.

I hope soon to hear the glad tidings that national banks are no more, the robber tariff a thing of the past, that monopoly and trusts are throttled with a death grip, that liberty, fraternity, and equality are the ruling powers. Then, and not before, will the strikers, rioters, dynamiters, and anarchists, cease to rise up in bloody rebellion against the now ruling power, the "almighty dollar."

I am also glad to see the mothers, wives, and sisters informing themselves on these questions, as the little boy at the mother's knee may learn the true principles of a "government of the people, for the people, and by the people." Home is the grandest field of operations that we should desire, and our sympathy, interest, and understanding will add more strength than a ballot at the polls. We should be contented with the compliment already paid us when it was said: "The hand that rocks the cradle is the hand that rules the world."

Joys of home life; woman's sphere

49.   July 5, 1888. Minden, Rusk County. Allie S.

EDITOR MERCURY: I have been reading the *Mercury* a very short time but I have long been interested in the farmers cause, and, as I know nothing of politics, I will leave that subject to those who are better qualified than myself.

I read a letter from one of our lady correspondents concerning Mother,

Home and Heaven; I thought I would take "home" for my subject. Home! What a world of meaning there is in that little word. When we are absent for weeks or months from the little place we call home, what a consoling thought it is to have one kind voice to welcome us back. That voice is our mother's voice, one that has been dear to us since we can remember. Those who are blessed with good homes and with both father and mother to love should be very thankful for so many of us have only one parent left us, while others have neither, to love. There is probably not a man or woman living who does not feel that the sweetest consolations and best rewards of life are found in the loves and delights of home. . . . Yours truly,

Morale boosting

50.   July 5, 1888. Polk Creek. Aunt Huldy.

EDITOR MERCURY: Are we as sensible to our state of bondage and servitude as the situation demands? I fear not. For we have borne it so long that it has almost become a second nature. We have indulged in a Rip Van Winkle nap of many years and our minds have become so thoroughly impregnated with somnambulistic tendencies that we have almost become indifferent to our condition but the time has come when we must awake from our slumber. . . . Awake! Hear ye not the anvil ringing? Shall we lie supinely on our backs until the enemy shall have bound us hand and foot? Is life so dear or peace so sweet as to be purchased at the price of chains and slavery? No! No! Where the God of day salutes our waking eyes is a little cloud the size of a man's hand and yonder where he bids us a smiling goodnight is another, and yonder, the home of the cruel North wind is still another, and in the South there is another one. They are the homes of the Farmers' Alliance and may they grow and flourish and spread until they join hands and with unity of action descend upon king monopoly and beat back the invading foe to its own domain. Then we will resurrect liberty, justice, and equality which the monopolists have crucified and buried and placed their seal upon their tomb. They will arise at the sound of the Alliance trumpet call, Phoenix-like from their ashes and restore our downtrodden and beloved country to its pristine glory. In ancient times there was a very wicked king who saw that the children of Israel, who he had in bondage, were fruitful and increased abundantly and waxed exceeding mighty, and he said unto his people "Behold! The children of Israel are more and mightier than we, come let us deal wisely with them lest they join unto our enemies and get themselves up out of our land.["] Therefore they set over them taskmasters. But the more they afflicted them, the more they grew and multiplied. And he charged all his people saying "Every son born to the Israelites, ye shall cast into the river." And there was a woman who hid her infant son three months and when she could hide him no longer she made an ark for him and put him by the river's brink. He was rescued from the monsters of the briny deep and reared by the hand of his own mother, under whose care he grew strong. When he came to years of maturity, with the rod of God in his hand, he delivered the people out of their bondage. Now, brothers and sisters, we are in bondage under king monopoly who has set over us taskmasters to afflict us with burdens and make our lives very bitter. But I believe that our cry of oppression has penetrated the azure vault of Heaven and reached the ear of our merciful and compassionate savior, who has sent us a little Moses, in the shape and likeness of the Farmer's Alliance, to affect our release.

Let us be as wise as serpents and as harmless as doves. Let us pray daily for wisdom and knowledge to guard our heaven-born gift from his foes. . . . The more we are afflicted the more may our noble Alliance increase and multiply, and when our infant Moses comes to years of maturity he will lead us up out of our bondage and the sea of monopoly will be cleft in twain by the glorious principles of our order and we will cross over on dry land while our enemies will be submerged by the returning waters.

P.S.—Brother Fat-and-Go-Last, I feel very much flattered by your complimentary remarks and am much pleased with your good opinion of me. I have no daughter but have a niece who answers your discription [sic] perfectly but do not know that she will accept the privileges you so generously offer. H.

Out-of-state letter; prosuffrage; prohibition

51. July 5, 1888. Sault Creek Alliance, Indian Territory. Eva J. Sims.

EDITOR MERCURY: As you have favored me by allowing me space in your paper, I will intrude again.* I see a letter of May the 17th from brother John Goode Hope. He writes my sentiments exactly; it makes me feel so bad to think Congress will give big men's wives immense sums of money when they are really no better than thousands of other poor widows who have to cook, wash, or do anything they can to make a living, and who are taxed partly to raise that large pension for those big men's widows. There is no justice or Christianity in such laws. I do not blame the poor, hard-working class of men for trying to stop these laws while their wives and little ones are not comfortable. I tell you, voting brothers, if I voted I would not vote for a single man who now holds an office. . . . Those we now have, have failed, and I will tell you, they are trying so much to make just such speeches as they think will gain your voice. But take a weak sister's advice and beware. . . .

Now, Sister Ann Other, I wish I could put my thoughts in words as you do for I am of the same belief. Some of the sisters try to make us think it is a disgrace for a woman to vote, but they have failed to do so for I felt like voting last August for the prohibition for I thought if we ever voted for anything, it would be to put down whiskey. I do not feel I was any more disgraced to go to the polls and vote than I would to go to any other big gathering and not half so much as when I attended a circus, for I do not think they are fit for a nice woman to go to. This day and time, women clerk, work in telegraph offices, and a great many other public places and if voting is a disgrace, those places are disgraceful too. . . .

If I could write anything, or do anything to help the Alliance brothers and sisters, I would never tire, but weak thoughts can't be of much value to the cause. Nevertheless, I cannot help saying something.

Previous letter not found.

Suballiance report; economizing

52.   July 5, 1888. Burns Station, DeWitt County. A Farmer's Wife.

EDITOR MERCURY: As I have seen nothing from Burns Station Alliance, I thought I would write a few lines.

This Alliance consists of about sixty-five members. They are all the very best of people but I tell you, Mr. Editor, we need someone to stir us up; we need a good lecturer. We have a very good lecturer in our lodge but what we need is someone like the state lecturer Ben Terrell, whose mind is stored to the brim with information, to rouse us and make us know and feel our duty. I am satisfied that we could do more if a great number of us took your valuable paper but am ashamed to say that I don't think there are but three numbers taken in this Alliance. . . .

The mass meeting of June 9th was well attended and some good was the result. I hear that our little Alliance at Burns Station marched away with the banner, that is to say, contributed more to the Exchange than any other Alliance in the county, which is a great credit to us, for we are most all poor, but honest, hard-working people. . . .

Debt is what is ruining the farmers, preventing us from being independent men and women. Let us shun it as we would the viper. We should practice economy and once getting rid of that tyrant, debt, then we will be able to battle for the cause. We may have to deprive ourselves of many comforts just now, but let us hold fast together for now we can see faint streaks of day dawning and soon we should be able to bask in the midday sun of prosperity. If we do suffer privations, what matters that to us? 'Tis the rising generation we are trying to benefit. Do we not all see that every year it is harder for the poor man to cope with monopolies and corporations of the rich?

We have fine prospects for a crop in this section of the country. Respectfully.

Alliance with labor; moral training of children; woman as helpmate; curse of Eve

53. July 5, 1888. Lavaca. Mrs. M. E. Ussery.

EDITOR MERCURY: I see you have correspondents from many counties in the state but seldom anything appears from Lavacca [sic]county. I know we have as wide-awake, thorough-going Alliancemen as can be found anywhere in the state and all seems to be a unit in everything pertaining to the grand order. All that is lacking to bring about the proper reform is a platform built by a united labor organization big enough and broad enough for all to stand upon. We are oppressed and taxed from the cradle to the grave. For twenty long years, in every stage of this oppression we have petitioned for redress in the most humble terms; our repeated petitions have been answered only by repeated injury; we hold these truths to be self evident—that all men are created equal; that they are endowed by their Creator with certain inalienable rights, that among these are life, liberty and the pursuit of happiness. We have in our order good honest members who belong to different political parties and no member has the right to abuse the party to which he belongs and thus hurt a brother's feelings and cause division and arouse prejudice which we are organized to suppress.

Sister Rebecca, your ideas and mine are the same. Let us give the hours devoted to politics to the moral training of our children; the idea of a refined lady going to the polls is absurd; if our good men can not run the government, I am sure we can not. . . . The true elevation of woman and her restoration to the place she occupied in the beginning is assured to every Christian woman and enables her to aid in restraining vice and correcting evils. Ambition will lead women to neglect wifehood, motherhood and all the nameless graces that adorn women. . . . In women is the strength to overcome evil, strength to endure, strength to resist the enemy of our souls. But for Adam there was not found a help mate for him, and God made woman and brought her to him. Women under condemnation for a violated law must suffer the penalty until she is redeemed from the curse at the resurrection. Our Savior and the angels liberated women. The angel said to the women, "Go tell his disciples that he goeth before you into Galilee." Thus, the glorious news, a Savior is risen, was to be carried to men by women. . . . The prophet Isaiah says, "Behold a king shall reign in righteousness." Then says, "Rise up ye women that are at ease, many days and years ye shall be troubled until the spirit is poured from on high, which took place on the day of Pentecost.["] And now it remains for Christian women everywhere to rise up and do the work of righteousness and fulfill the prophesy of Isaiah. Let us read the *Mercury* and feast upon its precious truths. Four of my family belong to the Alliance—two boys and two girls. . . . I will close by wishing success to the *Mercury* and all.

Example of humor

54.   July 5, 1888. Lavaca. Mrs. Jeremiah.

EDITOR MERCURY: There I dropped my slipper off at the door so as I could slip in without arousing the suspicions of the waste basket keeper. I'll try to get out before he looks up. I don't belong to the Alliance. [Mr.] Jeremiah don't and don't believe in it either and he says if I do "jine," he'll leave me certain. Well, I think it is a good thing anyway and I wish you all success. I don't know that I ever will join for (is it the Bible that says) a house divided against itself, will not stand; and my dear Jeremiah says he can't see the good the Farmers Alliance will ever do. Some of your members say the Alliance is next to the church. Well, I am a strict member of the church; (but Jeremiah don't belong). You see I joined that before he had any claim on me, but bless his dear old red head, he says he's glad I do belong, and I would not have me be any other way than just as I am.

Getting angry

55.   July 5, 1888. Red Oak, Ellis County. Poor Gal.

EDITOR MERCURY: A new one knocking at the door for admittance. Not that I have anything great to say but wish to let you know that there are some living, energetic, push-ahead Alliance people down here; they think and say much; quit their plowing early Saturday at noon, ask their better half to hurry up dinner. She will say, "Why, hubby, what is the matter?" "Oh, the Alliance meets this evening, didn't you know it?" "No, sir, for I don't belong and of course I could not think of anything and go to the mill too."

Now you see how green I am in the mysteries of the order but I will show which side I am on, as the old woman did when she shouldered the broom and started for the army. I feel, see, and hear so much about the downtrodden farmer that I sometimes wish I could finish splitting myself up and make a dozen men out of myself and join the Alliance that many times, and that my tongues were loose at both ends, so that I could cry out, down with monopoly and the middle men! If it came to the worst, I would have fists enough to hit extortion, strike monopoly, punch the middle dude who gets what we ought to have, plug a dart at the cotton buyers, who say, "I will give you seven and a half cents a pound," and punch the ignorant farmer for letting him have it, and with one mighty jump, leap square down on debt, doctors, and lawyers, and there hold them like grim death to a dead nigger, until they were willing to practice for farmers in the neighborhood of living reason. This is written in rather coarse language for the ladies department, but my very soul is stirred and prompts me to say what I have said.

Suballiance report; morale boosting; segregation

56.   July 5, 1888. Austin County. Country Girl

EDITOR MERCURY: I see letters in the *Mercury* from all parts of the United States except from our Alliance, No. 3152, so I thought I would write a little to let you know that we have a small lodge here and Sempronius. We are small in number but great in faith. Our lodge numbers about thirty members. I sincerely hope we will be among the first to shout victory when the time comes.

I was in Bellville on the ninth, and I heard one of the merchants tell an Alliance man that "the Alliance would break, it had to fall." I hope the day is not far distant when we will show him that the Alliance "don't have" to fall. The Alliance man told him that the bankers and merchants were trying to break down the Exchange, but we would show them they could not do it if we had to do "without bacon all next week." I also heard the same merchant speak wrongly of our county president. I hope the day is near when he will be sorry for what he said. He did not know I belonged to the Alliance.

My brother who lives in Nebraska writes me that the Alliance has been started up there. I do hope it will continue to spread until every farmer is a member of our grand organization. I am with [contributor] Bro. John Goode Hope when it comes to making a separate car for the negroes to ride in. I think if the south owned more of the railroads we would have our own way. There was some talk last fall of the Alliance starting a school in every county. Has that idea been abandoned yet? With best wishes to the *Mercury*.

Building the Alliance; class consciousness

57.   July 12, 1888. Denton County. Mrs. Ettie Lee

EDITOR MERCURY: Having been appointed at our last meeting by our worthy president to contribute to our paper, I ask a small space in your columns.

Fairview is situated immediately on the line of Denton and Collin counties, in a beautiful and fertile country, and our lodge is composed of members from both. We were organized something over two years ago with seven charter members and now number fifty with two or three applications at every meeting.

The male members have purchased a thresher and built a gin which they built jointly and run in all harmony. The lady members seem to be taking a great interest in the order and think they will give renewed strength to the cause. . . . It has been said by the merchants that this is the strongest organization that has ever existed among farmers and must be crushed. No. God forbid! By everything we hold dear, let us stand by these principles with so solid a front that the combined world may not break it. Our cause is a just one. . . . And to strengthen our order let us increase the circulation of the *Southern Mercury*. May the day speedily come when we may be able to place the *Mercury* in every toiling hand in the United States. . . .

I think we have some as solid men in our lodge as the world can produce, and our president is the right man in the right place. And sisters, we can be of great help by economizing; to encourage our hard toiling husbands; they have many burdens to bear, and by putting our shoulder to the wheel we will lighten the burden for both. Those great rich bugs think us a poor ignorant class than can't defend ourselves but I presume they will think we are awake to our cause from the way we rallied around the Exchange.

I tell you sometimes I feel like shouldering a musket, if I were a man and need be; but if the Alliance will but stand as a unit, we will gain the day without the musket. For fear of worrying you, I will close although I feel I could write columns without tiring, if I could express myself as I would wish to, but as I can't I will abide my time by thinking.

Education

58.   July 12, 1888. Colorado County. S. L. S. Waelder.

EDITOR MERCURY: I have just finished reading your letters in the *Mercury* which makes me wish to converse with you this afternoon through the medium of our educator. It is not about politics or women's rights but upon a subject of far more importance—the education of our children. To those poor farmers' wives who like myself, have to depend on poorly conducted public schools, or where we have only three or four months school in a year, I would say we can do much toward educating our children at home. But you will say oh, I haven't the time or the patience. Well, I am not celebrated for patience myself and as for time, I have as much as any woman who does all her own work, with a family of six to care for, and yet I should like to tell how I have succeeded as it might encourage some other poor mother to teach her little ones at home. My oldest one is seven years of age and has been learning at odd times, or when I have had time to teach her, about one year and a half, and she is writing and spelling and is ready for a fourth reader. If you will only try for a few months you will be surprised at your success. You will have saved money, and your children will be better able to go on with their studies when they are old enough to attend schools. I have heard people say they did not wish their children to learn more [than] they knew. But why should we deprive our offspring of a thing so essential to their prosperity and happiness? We know that our greatest public men have come from the farm and if we would have justice done the laboring class, our public men must in the future be chosen from among the common people. Let us then prepare our sons to honestly and intelligently fill any position they may in the future be called upon to fill, and our daughters to be useful as well as ornamental. We can do much for ourselves also although the golden hours of youth have fled and some are in the wane of life. Yet by devoting more time to reading and thinking, we may cultivate our intellect and in the course of time we may get our minds beyond the kitchen and the cotton field. Let us all subscribe for and read our paper, for it wields more influence for good, and is the best educator the farmers can obtain. . . . Who would not have their hearts filled with tender feelings and their minds with nobler thoughts after reading Charitie's beautiful words, or who could fail after perusing Marie L.'s contribution, to get about their daily avocations with cheerfulness?

Banks

59.   July 12, 1888. [No location.] Mrs. N. I. Rankin.

EDITOR MERCURY: The tenth plank of the Democratic state platform announces that the Democratic party of Texas is opposed to rechartering United States banks. According to my understanding, there is not a single United States bank in existence and has not been since Jackson vetoed the bill rechartering the U.S. bank in 1832 and withdrew the public money from its keeping in 1833. He said it was a power too great to exist in a free government, for its wealth would become so great that it would buy, bribe and force all legislation, both national and state to act in the interest of the bank which is just what the present banking association has done.

Is not our present banking system a national bank association and not a United States Bank? Am I ignorant or were the delegates to the great Democratic convention ignorant?. . . . Is it not more probable that it is a scheme originated expressly to deceive a trusting people, for they know well enough that Cleveland has never uttered one word against the banks and cares no more for the Democratic platform of Texas than he does for the croaking of a frog in a mill pond, and he dictates, as they well know, all national legislation at present. Everyone knows that the Democrats helped with all their might to give prolonged life to the banks, for did not a majority of Democrats, both in the House and Senate, vote to recharter the national banks? There has been no bill introduced commanding the greatest autocrat of the world, the Secretary of the Treasury, to pay for the bonds which have been due since 1879. Two hundred and fifty million were made payable in 1892 and seven hundred and eighty million were made payable in 1907, unless greenbacks were at par with coin in the market, or, unless bonds bearing the lowest rate of interest were at a par with coin in the market. Both these circumstances took place in 1879 and yet there has been no demand by the democracy of Texas upon their representatives for the payment of these bonds.

Did not the leading members of the convention attempt to mislead the unsuspecting people by using the term, United States bonds, instead of national banking association, hoping to hold by miss-used terms many who were driven from sheer necessity into the ranks of the reform party, which unequivocally condemns the entire banking system. The people are tired of paying fifty millions a year on bonds that are past due and hold our present Congress and President and Secretary (of the Treasury) responsible for the great robbery that is robbing our little ones of every comfort which childhood should know. There is no autocratic power known to civilization as that of the Secretary and he should be impeached for not using that power in the interest of the people, and Cleveland should be impeached for placing such a man in so important a position, and yet the democratic convention attempted to deceive the people by saying they were opposed to rechartering the U.S. banks knowing full well there were no such banks in existence. If my position is true, surely this is sufficient to drive all who are in favor of reform from the ranks of a party which deceives a people and which is supporting a president who, for four years, has never by word or deed shown that his sympathy was with the people.

Support for the Alliance; economizing

60.   July 12, 1888. Williamson County. Virgie.

I have been frequently prompted to write after reading some good letters in your excellent paper, and now after reading Brother R. A. Mitchell's, I will say to him through your paper I can bow to and shake hands with him in thought. A man of his principles can live anywhere.

What have I done? Called this gentleman Brother Mitchell. I am not an Alliance member, nor the daughter of one, but I am in hearty sympathy with them. Through the politeness of a neighbor Alliance member, I have the pleasure sometimes of devouring the sheets of the *Mercury*. I well remember the Farmers' Clubs that used to exist, how diligently they worked to support and uphold the farmer and the many pleasant meetings they had at home and in different states. Then, well do I remember the Grangers when they came thinking themselves a greater and better band than the farmers' club. They had their stay with us for a season. Then mightier than all these came the many Alliances and long may they wave. I have never belonged to any of these societies, though I am in sympathy with them I was a reserve to help. I have kept and quieted the crying babes while their fathers and mothers were attending their meetings. I have baked light bread, old fashioned wheat biscuits, fried crullers, doughnuts and ground coffee and packed the hampers full of good things for them to carry to their little home meetings. I have run entirely away from Bro. M. in the scenes of my county home of long ago. Pardon me and I shall finish my thoughts in Texas.

To Bro. M.: You see, I have emigrated as well as yourself. . . . I agree with the Bro's economy—live inside your means, get out of debt, and then keep out. Cash basis is best for farmers always. . . . Wives and daughters of the farmer, bear with me a little on woman's responsibility in money matters. Very few men have the time or patience to make a shilling go as far as it can, but women have. Especially a woman whose one thought is to save her husband from having greater burdens than he can bear. Surely there can be no greater pain for a loving wife than to see her husband struggling under the weight of family life, worked almost to death, in order to dodge the wolf at the door. All this might have been averted if the wife and daughter had known the real use of money and been able to keep what the husband and father earn. For any income is limited and you must teach yourself to live within it. . . . My thoughts run faster than my pen. I have not yet said what I want in this letter, but fearing the editor would have to call on help to page and chapter this, I shall stop before I'm through.

If, Mr. Editor, you think this letter worthy of space, please publish it.

Love of nature; a booming Alliance; mutuality

61.   July 12, 1888. Corn Hill, Williamson County. Birdie.

EDITOR MERCURY: Although my last communication did not make its appearance in your columns, I will not despair, but will try again. As I am now seated, pen in hand pondering what to write, I hear in the distance the sound of the reaper, reaping the golden grains as now and then a gentle breeze is wafting to my window. Waft on, ye breezes. You are welcome this warm June evening. Oh, these showers, these perpetual showers that cause the farmer to wear a long face now that he is trying to save his grain. It rains, it showers and still it rains. No more do we hear the cry of dry weather.

Once more bright anticipations are filling the farmer's breast of a glorious harvest and successful crops. He walks more briskly, smiles more brightly and holds his head erect. And the young men, oh, they are far more handsome; how bright and cheerful they look when they enter our lodge. I wonder how it is that the girls are smiling. Oh yes, by the way it is leap year; perhaps girls, some of us may make our fortune this year, who knows?

As I look from my window and see the gleam of the golden grain, the wave of the corn, and hear the music of the reaper, I feel we should be thankful. The cool breeze is softly coming and going, laden with the perfume of sweet flowers and the songs of birds. What is so lovely to the eye is nature, with its lofty trees, sparkling waters and carpet of land so verdant and green. God in His majesty and power has made all things complete. Art, thou art beautiful, but in no way can be compared to nature. You come and then vanish, but nature is with us still. The Alliance here is booming, members being initiated every meeting. The ladies are coming in quite briskly, both married and single.

Charitie, I'm glad that you have deigned to recognize me in this family circle. I feel quite complimented by the pen-picture you drew of myself. Yes, I suppose I am hog-bright and indeed I am very saucy. I am also, I am sorry to say, rather fat. So you may call me "fat and saucy." I would like to send you an image of myself to adorn your album and would be delighted to receive one of yourself. Here is the picture in my mind of you: a bright, sweet face with a kind, motherly greeting which speaks of a noble soul and pure heart. . . .

I will now say goodbye, for my last must've found its way to that dreaded wastebasket, and this may be doomed for that same sweet resting place. Kind editor, I now make my bow. Your Poor Birdie.

An example of Alliance history teachings

62.   July 24, 1888. Ennis, Navarro County. Ann Other.

EDITOR MERCURY: Away back in the twilight of time, we see mankind on Earth wandering, obtaining sustenance from such provisions as
nature furnished to their hand, living in caves or wild rocky recesses. . . .
Gradually, we see the advancement in their modes of living; then slowly the
idea of family is developed, which is the first step in civilization and government we can trace. From families we see developed the chieftain or patri-
arch of the family until we reach the light of written history recorded in
Greece. . . .

    To trace government in all its peculiar forms and failures would be too
tedious for these pages. But in the advancement of civilization, the searching back and forth of warlike tribes, there necessarily came a mingling
of ideas and customs that generally work for the advancement of mankind.
. . . We see nations and institutions gradually unfolding[,] passing through
a period of childhood[,] youth, of vigorous organic action and final decay
to give place to those of higher development until we see kingdoms and
republics established, flourish for a time, and advance the people a step
further in civilization until those in power acquire immense wealth to the
oppression of the governed and then begin their crumbling and decay.
Note, for instance, the vast Babylonian Empire, the wealth and energies of
the richest and most popular part of Asia as then known were employed to
build up the great capital and improve the province, a dominion so gorged
with booty wrested from others could not long last. Far back in the dim
twilight of time, Thebes, "the city of a hundred gates" was a colossal capital. Yet before history begins in Greece, Thebes had her youth, her long
period of glory and her almost superhuman palaces had passed their grandeur and crumbled into decay. . . .

    The instinctive and resolute refusal to accept a centralized government
of the Greeks was an important history of man in a civilized or organized
state; it was directly opposite to that of Asiatic and African civilization, and
left the Greek race open to a mental development which made them the
benefactors of the human family. Hence we have our independence of state
government allowing a fostering of the arts never excelled to the present
time. . . . Then by the advancement of civilization westward, we have the
Roman Republic founded by a band of adventurers. . . . But gradually
again, we see wealth creeping into high places, and the descendants of the

first people became the aristocracy and the common people formed a class called the plebes.

When we see with what greed those in high places are grasping the wealth of the nation; when we see vast corporations fostered and protected by the nation; when we see the bonds issued by the nation and bought up by the capital at sixty cents on the dollar and then so protected that the nation has retained no power by which she can pay them off at their face value at such time as it may become convenient, when we see these same bonds now demanding one hundred and twenty-five cents on the dollar of the producing population; when we see this same population stifled and clogged in their efforts to alleviate some of their hardships by this same banking system that our nation is fostering, then it is time for the people to cast their eye on the rise and fall of other governments and see that theirs does not meet the same fate.

As the patronage of the government has increased, the presidents have used it so as to enormously increase the power and prestige of the executive, while the legislative branch has been dwarfed almost to insignificance. When we see our senators voting $250,000 from the public treasury for themselves to visit Paris, it is time the common people inquire how that would benefit the people whom they pretend to represent. When we see them voting to Mrs. Garfield $20,000 of the people's money and then $5,000 per annum besides, it is time to ask how long before we will have the aristocratic title added. . . .

The war is soon to be fought over again against centralization of wealth and power in government, against railroads and all other combinations, a war with ballots, not swords. Where will you fight? Will you do your own thinking or give your oppressors another four years' hold on you? . . . .

Questioning the woman's sphere

63.   July 24, 1888. [No location.] Sallie Beck.

EDITOR MERCURY: Once upon a time a candid representative in our national halls was urged to reply to a caustic attack made on him instead of his pet bull by an opponent. The old man explained that he really could not as it "always strained him to kick against nothing," So I think it would be with Mrs. Ann Other in trying to reply to the . . . opponents of women suffrage. Life is too short to waste any of its precious time in [obliterated] to the strong minded trouser-clads. It is an humble old maid's opinion that it is no greater crime to wish to help manage affairs by casting a vote, bespeckled and blue stockinged, than to aspire to obtain a controlling influence by the aid of soft arms, shy blushing glances and the blandishments of "killing" toilets. The time is past when such rubbish of some of our "egalite" sisters would . . . claim even a moment's attention. Common sense and education, of course, is powerless to prevent such devotees from bowing their soft heads and hearts in enchanting humility before their chosen lords (I am always puzzled to know why any sensible man or woman—(or deity)—wants to be adored or looked up to) but happily will fit the vast majority for a wider range of vision, endow them with logical habits of reflection, discrimination, judgement and administrative ability, a noble and dignified heart, intellect and outward bearing so that in any capacity either as homemakers or assistant homemakers, they will be superior to the shallow-brained, pink-cheeked embryo termagants whose credulity is equal to believing that the moon is made of green cheese if the superior biped called "my husband" only declares it.

An Alliance encampment

64.   July 31, 1888. Americus, Marion County. Mrs. V. A. Taylor.

EDITOR MERCURY: Variety is the spice of life so I concluded this time to send you a short letter describing the events of last Saturday, viewed through the spectacles of an Alliance picnicker (to wit, myself).

First there was the hurry and bustle of the morning's packing provisions, placing baskets and children in the wagon so as to consume as little space as possible for we must take in friends on the way until we are pretty thoroughly jammed. No inconvenience I assure you however for our sub-Alliance which had been invited to join the Lasater Alliance in a day of general boom, fun and frolic must be well represented, hence the cram in all available vehicles. A drive of eight miles over rough roads, under a blazing sun did not in the least damp the ardor and enthusiasm and we arrived there with keen zest for the enjoyments of the day, meeting old friends and forming of new acquaintances under the auspices of being united in fraternal love.

I look upon this Alliance movement as the most potent abettor of Christianity that has ever originated, but hold! I am not going to moralize just now. The program of the day was first music; second, essay on the principles, aims and possibilities of the Alliance, by your scribe; third, lecture by Bro. Macready who was sent to us by Dr. Macune; and I have only to say if the Dr. is as successful in running that Exchange as he is in getting hold of good material for speeches, it is bound to succeed; fourth, dinner, and that in quality and quantity all that could be desired. After dinner, music, then as he expressed it a sort of "fill up the time talk" by Bro. D. R. Hale, but let me whisper in your ear that those are the kind of "fill up talks" it pays one to listen to. His happy hits and telling anecdotes fill us with mirth and enjoyment while his unlimited zeal fires us with enthusiasm for the cause. Next, short speeches from the candidates for county office and there seemed to be less palaver this year than ever before. I believe that class of office-seeker is becoming extinct or do not dare to show themselves among Alliance people.

Toward the end, I allowed certain side issues, viz. music and dancing, to divert my attention from the graver questions of the day, but I had an excuse. I took my little ones where for the first time they might behold displays of the terpsichorean art; not that I cared to witness, oh no (?) but like school teachers and preachers who have to carry the little ones to circuses and menageries, sacrificed my wishes in order to please and interest the children.

The sinking sun reminded us of the weary miles we had to plod upon our homeward way and bidding goodbye to friends departed with the kindest of feelings in our hearts, our loyalty to the Alliance strengthened.

Distrust of traditional press; dislike of Pinkerton police

65.   July 31, 1888. [No place.] Western Reader.

EDITOR MERCURY: In your issue of the twelfth of July, the *Dallas News* receives a merited rebuke. For years, the *News* has realized the gradual enslavement of the American people, yet not one call for a "halt." Now, of course, in these election times the *News* as well as the *Atlanta Constitution* pose as mediums of lofty conservatism, political morality and "the final hope of the republic." The truth is that whether these journals pipe "reform" or sing in their old falsetto, they can no longer obstruct the forces that destiny is marshalling in behalf of the great majority, the working people. In the Old World, in new America, a grand revolution is going on and the day is approaching when the chains will fall from the long manacled form of prostrate labor. A remolding of social and political institutions will enable the working classes to enjoy the advantages they create, but [which] are now wrested from them by licensed avarice. The agricultural classes, usually the most patient, have at last been touched by class consciousness, and are realizing their capacity for organized resistance. . . . The system of competition now so generally practiced by our modern corporations is slowly murdering democracy and establishing economic slavery. The *News,* while applauding the New York courts in deciding that the laboring men have no right to use the boycott, should also suggest some defense for the employee of railroad corporations, against whom the blacklist is used. . . .

The successful, the rich, the unscrupulous, exhibit lamentable lapses of memory and a fatal forgetfulness of the lessons of history. It does not concern them to know that the avenging masses in the French revolution were literally starving and were at length maddened into blind revolution. Evil can only rise to a certain height, it then becomes reactionary. No true reform can come from beings tortured by the ills of poverty and wretchedness. A starving body implies impoverished brain and moral degradation. True revolution, or more properly, evolution, is inaugurated by the high-thinking laboring classes, trained to a consciousness of their wrongs, their strength and the power which destiny intends them to wield. . . .

It was a real reformer, not Bro. Claiborne, who said, "no nation can be better educated than fed;" so it is unwise to follow the Alliance sisters advice to live on corn, bread and water. Refreshments should begin with the rich and bestuffed drones whose dyspepsia is the result of over-consumption. Should all the farmers in every state in the Union begin now and practice in the most rigid, stinting, starving economy, it would not loosen one single chain now binding them. A liberal education, generous diet, comfort and progress in all surroundings will develop a class capable of solving the problem now puzzling our social world. All forms of tyranny whether ecclesiastical, political, or commercial obstruct natural processes . . . and provoke disturbances. The domination of capital in this country with its attendant evils[,] such as an army of Pinkerton "thugs," truckling satellites, a subsidized press, extreme poverty (and its inevitable sequence, intemperance) is so grave as to threaten democratic life, that wisdom and high courage must guide the reforming class in its efforts to overthrow the danger. . . . Government and corporate monopolies are too friendly, soon they will unite and merge into one. The Pinkerton army is already as large as Uncle Sam's, better drilled (for their honorable work), better paid, better equipped (minus conscience and heart). A change is imperative if overworked judges, lawyers (with ready-made judgements), new prisons, and instruments of judicial murder are not desired. . . .

Defending the woman's sphere

66.   July 31, 1888. Bexar County. Corn Bread.

EDITOR MERCURY: I have seen so much said about "woman's rights" I thought I would beg admittance to you, dear paper, to say a few words. Although I have not been one of you, yet I feel a deep interest in all you do; for does not a vow which is made before the high heavens bind us? We are the housewives, the makers of the home, and the home makes the nation. It puts me all out of patience to hear some of the ladies talk about their "woman's rights." How can any true wife and mother walk up to the polls on election day amid a crowd of gaping men, perhaps some of them drunk and some of them using slang. I don't mean all when I say some. You have no right to do such a thing, dear ladies, that is your husbands' and brothers' and fathers' business, not yours. Then you must know that if you are to be a man's equal in these things you must help to make the living. My husband is a farmer and I think I would much rather be a house-wife than be a "woman's rights" woman: not that I do not believe in us all having our rights; if you only knew it, we have more rights than a man has, "the housewife makes the home and the home makes the nation."

Dear ladies, are you not the counselor of all your household? Do you not know why your husbands object to your going to the polls? It is be-cause as a masculine woman you are no longer the dear little girl whom he promised to love, honor and cherish. Be contented as we are and make the home pure (if the men can't make the laws so) and stand by them. The ladies had better keep out of politics.

If this don't offend the Alliance I will come again.

Mention of Adam and Eve; woman's sphere

67.   July 31, 1888. [No location.] Anna Rester.

EDITOR MERCURY: When God made this world, he made a garden and put Adam into it to till and dress it. He also gave him a woman to help and in that way they obtained a large portion of their support. From that day, and the days when the noble Rebecca herded her father's sheep and the fair maidens of the land carried the water and ground the mead, has woman ever been found by her brother's side, helping with her own hands, her soft words, kind advice, her spirit of meekness and cheerfulness have mingled sunshine and happiness to the toils and labor of man. And further

Farm family picking cotton. Courtesy Library of Congress

down the lane of life when the constant knock of the loom by day and the buzz of the spinning wheel by the bright light of the fire in the long winter nights filled the demands of the clothing department, peace, happiness and cheeriness characterized the circle of farm life. And why not woman in the nineteenth century while wealth and monopoly have driven her natural sphere of peace and quiet in domestic life to the corn field and cotton field, there to take her share of the labor with the hard-banded man of strength to make a common support—and now the burdens are grievous to be borne—the noble order of the Alliance stands up and asks for ways and means of relief from these intolerable burdens; and why not the daughters of the land be invited into the councils of the wise, to do as her mission has always been, to cheer with her presence and encourage with her smiles and soft words the great work of reform.

May our Father speed the day when, through the great efforts of this order, the daughters will be sent away from the fields to more quiet and pleasanter duties of household life . . . .

Men, too, should practice economy

68.   July 31, 1888. Ona, Robertson County. Ada Williams.

EDITOR MERCURY: As I have seen nothing from this place, and as we have a good Alliance here, I will just write and say what I think about it. I do not belong to the Alliance but all the rest of the family do. . . .

I, like the "Texas Girl," think the men should practice more economy, they will preach to their wives and daughters about economy, saying "it seems to me like you could get along without that," and all such expressions. Why should women use all the economy while men go and buy on credit while their wives and daughters strive to save and stint. More than half of the poor farmers' wives are mere drudgers but, hurrah! the time is coming when they shall be above want, when the merchants' wives will not be more tenderly nourished and succored than the wives of the farmers.

On! brave Alliance men, on! to the fields of success and independence. As long as the Alliance has brave, earnest workers striving to their utmost to bring out the farmers from under the yoke of the depression caused by the national banks and monopolists, and the time must and will come when these brave workers must succeed.

Now, Mr. Editor, if you think this from the pen of a young aspirant is fit to publish, why, publish it, Texas "Puella."

Image of the Alliance as a small, sea-tossed ship; questioning the system

69.   August 14, 1888. Reprinted from a talk given at Elm Springs Alliance, No. 603, Farmers Branch, Dallas County. Mrs. H. M. Calmes.

No other organization ever instituted has aspired to the development of mankind. The promotion of universal benevolence and all legitimate enterprises as the Farmers Alliance, North, South, East and West, united by true brotherhood, allied by the golden chain of love and duty. The magnitude and ability of this noble order are almost beyond the comprehension of human agency, as by the combined strength of thousands working in unison, almost any undertaking may be accomplished. So determined are its efforts, so great its ability that we are fast realizing the purposes set forth in our constitution by developing the mental, moral, social and financial interests of the agricultural classes, constantly striving to secure harmony and good will among all mankind and brotherly love among ourselves, and at the same time endeavoring to suppress personal, local, sectional and natural prejudice, all unhealthy rivalry and all selfish ambition. . . . Hard pressed as we have been by opposition, goaded almost to desperation at times to make our yearly income meet the bare necessities of life, realizing each year that the poor were growing poorer and the rich richer, we were foolish enough to believe that the poor farmers were unable to avert the pending shipwreck; so with stolid indifference and dull apathy, akin to that which takes possession of a condemned prisoner from hearing his doom pronounced, we resigned ourselves to our fate and toiled on for self alone, hardly caring if a neighbor were sick or in distress. Can we ever feel thankful enough for the glorious light that has dawned upon our lives, revealing to us the better way? Now twice a month, instead of brooding at home over our misfortunes, we repair to our place of meeting, prepared to sanction any call of duty lending to the material advancement of our order. Then is a brother sick, is a brother in distress? Avaunt, thee selfishness! Love and charity to the rescue. . . .

While developing the more generous elements of our natures, our minds have not been dormant, so busily engaged have we been in searching to [find a] way out of our financial embarrassments. . . . Why have we so blindly staggered on in darkness? Why have we so long paid such exorbitant rates to middlemen for transacting our business which we are in every way qualified to take charge of ourselves? The amount, yearly, wrested from the laboring classes by speculators and middlemen is appalling. But no longer are the ignorant farmers to be deluded, duped and gulled. . . . We have no need of shipping our cotton and wool thousands of miles to be manufactured when we can manufacture them ourselves; no need of shipping our grain or selling at half price when we are capable of grinding it ourselves; no need of paying [the] agent one hundred per cent on our farming implements when the material for their construction flourishes on our own land, can be cut with our own axes and by our own hands converted into the very best implements in the United States.

What grander, nobler achievement can be conceived than our Alliance Exchange. . . . ? Our vessel is built for rough sailing, planked, spiked and rigged with integrity, industry, and perseverance and is commanded by brave, strong and honest men. Yet there are times when the waves of opposition roll high above us, threatening to submerge us; times when every timber in our noble vessel seems strained to its utmost and is lurching and quivering 'neath its terrible pressure. . . . We hear through the tumultuous beating of the storm the voice of our noble commanders bidding us to stand by our posts in the face of every danger. . . . Do we hesitate? No: inspired . . . we send back the shout, "We are coming." By the grace of God we will not betray the trust reposed in us. . . . As we lay our hands to the wheel, bringing every energy to bear while breakers dash wildly[,] on we rise. . . . triumphantly, to the surface of the foaming billows unharmed by all the conflicting elements through which we have passed. A flood of golden sunshine is now revealed through the rifted clouds above us. . . .

An Alliance supporter

70.   August 14, 1888. Wilson County. Fay Forestelle.

EDITOR MERCURY: I am not a member of the Alliance although the movement has my warmest sympathy and best wishes. Why? Because I do not believe it is an advantage to the order to drag an apparently cold, indifferent member along, and were I to join the Alliance I could not attend the meetings or take any part in the proceedings thereof, and that would cause me to appear cold, or at least lukewarm. I fear I should be a dead weight because I am the mother of seven children, most of them mere babies; we live a long mile from the place of meeting and I do not think 'twould be right to leave my babies at home, nor yet to bring them to the lodge. My husband is a member, has belonged since the order was first organized in our neighborhood. I venture to assert that this valuable friend and instructor of the farmer and the farmer's wife—*The Mercury*—has no more eager and interested reader than myself. . . .

Prosuffrage; prohibition

71.   August 21, 1888. Red Oak, Ellis County. Poor Gal.

EDITOR MERCURY: As I failed to raise the spunk and ire of the members of this our (Griffith) Alliance into writing her up, I come again, not with anything airy but a little common sense talk. First, let me say to Sister Cornbread, had she seen her husband and sons, if she is so fortunate as to possess the same, after spending all day in town, being treated by so many friends seeking office, coming home totally unbalanced, reeling, staggering, swearing, thinking the wife and mother a robber, while she tries to get their clothes off and put them into a nice warm bed before any one outside should suspect the disgrace, I think she would say, woman's rights out of the other side of her mouth; vote to put down whisky, vote to keep thieves from ruling us, vote to fight the foreign moneyed cliques, vote to keep our sons from being peons; yes, she would say let me vote till I die. Anna Rester, you speak my sentiments to a dot. You certainly know a woman's sphere. I too can't see where the disgrace comes in, when by the side of her husband, brother or son, she goes to town and puts in her vote. And don't we have protection from Uncle Sam, as well?

The Alliance picnics, so far, have done credit to the noble order. . . . I have been taking the *Mercury* in broken doses nearly six months. I feel better, think better, see better. . . .

The hypocrisy of the traditional press; defending the farmer

72.   August 21, 1888. [No location.] Western Reader.

EDITOR MERCURY: The *Dallas News* displays acute sensitiveness in behalf of the jeoparded (?) interests of the railroads in this state, and is disinterestedly looking (a leedle odd) to see that neither Mr. Terrell nor the Farmers Alliance shall be the least unconstitutional (!) in their efforts to stop the abuses of these overgrown monopolists. The *News* does not deny the existence of the abuses. Oh, no! But for Lord's sake, be careful, dignified and slow about getting out of trouble. The people of Texas can never be sufficiently grateful to our Chesterfield guardian, the *News*, for impressing on our minds our good governor's sage plan for relief, which is "to force the railroads into competition"! Of course, our witty governor meant this for a bit of sarcasm, well knowing that no one can force Jay Gould. . . . Thus hopelessness is slowly penetrating all the industrial classes. Money is power, crushing alike individuals and masses with impunity.

A rich manufacturer or any disinterested being who devotes large wealth, inherited estates and high intellect (vide Godin and Beauciant of France, Count Leo Tolstoe *[sic]* of Russia) to devising and practicing methods of uplifting and dignifying and glorifying labor are called cranks and fanatics. Instead of assisting them in their noble efforts, those in power and place scorn to examine their plans, refuse to note the results, and like bigots cry out, "Utopia!" "Revolution!" To love others more and better than we love our own Deity-stamped corpus is considered impossible by their mole-visioned self-worshipers. To pity the miseries of the poor and degraded, seething in the slums of all our large cities, to feel compassion for myriads suffering injustice and tyranny in every land, to waste time in trying to destroy the cause of this vice and misery is sheer nonsense in the opinion of those who fatten by this present system.

That the producer of all wealth of the world should aspire to enjoy some of the leisure and pleasure which their labor affords and buys; that "clod-hoppers" and "horney-handed" grangers should desire to rake the "hayseed" from their locks, erase the corns from their toiling hands, enjoy daily baths and meddle in politics, is quite horrifying, and few old fashioned democrats or "grand party" republicans can stand the shock of such temerity. When education becomes more general, when unity and organized cooperation among all labor becomes more universal; when the victims of injustice realize that they have only their chains to lose by united uprising; when only men representative of our interests receive our suffrages, instead of politicians (so biggoted that if a woman dares criticize she is accused of not wearing gowns), then perhaps Justice may lend us an ear, Capital and its tools realize their suicidal policy and Farmer Claiborne stand agast at the beneficence of the eight-hour law. . . .

73. August 28, 1888. Reprinted on the *Mercury's* front page from a speech delivered at a meeting of the state Alliance. "Little" Jennie Scott Wilson.

LADIES AND GENTLEMEN: Thousands of friends and enemies to the Alliance have prophesied that the Alliance would suicide. One fearing that it would; the other, hoping and confidently believing that it would. But today the mists have cleared away and every intelligent Alliance man recognizes that it is founded upon a solid careful basis, and that it has taken such a hold upon, and has been so implanted in the minds of the sturdy farmers of our sunny Southland, that it will live, spread and prosper despite opposition or political scheming. It is true that the leaders in this mammoth and overshadowing move now being upheld and supported by the honest yoemenry of the land, may make some unintentional mistakes but there is a deep and abiding determination among the great masses of farmers to no longer submit to the present monstrous system of . . . misrule and open-daylight legalized robbery and oppression. . . . Some of the wide awake enemies of the Alliance tell us this movement will result in war, that it reminds them of secession days when the South was going to whip the North and gain her independence. Is there any comparison? The Southern states seceded from the Union but the Farmer's Alliance has not seceded from anything. We are only claiming our rights and fighting for them under the same old national stars and stripes. The war between the states was fought with cannon and musketry while this war is being waged with pen and thought. In the war between the states, there was blood stain all over the land while in this war the only stain is ink upon paper. The Alliance is fast assuming gigantic proportions whose influence is felt all over our country and the great monopolies of the land are trembling when viewing its increasing power. The Texas Alliance headquarters at Dallas already do a monthly business, I believe, of over $200,000 in filling cooperative orders. The order is now running large flouring mills and ginneries and expects to establish many more local ones throughout Texas. There are over 200,000 members in Texas today and the membership is experiencing a healthy growth.

Some say that women have no business in the order. When Columbus braved the perils of unknown seas to add America to the world, whose hand was it that fitted him for the voyage? A woman, Queen Isabella. Every effectual man who has left his mark in the world is but another Columbus for whom some Isabella in the form of a mother has laid down her comforts, yes, her chance, her jewels. I would suggest to all those who think ladies are out of their place in the Alliance and have no discretion and are given to telling all they know or hear, that they had better read up a little and be less explosive themselves in the lobbies of convention halls. . . .

Woman's sphere; suffrage; concern for working-class women

74.   August 28, 1888. Ennis. Ann Other.

EDITOR MERCURY: Somewhere near three thousand years ago people were divided into class or castes, the son being obliged to follow the occupation of the father; and all branches of business and industry, public and private, were arranged in a most methodical manner. But in tracing institutions of men and government we find man outgrowing the idea of their capabilities being limited by anything short of their physical endurance, and finally this capacity came to be recognized more as the ability of the mind rather than physical endurance, and for more than two thousand years has he scorned the idea of being born with the obligation to follow the trade of his father or limit the scope of his action by anything short of this sphere of his mind. And now, after three thousand years of development and advance, men still claim to think that woman is born to the trade of her mother and has no right to step beyond her "proper sphere" of the kitchen and the household.

If independence of thought and action is good for the development of man, why would it not be for women? Can we have the full development of mind in children when mothers are trammeled by inconsistent laws and dictates of fashion, and society that dictates to her in dress, in thought and in action? Has not a slave mother produced a slave offspring? And when we see laws passed by men alone, have we any right to wonder they are not always just to the silenced element they govern? Have women an equal right (with their husbands) in law to their children? Have women a right to property acquired before marriage, and have they an equal right with the husband to that acquired after marriage? Some years ago in one of our states, a man married a woman worth fifty thousand dollars; he invested her money and at the end [of] the year died, leaving her by will fifty thousand dollars, as long as she remained his widow, when, in case of her marriage, it was to revert to his relatives; but thanks to a Divine Providence, women's rights have stepped into that state for enough to change that "just law of good men. . . . "

In Wyoming Territory suffrage has been established since 1860[;] and in 1885, Governor Warren wrote, "Woman suffrage has not lowered the grade of public officials in our territory. On the contrary, our women consider much more carefully than our men the character of our candidates and both political parties have found themselves obliged to nominate their best men in order to obtain the support of the women. . . . Opposition is substantially confined to three classes: first and chief, that immoral element which sustains and is sustained by the drinking saloon, the gambling house; second, a much smaller element, the 'high-toned' class which finds delight in the frivolities of fashionable life; and third, a small but eminently respectable element, that is bound by traditional notions of man's superiority and 'woman's sphere,' and lies curled up upon itself altogether like a chick in an eggshell who ought to hatch but doesn't. To this last element belong those who think they read in the Bible a divine right of man to rule over women."

And now let me ask if she shall shut our eyes to the vast fields of intellect that man has opened for himself, but still excludes women? . . . When the teachings of Christ shall be fully understood, then will it be clearly seen that his mission was the emancipation of women and slaves, and to teach the equality of the whole human family before God. . . .

The country needs a Golden Rule in religion and patriotism when one class of the community heaps miseries upon the other class because of unwillingness and stupid capacity of the one to put itself in the others' place. Most of the miseries of the world have their cause here. The condition of the 3,000,000 women in the United States, who earn their own living, should be considered in the light of the Golden Rule. Those who are in bonds should be remembered as if we were bound with them. I beg satisfied ladies of fortune and gentlemen who boast of the perfection of "woman's sphere" and our Christian civilization to imitate Christ by going among the people of want and there learn the lessons of needed change. Go to the stores and shops where the products of woman's work is sold and watch the merchants pass the lives of women over their counters in every package of ill-paid work they sell. Go and learn how helpless women are driven to lives of shame and then despised by the class of persons who have lived off their labor and their tears. Then sit back in your easy chairs and cry against the ballot for fear it may sully some hands too indolent to use it for the emancipation of the down trodden.

Oh, may the day hasten when all women shall understand the laws that govern them and is grinding the faces of the poor. May the time come when men shall intelligently understand the franchise and exercise the same in an intelligent manner. When we will no longer hear of such arguments as I heard a man make a few days ago when the subject of suffrage was broached. "Let my wife go and pitch millet all day as I have and I will take her place in the house and she may do the voting." Oh, depths of logic! What deep reasoning faculties such arguments indicate! But suppose the ability to pitch millet all day or other manual exercise were made the test of franchise. How many men would be excluded and would not many women, especially our strong foreign women, be admitted on these principles?

Hardship

75.   August 28, 1888. Corn Hill. Birdie.

EDITOR MERCURY: It seems that my mind is wandering from the present to the future but a shadowy veil envelops the future keeping it always out of view. What does it contain for me? For you? Will our efforts in life be crowned with success? Will we wear a garland of flowers, emblematical of success and happiness. . . . Or will it lead to bitter disappointment and woe? Shall our blossoms be crushed forever and our hopes decayed? Will these burdens ever be removed? . . .

How can we be happy when we toil so from day to day? Our fathers, mothers, brothers, all that is dear to us getting farther away. Fathers and brothers toil until when they come in from work they are too tired to talk or enjoy home with its softening influences. Mothers and sisters cannot bring any hope to the taxed and overworked brain. Mother thinks, how can I tell him there is no meat in the house, lard or coffee when he has no money and don't want to go deeper into debt? She looks at the children and wonders how shall we support them, educate and clothe them? The daughter wants a new dress as she has been making out with her old one but she looks at her father and thinks she must wait longer before she asks, and still she waits.

There are hundreds of families in this condition, dear readers; do you not know families in this condition? What is the cause? Not idleness. What is the remedy?

We are needing rain now very badly, but it looks quite threatening; think it will come soon.

Mr. Editor, the 9th was my birthday but I will not tell you my age for fear some one might guess who signs her name.

Tongue-in-cheek; Eve; prohibition; suffrage

76.   September 4, 1888. [No location.] Old Woman.

EDITOR MERCURY: As you[r] paper seems open for wimin as well as men, I thought I would write a letter. I read the *Mercury* and liked it, too; but I don't belong to the Alliance. The old man does; you see we can't both lose time to attend the meetin's, so he goes while I stay at home and economize.

Well, sir, I think the Alliance is doin' a heap of good, if them fellers in Dallas don't skeer the poor farmers and make them lose confidence in the leaders; but I guess that would be hard to do, jedgin from the way they rallied to the front when a call for help was made. I know this old man went to mass meetin' and helped all he could. I heered they had a big time, and I heered they had the candidates mighty bad, and I know they had something mighty bad, cuz the old man didn't get in till the roosters was a crowin', and I smelt somethin' cranky on his breath, and I seen him castin' up accounts, too.

I hear a heap of talk about prohibition and wimin votin' and all that. Now, the ones that want whisky howl about sumptuary laws, and all that. I want to know if there ain't some way to get rid of the s'loons? I hear 'em [say that] some of our poor farmers go to town and go in them s'loons, and the candidates "set 'em up." And by the time they are ready to start home somebody has to set 'em up on their hosses or in ther wagin. And they say what they give 'em makes one quarter look like two. I reckon that is why they git home without money. I want to ax one thing. Can't they get at them s'loons at the head of cruelty to animals, or somethin' of that sort? Now, I will tell you what I heered about one of our biggist lawyers. And they say it is a fact, and he has got mighty big aspirations, too. He went into one of them s'loons and got so drunk he thought he was a hoss. And he went out on the street and went to a wagin that had some fodder in it, and he tried to eat it hoss fashion; he stuck his head clean through the top of his hat and pulled the brim down on his shoulders for a collar. Now, is such a man as that fit for office?

There is a heap of men don't want wimin to vote nor have a hand in government affairs. Some try to make out they hain't got sense enough, and has got no right, and all that. They never think that they owe all their knowledge to wimin. Yes, sir, they wouldn't have no more sense today, than a goat if old mother Eve hadn't eat from the tree of knowledge; and when she eat it, she knowed Adam was a fool. And then, womanlike, she wanted him to eat and he be wise too. Then, after all, the curse was put upon the woman, and, sir, she has been "cussed" ever since. No more from your friend til' death.

Suballiance report

77.   September 4, 1888. Pilgrim Lake. Aunt Belle.

EDITOR MERCURY: I will proceed to write you a few lines to let you know what our brothers and sisters are doing in Pilgrim Lake Alliance. Our Alliance is not so energetic in its actions as a great many others we read of in the *Mercury,* but we hope to do better in the near future. Our member-ship increases every meeting. It seems that the ladies are taking a great interest, as they are joining rapidly now. Our alliance has about forty-five members.

I see so many nice letters written by the ladies, I thought I would surprise our brothers and sisters when they look through the *Mercury* and see a letter from our Alliance. I think a good dose of the *Mercury* every week in our Alliance would be of great benefit to some of our bilious members. You know that when a person gets real bilious that mercury is the only thing that will cleanse their system. . . .

We are enjoying a fine rain today. Some think that cotton will make the second crop if worms do not come. Some have picked a good deal of cotton already, in spite of the extreme hot weather.

We have had a great deal of sickness in our country this summer, mostly of a malarial type; some congestion. . . .

Woman's sphere

78.   September 4, 1888. Lavaca County. Emma L.

EDITOR MERCURY: I have become so attached to your paper and especially the Ladies Department that I can no longer resist the temptation to write again. Our corner is a real work of pleasure and information, such as ladies actually need and enjoy. Thanks to the kind editor for tendering to us a page in his most valuable paper. Hope he will never regret his liberality. Let us all write what they think will be encouraging and edifying to each and every one.

Sisters, let us try and make our page interesting and quit writing so much about women suffrage, for I can't see how it would make things any better. Their vote would be divided the same as men's are. I think we have enough to do to attend to our home affairs and the moral training of our children. I, for one, am willing to leave the ballot box with the men. If we could only have what rights are properly due us we would do well enough without holding office and voting. If men, with all the power and brains, make mistakes in the management of the government, what would woman in her weakness do?

Seclusion lodge gave a barbeque on this 27th of June, which was a happy, profitable day in the history of our lodge. We had invited Bro. Ben Terrell, lecturer of the National Alliance, to speak. There were 800 to 1000 people listening to his humorous but instructive talk.

I think I might say our lodge is on a boom. Most all took stock in the Exchange and there are applicants for membership at every meeting. Our president is a whole-souled Allianceman, ready to do all in his power to help keep the Alliance wheel moving.

The crops in our county are not so good as was expected a month ago, owing to the dry weather we have had recently.

Reference to previous letter from Mrs. Jeremiah; antisuffrage; defending the farmer

79.   September 4, 1888. Dallas County. Dianecia Jones.

EDITOR MERCURY: Well, as we are having a refreshing shower. I can't think of anything else to do but give you some more dots from these parts, although it seems as if you don't care about dots up here, as my last was cast in the waste basket.

What has become of Aunt Huldah and the other of the good writers? Surely they have not been filling the greedy old waste basket.

Woman's rights! Now sisters, let that question rest. As for my part I don't think it would improve things for the ladies to vote. Let us allow the men to make laws. We can certainly live by their laws if they can. As to woman's suffrage, that is something we will never get in this world. I say look up and trust for our rights in a better world. Mothers, let us try to raise our sons to make good laws and not be afraid to work. Shame on the farmer's boy who goes out to plow with a handkerchief round his neck and gloves on his hands. A word to some of you Alliance mothers. Don't teach your daughters to frown on the sunburnt lad and say, there is a nice young man; the sun don't shine on him; he is smart enough to make a living in the shade. But teach them that farmers are honest and not afraid to work to make an honest living.

Now a word to all. It may not interest you free farmers, who never lose a day to go to a speaking or a picnic. You and Jeremiah can't see any good in the Alliance. You sit back and let the dude spit on you and laugh at you for taking it. Listen to the big bosses: We ain't scared; the poor old ignorant farmers won't stick together; they can't do anything. Now come out, you farmers, and don't have that flung in your face any longer, and show them that you stick as tight as old Aunt Jemima's plaster.

Well, I don't belong to the Alliance but not for the same reason as that Mrs. Jeremiah but because I haven't had an opportunity of joining. But at last Cedar Hill has opened her doors to us. . . .

I have been told the reason George Washington never told a falsehood was because his wife never asked him any questions.

Letters beginning to grow scarce

80.   September 4, 1888. Concord Alliance, McLennan County. Country Girl.

Tap, tap, tap. Mr. Editor, will you kindly open the door of the ladies department and allow a new-comer a few moments' chat with the sisters.

Attention, sisters! What is the matter with you all? So many of the good contributors have ceased to send in their spicy letters and we miss them so much. Come to the rescue, some of you gifted talented farmers' daughters; our page is almost half full of advertisements which will never do. What has become of Ann Other? I am afraid that she is asleep and will have one of those fearful dreams of hers. Oh, Charitie, how we miss you, Rosa Lee, and many others.

Our Alliance is on a standstill, but we hope that when the weather gets more pleasant and sickness subsides that it will do better. I expected that you would hear from our Alliance right often, as our sister, "Farmer's Daughter," wrote such a nice letter some time ago, but alas, her letters are few and far between.

Advice to farm boys

81.   September 11, 1888. Ennis. Ann Other.

EDITOR MERCURY: To the Ox Driver [a contributor] and other boys: Yes, dear boys, what will become of you? Where are you drifting and what kind of old man do you intend to be? I dare say you will be fully good enough for those young ladies who you think are "sticking up their noses" at "farmer boys" and looking for the "ten cent dudes." But let us stop and consider for a few moments. Do you never do anything you would be ashamed to have them know? Are you always as choice of your company as you would require them to be, to be good enough for you? Is there never any time when you are out with the boys smoking, drinking and indulging in low class stories what for the world you would not want mother or the young ladies know? Is your mouth always clean and the breath sweet as nature intends it should be without the assistance of cloves and cardamom seed? Do you know that tobacco is, according to all our best scientists, to be one of the strongest leaders to strong drink? It destroys in a great degree the vigor of the mind; dulls, by its narcotic poison, the quick sensibilities for purity and virtue; makes a slave of the appetite and a filthy casket for the soul . . . ? Instead of spending forty or fifty cents for that pound of tobacco that will last you, you know how long for I do not, take it to a bookstore, but stop, those lying on the counter so handy are not the ones I want you to look at. You might better spend your money for tobacco and ruin your health than in that "yellow covered literature" and ruin your mind. Look instead for the "Alta editions," beautifully bound in blue and gold, many of them are the lives of our greatest men, Washington, Jefferson, Patrick Henry, Clay and Webster, and also at the books of travel, of foreign lands. . . .

I hear you say, "but I don't have the time to read." But stop and think: Where and how do you spend your Sundays? Of course you will say you go to church, but does church last an entire Sunday? How is the rest of the day passed? Do you pay attention to what is said? I think there is not a clergyman in our land who would not prefer to have you stay at home and read and study one of the books I have mentioned to having you attend church simply to cast your eye over the audience to pick out the best look-ing girl and wonder if Jim could cut you out with Annie since he had this new suit of clothes. . . .

But I hear someone say he is so tired when he comes in he cannot read. Let me say to the young, if you are healthy and your diet is wholesome, not too much of fat meats and strong coffee, this habit may be overcome. With persistent use, the mind becomes strong and no need to leave the farm to cultivate it. With the old, nature demands more rest and long inactivity of the mind bends it like an old oak tree that has stood for many years with its head bent to the winds of adversity. But even bent minds can be made to take on some of the finest fruits of thought by persistency and vitality of the individual. . . .

The gullible farmer

82.   September 11, 1888. Bexar County. Corn Bread.

Please allow me to address my brothers and sisters of the Alliance through your paper once more. I hold vanity as an excellent quality; it stiffens the back, holds a man up and reinforces that prime element, pride. Let farmers take the hint; it matters not that we be highly cultured; for many a man who cannot read has more gumption than the average statesman, scientist and professor. I do not want to impart a lesson of stalwart vanity but we ought to feel our worth and weight. We are not near so smart as some but the smart ones are mostly shallow. Raw statesmen, small-bore lawyers, chronic office-seekers, snobs, toadies, fops and railroad wreckers are not as good as we[,] though immensely more showy. We make statesmen and we unmake them. The sharpers have used us a long time and found us very profitable; but as we suffer, we learn. There are men so prematurely keen that they cheat you instinctively, unconsciously. . . . It is wonderful how many of us are afraid of buggaboos and how we defer to the rich who have robbed us. . . .

But there is a monster in our path that is not a buggaboo, but a real devourer, worse than the devilfish with thirty-foot tentacles. Protection stands before us, brazen and audacious, demanding that the poor whom it made poor shall protect the rich, the same as the lambs protect the wolves. And the working people protect the band of greedy rascals who have robbed us twenty years or more. It has hordes of gold gotten from us through unjust laws that it worked upon us through congress. Members go up to do our work, and the cunning men beguile, bribe and seduce them to give them laws to take our earnings. . . . So brothers, be careful what you are doing at the polls when election comes off. Yours.

Farmers and politics

83.   September 11, 1888. Weimar. P.

THE FARMER IN POLITICS

Whenever a farmer utters one protest against his wrongs or attempts in any way to clear his garments from the mud with which the privileged class have so ruthlessly bespattered him, you hear something like the following: "The farmers are running into politics; there never was an association of farmers that was not broken up by political aspirants. The average farmer is easily fooled, and is so unsuspecting that he is drawn into the political net before he knows it. The Grange and the Alliance all die of the same thing."

Now, what is the same thing? . . . It is to be hoped that no reasonable being, no thinking mind belonging to the laboring class which desires to be a competent judge in its own behalf . . . can be so hoodwinked. Trust companies, cotton monopolies and other varied monopolistic tyrannies might tell us, if they would, who forges the chains that so manacle these bodies that they die of inertia. Are not these combinations fostered by our government? We may be fools and unsuspecting, but we are not such fools as not to see the rottenness of a government that is scorching us to death by the sirocco breath of class legislation. Pray, who is to grapple with and strangle to death these thieving combinations of power? If farmers and other laboring classes do not?

Yes, of course the farmer is running into politics. . . . Who has a better right to find out what is the matter with this political net than they who are being strangled to death in its intricate meshes? Have we not a right to know why they who toil not, are clothed in purple and fine linen, whilst the toilers scarcely know sometimes whether they will be clothed at all. . . .

Every organization that has for its object the good of the laboring class may die, crushed beneath the mighty monopolies, which say, you shall not live: for it depends upon the laborer to show the monster tyrant that he will live, or to his funeral pyre light a torch. . . .

General Lee is said to have given as the cause of the failure of the confederacy, "That the southern people were not half in earnest." If the Alliance fails, it will be from the same cause; not sufficiently in earnest to walk boldly into the strife of the politician and strike left and right until the last armed foe expires. . . .

Farm life; women in the field

84.   September 25, 1888. Live Oak County, Oakville. Lucretia M. Dunn.

EDITOR MERCURY: Please allow another sixteen-year-old girl a little space. I enlisted a short time ago in Lebanon Alliance No. 3612. Our lodge is in Live Oak county, east and nine miles from the town of Oakville. It was organized a little more than a year ago with thirteen charter members; now it numbers sixty and others are still coming in.

Our neighborhood can't be beaten in this state, either morally, socially or religiously. We have no lawyers, gossips or other chronic disturbers of the peace among us and harmony reigns supreme. In the first place, we have local option, and none of us are rich to excite envy, and none so poor as to create suspicion. When we go to church we take our dinners and are a social between religious services as though we were at a picnic; but when the hour for service arrives, we all gather into the church house and listen to the sermon; none stay outside to gossip.

This is a happy community, but human nature is here all the same, for I don't think there is one in the vicinity but would change places with the czar of Russia or Jay Gould; but would it be wise for us to do so? As we are, we really have plenty. We go when and where we please, and never think of the assassin's knife or the nihilist's bomb, while the czar and the millionaire—although they live in fine palaces surrounded by guards and every luxury that wealth can procure—are always in fear that they will be assassinated. . . .

Crops, corn and cotton, are very good here; so nearly all the girls in the neighborhood don their sun-bonnets and gloves and spend the day picking cotton. Our cotton has averaged a thousand pounds per acre and there are a great many matured bolls in the patch now, but I'm sure that my cotton picking will be finished when they have opened for within the last ten days worms have appeared and completely destroyed the leaves.

Farm boys

85.   September 25, 1888. Cotton Wood Alliance. Milk Maid.

EDITOR MERCURY: I've come over to have a chat with you "about your neighbors," you say—eyeing me rather dubiously, thinking perhaps that I ought to know that gossipers are not admitted to our band. Oh, no, my neighbor's affairs never bother me. I am busy with my own. About politics, someone suggests. No, sir, or ma'am; you are wrong, Oh, I know, it's about how you cook, bake and wash dishes, for I know you are a farmer girl from your appearance. Wrong again, if I am a farmer girl, cook, bake and wash dishes, I would not be so unkind as to take the valuable space allowed me in the dear old *Mercury,* for such nonsense as would neither interest nor instruct its readers.

Ox Driver wanted to know what is to become of the boys growing up on the farm. . . . Some of them have talent and will make use of their time, perhaps will be President or fill some office of rank. . . . Others will neither get an education or anything else but will drag their lives out on the farm and never be worth anything to themselves or anyone else. . . . Do not think I am running the farmer boy down, or am prejudiced against them all, it is those who idle around and live off their parents' labor and do nothing to help them. I love the farm and don't think I could live anywhere else. It is the safest and surest of occupations. . . .

I hope the day is not far distant when farmers will have gained the victory, and then you who have become discouraged and quit the business will wish you had remained with the honest farmer. I heard a young lady say the other day . . . that she did not want any "ten cent dude." It is the farmer boy who has the pony and rides around with a six shooter about him and imagines himself larger than his father that the girls turn up their noses at. . . . I am sure he eats what his father earns by the sweat of his brow. Away with such farmer boys. Let the girls turn up their noses at them and away with ten cent dudes. I think young men who are not afraid to drive the ox and till the ground ought to be encouraged, and if they can't make the ends meet, we should help them get an education. Farmers need education as much as any people. . . .

Charitie returns; mother love; mutuality

86.   September 25, 1888. Ruston, Louisiana. Charitie.

EDITOR MERCURY: A bright sunny evening, a clear blue sky with a few clouds floating around, welcome after a week's rain and misty weather. There is just a breeze enough to stir the green tops of the grand old pines that stand in every direction, as they doubtless have stood for hundreds of years. Silence like a gentle spirit is brooding over the earth—only the sound of the piano breaks the stillness, as "Olla" (my daughter), plays and sings, "Mother Childhood, Friends and Home." 'Tis such a time when meditation walks abroad and holds communion with the soul, as I sit before an open window thinking what shall I write after reading so many good letters from my brothers and sisters in the *Mercury*.

How few of us are so swift to discover beauty in everyday scenes around us? It is indeed true that the art of observing "little things," and extracting pleasure therefrom, is a great passion and ought to be cultivated. Whether it be mountains, streams, valleys or a bed of beautiful flowers, they never quite depart from our existence. . . . Marie Labouchere, I am a wife and a mother, I have several bright boys and girls, I will leave it to them to give me praise. They never weary while I weave to them bright memories of happy bygone days.

It was at the request of one of my daughters that I wrote "Mother Childhood," as she wished to preserve it in her scrapbook. My childhood home she has never seen, for that home was in South Carolina. Ah! What contrast the clear sparkling streams of Carolina with their pebbly banks and bottoms present to the muddy creeks of Louisiana. But I have a pleasant home here, I have formed many new and pleasant links in the chain of friendship here but none so strong and endearing as those of my childhood. Yes, as I write, I can see the whole scene rise before me like a vision. The old home, the tall trees standing in the backyard, spreading their branches protectively over that quiet home. And there my father sits under them reading the journal or some good book—brothers, sisters, all the family just as if it was yesterday. With what power does little things bring back to us memories that have long slept. All of joys, all of sorrows that our hearts have known is there before us with the vividness of actual existence. My mother died when I was eleven years old, from that time until the time I was married, I knew not a mother's love; I had none to give me that love and sympathy that a child so much needs. I have not forgotten how I longed for a mother. I would think if I only could have my own dear mother for one hour, I would lay my head in her lap and tell her all my troubles, feel her hands stroking back the hair from my forehead, and her lips press mine with a loving kiss. I can see her now; still in death and a white rose lying on the cold still bosom, that pallid face. "Mother, in my heart, thine image long shall be, until in heaven at last I shall meet with thee."

By memory we live the past over again, and in bestowing that gift, God hath more than doubled our existence. Memory is a gallery where we may treasure the unfading beauty of countless pictures; the face[s] of those loved and cherished ones who have long since be[en] dead, are enshrined therein and friend[s] asundered from us by stream and valleys, time and distance, remain photographed on its walls forever. Marie Labouchere, write often, for all of your letters will find a place in my scrapbook. I have many a friend and relative somewhere in that big state of Texas; won't some of them remember me and send me a letter?

Yours, truly,

Mention of a third party; questioning the system

87.   October 2, 1888. No location. Hope.

EDITOR MERCURY: The *Dallas News'* unfair remarks about our es-teemed president, Evan Jones, were as untrue as biased. How absurd for the news to declare that democrats "never hold a caucus." The dictionary defines "caucus" to be a "preliminary meeting held for political purposes," and can the *News* assert that the Democrats never held caucus meetings with closed doors in Washington. . . . The caucus convention held by the Cleveland democrats in Dallas in their style of management, reminds one of [the] lo[o]se and easy way in which similar dominating caucuses are conducted in the republic of Mexico. . . .

Farmers need not hesitate to espouse the cause of labor, no matter how "insignificant" may appear the origin of the party carrying its banner. The original leaders of the abolition party were threatened with death (one was hung) and suffered just such hatred as now abhor "the third party."*

All laboring and industrial classes have everything to gain and nothing to lose by a third party. In the opinion of those who flourish by the present system, it is audacious for its victims to protest; . . . a syncophantic cringing devotion to corporate interests pervades all the friendly counsels these journals bestow on us. . . . See how boldly nepotism flourishes here in our own state. Senatorial relationship is worse than a grasshopper plague here. The conduct of our representatives declare[s] them to be our enemies, and how can we expect our enemies to advance our interests? . . . Deceived by the apparent prosperity attending the advent of railroads into a country trammelled by party traditions, worshipping Jeffersonian idealities, farmers timidly shrink back into the folds of the two big parties, consoling themselves with such words as "cannot be avoided, must be quietly endured." Would the immortal Jefferson, who wrote from France that it were better for all nations that the French Revolution had been, even though only one man survived, provided that man were a free man, would he now lead the party so hypocritically claiming him? Could his intrepid spirit again become incarnate? Would the martyred Lincoln be proud of the degenerate monopoly-fattened party he once inspired so grandly? . . .

Abolitionist and editor Elijah P. Lovejoy was murdered by a mob in Alton, Illinois, in 1837.

Farm life; the plight of the farmers

88.   October 2, 1888. Cornhill. Birdie.

EDITOR MERCURY: Here I come again, asking admittance into your charming circle. It is so nice, Mr. Editor, to talk to you and your numerous correspondents that I can't resist the temptation to have one more chat. If I am intruding or asking too much, just cast me off but not in the wastebasket, if you please.

It is raining today and I expect some of the farmers whose fields are gleaming with snowy whiteness are fearful of losing some of the fleecy staple. We fully realize the rush of the season is upon us, the busiest time of the year for the farmer. It is real lovely to look over the fields and see the green meadows with snowy whiteness in the sunlight, yet one tires of it when compelled to gaze on it from morn' til night. Oh, why do the farmers perish in raising so much cotton, when they work in it nine months of the year, and then what do they receive for their labors? Not enough is realized from the proceeds to sustain them while cultivating.

So much has been said about economy. Mama said she is sick of that word, for she has heard and practiced it from childhood and to economize any more would be to do without anything at all . . .

What has become of "Texas Girl"? I liked her so well. I fully endorse what she said about the men; let them practice as well as preach economy. . . . Mr. Editor, I wish you would let me in your sanctum and let me help you with these numerous letters. I really think I should like to be an editress. Don't you think I could learn?

I am still the lonely,

The scarcity of letters; pride in fellow writers

89.   October 9, 1888. Fanbion, Burnet County. Sallie Pangle.

Looking over the *Mercury* of September 18, I see only three very short letters from the sisters. Why is this, dear sisters? Is it our fault that our page is being filled more and more, each week, with advertisements? Are we getting negligent or tired of writing and reading the interesting letters written by the sisters? Indeed I am not. The Ladies' Department is the dearest page of all the *Mercury* to me. I read it first and then I am ready for the letters full of good advice and teeming with knowledge which our farmers have never had any credit for having.

Why do not more of our aged sisters write? I enjoy reading their letters; they are full of interest to me. When I am reading one of the letters written by them, I feel that I am reading the true sentiments of a noble heart. While some of our young ladies write letters full of merriment, romance, and poetry, and others write words full of wisdom showing how deep into the fountain of thought the feminine mind can penetrate—letters from which we may gather many rich thoughts which none of us can read without feeling we are benefitted. . . .

Sisters let us not fall behind with our part of this grand work, our brothers have asked us to go with them, hand in hand, in this great effort they are making and let us try to fill up our page with letters laden with instruction and encouragement, not advertisments.

Death; mutuality

90.   October 9, 1888. Ennis. Mrs. Ann Other.

EDITOR MERCURY: How far removed yet how closely bound seem the sisters and brothers of "our paper," and I often wonder to how many homes has come the gentle, though unrelenting, hand of death as it has visited my home circle this summer; how, after weeks of patient and prayerful watching and faithful nursing, I have seen the little bud slowly fading, fading, and feeling that its little spirit was unavoidably passing from our care and skill; and then, all of a sudden, to be called upon to realize that another one of our home circle just putting forth the foot of manhood upon life's path with the strength of mind and moral vigor that promises to manhood's sphere one of its brightest and ablest workers—to all of a sudden see such a tree of Lebanon drop its branches and fall to the ground with the crushing weight it must bear to all hearts that love it; to go and witness the last sad rites the living can pay to the dead, this is sorrow, but then to return to your home and still see the death angel perched above your door, and to hear [in] your sad heart the cry for the return and know the answer of "nevermore," and then after another week's anxious waiting and prayer to lay another loved form in its little white casket and still feel that "He doeth all things well," this calls forth the heroic strength of a Christian nature.

We find comfort in the thought where they have gone there will be no hindrance to the full development of the beautiful minds with which God endowed them. They shall behold the beauty of the Lord and inquire in his temple and who can tell, who can conceive the beautiful lessons they shall learn as they wing their way from star to star, from one planetary system to another, to there drink in all the mysteries of astronomy with God's angels for guides and teachers, or to stoop to the lowly flowers of our fields and penetrate all the unacquired problems of botany and chemistry that has held mortal minds enthralled or perhaps, if their tastes directs, to study physical nature as developed in God's animals on earth, and there see where man's science falls short in penetrating God's laws, and perhaps whisper sweet messages in waiting, open ears, thereby helping medical science to unravel mysteries surrounding human ills.

In these hopes perhaps the waiting hearts may find solace and while each token that tells of the departed—the straw hat with its broken crown through which a stray curl once peeped, the violin and harp that once awoke sweet echoes in the old home corners, the locked chest with its boyish treasures, the chest of tools with its repaired knives and other mechanical inventions with which the dear hands last worked, to school books here forever closed for the studies to be taken up higher, or the tiny shoe which baby feet never soiled and the little white robes folded away as a mother's shrine, to be replaced by brighter, fairer robes to be worn in an immortal world; all these while they bring keenest grief to our hearts, we know in God's good time they will soften, until they will bring only pleasant remembrances, and we will thank God that they were sent even for so brief a time to bless and brighten our pathway.

If to any other homes of the sisters such grief has been sent, let us clasp hands over the space that separates the readers of the *Mercury* and with firm resolve, take up our burden and use every opportunity given us to improve our minds, realizing that is the immortal part.

Woman's sphere

91. October 9, 1888. An essay read to the Pleasant Ridge Alliance and reprinted in the Mercury. Miss Mattie Glover.

We have often heard that a brave man struggling with the storms of fate is one of the most sublime and moral spectacles there is. One of the most beautiful is that of a gentle, amiable and accomplished woman. One who performs her social and domestic duties with grace and dignity. If she extends her usefulness beyond the limits of her household and, by her examples and exertions, benefits the whole country, she at once becomes an object of public interest and people will point to her with pride. . . . In time past, people seemed to think that a woman could do nothing for the public interest or good or take part in public questions, unless she was very wealthy. It is different now, and we should be glad to see and know that women generally are taking an interest in public questions concerning the good of our country at the present time. . . . They are not only taking an interest but are using their influence more than ever before.

All women are not placed in positions to accomplish very great deeds, but most of them can and should prepare themselves more diligently for the performance of their more appropriate duties, such as the sweet and tender charities of life and a pure and gentle heart, which is a hundred times more valued by society than great and heroic deeds.

Women's rights

92. October 9, 1888. Bexar County. Corn Bread.

EDITOR MERCURY: There are some who profess to know it all. They think wisdom lives and will die with them. I am not of this class, and those persons will doubtless think it an intrusion upon royal prerogative for me to write upon woman's rights. Let me first say to sister Poor Gal that I have a husband and sons and I know their votes can't be bought for a drink of whisky, as she implies that hers can, and also know how to hurry them off to bed as though she has experienced the shame and tried to hide it for them by putting their drunkenness to the bed. I think she had better put them under the bed, or out in the street. I think she would rather be a housewife and be at home than [be] a woman's right's woman. I tell you there are enough dead heads at the polls without any more. . . . If men can't better the laws by their votes, I would like to know what good would women do . . . ?

A question of censorship

93. October 16, 1888. Prairie Grove. Alice.

EDITOR MERCURY: I was just reading the letter in the *Mercury* from a brother who says he dislikes "those novels" published in the *Mercury*. Now, brother, if you do not like them, do not read them. But do not try to deprive others of that pleasure. I like them exceedingly. I am very fond of reading novels, and I also love to read my Bible. As for being "light minded," I have the honor to say I am above that. I read all I can and do my work— my milking, washing, cooking, all the sewing for my family, including my husband's pants, vests, coats, and knit his socks, and I must say he is well pleased with it all. Brother Barnes, I think you are unduly prejudiced against novels. As for your children reading them, I think they will read them anyhow if they have any desire to—if not while they're young and under your control, then when they are grown up.

Slander

94. October 16, 1888. Extract from an essay read before Elizabeth Alliance, Savoy, Fannin County, and reprinted in the *Mercury*'s "Ladies' Department." Miss Mattie Taylor.

It is a well known fact that when you find a farmers organization you find a neighborhood where there is more sociability and less fault finding and that greatest of all evils, tattling, than in a neighborhood where they are bound together by no stronger ties than those which bind the human family. When they have each taken a solemn obligation to assist the others, they feel or ought to feel it their duty to protect their brother's or sister's honor as sacredly as if it were their own. Brothers and sisters, I do think that we should fight slander as much as we do monopoly, for while the latter brings a man down in his financial affairs, the former deprives him of what zeal he would have in trying to be a man and make a mark in the world.

What a common thing it once was for one dear friend to whisper to another, "Do you see that man? Well, my wife's sister's husband believes that he took a piece of meat from his smokehouse; but don't you breathe a word of it for the world." Well of course that dear friend has a particular friend with whom it is as safe as in the grave, and so on and on, till by the time the story reaches the ears of the accused, it is reported that he stole a whole drove of hogs. Then he starts out to settle the matter, and even after this is done, there is always someone to say to every newcomer, "I would not trust that man too far. He was once accused of stealing. It is true that he proved out of it, but still I would watch him." So you see the voice of the tattler, once raised again; a person injures him to some extent for the rest of his life. Let it be said of the Alliance that it does not tolerate such, and that instead of its members trying to attend to other people's business, they attend strictly to their own and let others do the same. We will certainly lose nothing by this course, but gain a great deal of interest.

See how much difference there is between the tattler and the man or woman who always speaks well of his or her acquaintances—while the one is dreaded the other is honored by all right minded people.

Suballiance report

95.   October 16, 1888. Leon County. Crickett.

EDITOR MERCURY: I am a stranger to you and your paper, but want to write a few lines from Wilson Chapel Alliance. We are few in number but the majority of our members are ready to go down into their pockets any hour they are called upon. Still there are a few who whine and twist their mouths, and say, "I will wait a while till I can see a little further." Now my dear Alliance brethren, this will not do. It takes money to run all machinery, and if you don't watch, the bearings will soon be out of grease.

They say the *Mercury* is good medicine. So it is, but we don't take enough of it down here.

It seems that the Mercury has been a sort of "regulator" sure enough, taken [in] large doses once a week, price $1. For sale at this office, Ed.

With the October 23, 1888, issue of the Mercury, *the "Ladies' Department" becomes "The Family." Most of the letters printed there appear to be written by young people. This "The Family" section, which is shorter than the previous "Ladies' Department," begins with a solicitation from the* Mercury *editors to the "good mothers and wives, the boys and girls—in short, the families of the country—that it will be glad to hear from them at any time. . . . the* Mercury *wants this page to be the pet of the fireside." This section also contains a cure for corns (apply liquor potassae), excerpted from the* American Home *magazine; half a column on caring for pork, under the heading "Domestic"; and a short historical account of the Revolutionary war hero from Vermont, Col. Seth Warner.*

Defending the farm boy

96.   October 23, 1888. Chapel Hill. Milk Maid.

EDITOR MERCURY: I read a letter in a late issue of the *Mercury* to "Ox Driver" written by Ann Other in which she does the farmer boys an injustice. I go to church sometimes and I see the country boys there—rich and poor, sober and gay. I see country crackers and city dudes. I never see anybody spit on the floor except the clerks from cheap grocery stores. They look as lordly as if they were Goulds or Vanderbilts. Ox drivers are ashamed to do so.

The absence of letters; feelings of mutuality

97.   October 30, 1888. Ruston, Louisiana. Charitie.

EDITOR MERCURY: I am a little on the sick list today and so have time to write. I miss many of the writers of the *Mercury* who used to talk with and to us, but each passing month brings many changes. Marriages, births and deaths file along together. Thanks that there has been but very little change in my life—only sickness.

Where is Rebecca, Marie Labouchere and bright saucy Birdie and many other bright faces I used to see? Ann Other, I sympathize with you and your sad bereavement but death comes very suddenly and often plucks out our brightest flower; but if we live as the Bible teaches us, death can do us no harm. I would very much like to receive a private letter from you as I am very anxious to become better acquainted with you; so that if we are not related, we may become very good friends, which is much better. . . .

Despite the presence of Charitie's letter in this Mercury *issue, by October 30, 1888, the paper's "The Family" section consisted mainly of cures, short letters from children, recipes, a light article on the "Finicky Fooleries of Fashion," and the following paragraph:*

Woman's Suffrage—from an essay read before Delta County Alliance by a good Sister whose name we failed to get. Brother Ben Terrell brought it up, but had forgotten the name: "I do not know what you think of woman's suffrage, but I think that Alliance women have nobler duties to perform in the great battle of life than going to the polls and voting. We can help you pick out your cotton crop, cook your three meals a day, and try to make home happy for a happy home ought to be the dearest boon that a true woman could crave. Do not our husbands bring home their hard earned trophies, be they great or small and cast them at our feet? Then why should we wish to meddle with politics?"

Occasional letters still were published.

Mutuality between writers; domestic happiness

98.   November 6, 1888. Grayson County. Marie Labouchere.

EDITOR MERCURY: In [a past issue] our much admired correspon-dent, Charitie, requested me to write often and honored me with the kind assurance that all my letters will find a place in her scrapbook. It seems strange that she and I, who are so far apart, should have been thus complimenting each other for Charitie's communications had already graced the tenth page of my book of literary clippings. Her feeling expressions indicating innate refinement and long-enduring filial attachment have found a cozy nook in this household. I should gladly converse often with the agreeable visitors on our page, but my domestic responsibilities have in-creased far beyond my expectations since the advent of our beautiful twin babies. I should like to have my readers feast their eyes on my interesting trio, as my husband stands before me now, holding a cherub on each arm while a radiating smile illuminates his paternal countenance. . . . I am happily domiciled on the broad prairie, but continued blessings do not prevent my heart going out in sympathy for the suffering and sorrow of whom we read. Sometimes a notice in a secular paper tells us of a baby having departed this life, and in my imagination, I visit that desolate home. How awesome is the stillness! The air is bereft of music, for the pretty homebird has forever ceased his earthly warbling. And the desolate dwelling no more resounds with the patter of little feet. . . . I see the bereaved parents stooping low to decorate the grave with rosebuds and white lilies while commingled tears bedew these emblems of youth and innocence which now adorn the new made mound underneath which lies a tiny case containing the waxen form whose dimpled hand will never again pat and fondle the warm bosom which nurtured it unconsciously for the premature tomb. . . .

Concerning farm boys

99.   November 13, 1888. San Saba. Rural Widow.

EDITOR MERCURY: Ox Driver, you say the girls turn their noses up at the farmer boy. Whose fault is this? Does the farmer boy, when he calls on the girls, discuss literature or the current news of the day, so full of vital importance to intelligence? Not a bit. He deliberately leaves his senses at home with his workday garments and in the full dress of folly goes out to look for a life companion. After the weather has been fully discussed, the piano is invoked. After this comes compliments in all the superlatives at command; this causes a deluge of laughter and reiteration with polite positiveness and declarations of sincerity. Then follows small talk—so small that no microscope could make it visible. Then he declares that he heard she was going to get married. This remark contains an amount of facetiousness that cannot be computed. Two hours are given to discussing these observations and then the intellectual banquet is over, and with a sigh, the youth of twenty (forty) goes home to complain that the girls turn their noses up at him. When the farmer boy acts like an intellectual being and treats the girls as such he will never be snubbed by she who has a grain of common sense.

N. G. Barnes, what is there in Charles Dickens' work to make one light minded? "He taught the world," said Dean Stanley, as he stood by his new made grave, "great lessons of the eternal value of generosity, of purity, of kindness, and of unselfishness." Scott, Thackery, and George Eliott [sic], who can read them and not feel benefitted? I hold it true that not to know

Shakespeare, the keen and mighty prober of the deep heart of humanity, is to live in a mental darkness most deplorable. I would not give my acquaintance with these men and women for the costliest gem that ever sparkled on a monarch's brow. Ann Other, I sympathize with you in your sad affliction, though I know but little of this messenger we call death. John Goode Hope, has the "obstreperousness" of some of our band frightened you away? And do you now view the conflict from afar? Buckle on your armour again and come back.

The tone of the Mercury *is changing. The issue of December 6, 1888, in its "The Family" section, carries a quarter-column from "a writer in a woman's journal":*

To wives: Be as kind and courteous to your husband as you were when he was your lover. Then you used to look up to him; do not now look down upon him. Remember that you are married to a man not a god; be prepared for imperfections. Once in a while let your husband have the last word; it will gratify him and be no particular loss to you. Let him know more than you do once in a while; it keeps up his self-respect and you are none the worse for admitting that you are not actually infallible. Read something in the papers besides fashion notes and society columns; have some knowledge of what is going on in foreign countries. Be a companion to your husband if he is a wise man, and if he is not[,] try to make him become your standard. Raise his standard; do not let his lower yours. Even if your husband has no heart he is sure to have a stomach, so be careful to lubricate the marriage yoke with well cooked dinners. Don't always be teasing him for money . . . Respect your husband's relatives, especially his mother. . . . She loved him before you did.

Criticism of the *Mercury* letters; response by *Mercury* editors

100.   November 13, 1888. Wortham. Belle.

EDITOR MERCURY: I have been reading the *Mercury* a good while and I think it the best paper for the farmers [that I] have ever seen. I admire all the letters written by the sisters except one or two. I believe they try to get off a little sentiment—Blue Eyes [a writer from Pickens, South Carolina, whose letter is not included here] and another one or two. Now I don't think they should write sentimental letters because it is the farmers' paper and farmers do not indulge in sentimental foolishness.

This would be a sorry world without sentiment, Miss Belle; for it is sentiment that makes us love our wives and mothers, sentiment that makes us good and true, sentiment that makes patriots and heroes. But there is a kind of silly sentiment—"puppy love," the old men used to call it—that should be rebuked. That kind of sentiment between immature boys and girls often leads to disastrous results.—ED.

Criticism of the *Mercury* editors

101.   December 13, 1888. Lavaca County. Mary Ussery.

EDITOR MERCURY: Now for an hour of delicious quiet and unalloyed pleasure said I to myself as I picked up my paper which is always so welcome. So I seated myself comfortably in an old easy chair—not that I am so diminutive—that I might enjoy my paper. I picked up my favorite, the *[Mercury]*, unfolded it with an air of intense satisfaction, glanced over the local column, turned the paper and the first thing my eye encountered was two columns and a half of "Advice to Ladies." That was quite enough for one evening, but then I found "A Little Advice to Wives" and threw it down in disgust and wished the person who was so very thoughtful of our comfort as to bother his ingenious brains with writing no less than eight or ten pages of foolscap of advice for the benefit of poor women is—well, no matter where. It is very pleasant to know we have so many kind and considerate friends, who are always willing to discommode themselves in almost any manner in order that we may have our share of advice; but too much must not be expected of us for it is not a woman's nature to listen all the time.

"What is sauce for the goose is sauce for the gander" is a maxim, though old, still true and according to that it is about time for us to be taking upon our shoulders the responsibility of giving a little advice ourselves. We are charged to be ready with a smile to greet our husband, father, or brother when he has been out. Were we to follow that advice, I fear we should be smiling a greater part of the time and sometimes at one or two o'clock at night, too. Another injunction is, "Do not be ready with a whole rigamarole of domestic troubles to relate to your husband or father when he comes home late at night wearied with his own affairs." Indeed! I think we poor persecuted women would willingly bear some of his cares for him. For instance, it would be a quite pleasant "care" to regale oneself on a sumptuous little meal and to leave poor Papa to an evening of quiet and rest after the cares of the day and the pleasant little task of clearing away the tea things and amusing the children till bedtime, you, in the meantime, sallying forth to see after his "cares," which consist in a delightful walk for a couple of hours of jollification at the club in time to be home at the early hour of one and of course, Papa will be at the door ready to greet you with a bright smile, no doubt greatly refreshed with his evening of quiet and rest.

Now, Mr. Editor, what would you incorrigible men think if in every book, paper and magazine you took up you would find at least half the contents were articles of advice addressed to the gentlemen? Perhaps you would know how to sympathize with us poor women. But I am more fortunate than some of my fair sisters, as the advice does not apply to me, for I am not a wife, nor am I likely to be until next year, or until, confidently speaking, when women have their rights.

Decline of the Alliance

102.   January 24, 1889. Guadalupe County. Mrs. P. H. Hall.

EDITOR MERCURY: I have not seen many letters from the ladies in the *Mercury*. I think they have lost all interest in the Alliance and that causes the men not to take the interest they would. I am sorry to say ours is not doing much now; We have our regular meetings twice a month but they are very poorly attended. We need a good lecturer to come and wake us up. One thing I have noticed. When the ladies attend our meetings regularly there was a very good turnout, but they have nearly quit going and so have the men. Now, sisters, let us do our part. We can go to their meetings and encourage our husbands to go. My husband never misses a meeting. Neither do I.

Education

103.   February 14, 1888. [No location.] Mrs. George R. Chase.

EDITOR MERCURY: The mother must do much toward the education of her girls, but she cannot do everything, nor can all mothers do equally well. Many a daughter will outstrip her mother, to that mother's joy, not regret. Let the mother, however, try to keep pace, to bring back once bright school days and to brush the dust and cobwebs from matters nearly forgotten. Follow Bacon's famous direction. Pursue a course of reading with congenial associates. . . . try writing out in your own words the information that has come to you through reading. Then write your own ideas. . . . Encourage the daughters to tread the path of learning as long as they will. If civilization pays, if education is not a mistake, if hearts and brains and souls are more than the dress they wear, then by every interest dear to a Christian republic . . . give the girls the widest and the highest education we have dreamed of.

Then, too, they ought to have the chance to secure a special education. Why should not an education practical in character be provided by the state for farmers' daughters as well as farmers' sons? Let not our girls look down upon the simple womanly tasks that bring joy and comfort to the household. . . .

Urging on the Alliance

104.   February 21, 1888. Devers Woods. Black Eyes.

EDITOR MERCURY: Will you permit a member from Oakdale Alliance to come in and chat with the dear Brothers and Sisters? I promise not to consume too much space in our dear paper. Now brothers of the Alliance, the election is over and to the surprise of a great many non-members, the Alliance is here yet. Now let us one and all see if we cannot keep it here. But we must be up and doing for our enemies are great. We must not sit with folded hands and wait for someone else to do everything. We must not get mad and say we will not have anything more to do with the Alliance just because everything does not suit us. We must forgive these little wrongs for we are none perfect. We must be ready to do what our leaders think best, for I am sure they will not tell us to do what they think to be wrong. Now dear sisters, let us all try to do what we can to help the Alliance to prosper. I know we can't do much but we can help keep our fathers and husbands out of debt this year. So with the new year let us see if we can't do something to advance the cause of the Alliance and I think at the end of the year we will not be found wanting. Brother Editor, wishing you and your host of readers a happy and prosperous year, I close.

Self-esteem

105. February 21, 1888. Tehuacana. Mollie Lamb.

EDITOR MERCURY: I am old enough to belong to the Alliance. I think the Alliance a good thing for the farmers, for if the farmers don't help themselves they won't get any help at all. Brothers and sisters let us stick together; if we do not we need not expect anything but bondage. Editor *Mercury,* this is my third letter to our dear old paper but I thought of what the reader says, "try, try again." We have got some true Alliance men in our lodge as can be but the ladies they don't attend worth a snap, but we can excuse them for we know they are simpletons anyway, that is what the men say about us. Mr. Editor you must not expect much from me. My oldest brother belongs to the Alliance. Success to the *Mercury* and "long may the Alliance roll."

Citizenship

106. February 28, 1889. Bexar County. Corn Bread.

EDITOR MERCURY: There is a very credible movement in several parts of the country to form clubs for the promotion of good citizenship. . . . In this government by the people, the majority of men take no more real part in governing than consists in voting for the men the professional politicians have named for them. The government seldom sifts down to the people but only to the caucus packers. The government is chosen by the caucuses, and people never attend the caucuses—only politicians as a rule do this. If these societies for the promotion of good citizenship shall teach men that the caucus and not merely the polling place is the direct point of contact between the government and the people, they will teach the first great lesson of citizenship. Another great duty of citizenship is thorough information about the political economy of the day. Our system of government is menaced by tremendous forces of socialism, anarchism and other disturbing elements. The disciples of the systems are not, as is generally supposed, ignoramuses and half lunatics. They are members who have made a lifelong study of the world's social and political problems. The anarchists recently hung in Chicago were learned men, doctrinairies, well-drilled specialists in the social problems of the day. These men are dangerous because they think they have found a tremendous injustice at the bottom of society, and they are doubly dangerous because in this belief they are right. It is the duty of all good citizens to recognize this truth early and to set about finding remedies for this injustice before these dangerous men find it in the firebrand the dynamite bomb. A fatuous faith in the permanency of our institutions is not patriotism as much as laziness. At no time is that eternal vigilance which Jefferson calls the price of liberty been as necessary as at the present.

Hoping to see this in print I will close for this time,

Alliance duties; loss of support

107.   February 28, 1889. Gillespie County. A True Sister.

EDITOR MERCURY: If there is anything an Alliance person should know and perform it certainly is their duty. When a member is once initiated, their first duty is to find out what is inside the constitution of the order that he or she may be able to define its principles when assailed by our numberous enemies. . . .

It is our duty to attend every meeting and give strict attention to every subject that may be presented before the body for consideration and study both sides of the question thoroughly that we may be capable to vote intelligently. We should not sit still and allow our brother or sister to do our thinking for us; if we do, how can we expect to improve intellectually?

It is too often the case that the majority of Alliance members fail to express their own opinions even if they have one, but let them get out and they can tell you exactly what they believe. If we would only speak our true sentiments either for or against anything while in convention, there is a chance, if we are holding to a wrong idea, to be corrected. . . . There are really members, many of them in this county, who believe the Alliance dead, simply because the *Mercury* never enters their houses. We must peruse closely its every page. It is our greatest source of information. . . .

Farm life

108.   February 28, 1889. Colorado County. Mrs. Maner.

MR. EDITOR: Down here in southern Texas, the Alliance has brought its knitting and come to stay; the clicking of its needles are heard in every neighborhood. We're winning, too. Outsiders have left off scoffing at us [and] that helps some. Our enterprising brothers started a co-operative store here which is a sure success. We are beginning to trust God and help ourselves.

This has been a wet, dreary winter. There is some cotton to pick yet; very little plowing has been done. Many cattle have died, I think more from disease than hunger, as we lost some and ours had plenty to eat. We have corn, potatoes and pork for our own use and some to spare. We keep our cotton seed to feed the cattle, and have milk and butter all year. We have several acres of Johnson grass from which we get more hay than we need. During this gloomy weather I've been busying myself repairing old garments, making quilts and getting better acquainted with my husband, who, by the way, is not near so attractive since he sits in the house and whittles, as he was when he only came in at meal time. The sum of human happiness is made up of little things.

Men must work and women must weep. Men will whistle and women must sweep. I'm going to have my share of happiness. I fill my lamp of love with the oil of patience and keep it burning brightly. Last night was Saturday night. After the work was all done, Ben sat before a cheerful fire drying the dampness of his clothes. Georgia in her own corner busied herself with some lace work, while I, too tired to knit, drew my low rocker nearer the lamp and sat down to rest and read. I selected a volume of Alden's Cyclopedia and read aloud extracts from the writings of Heroditus and others; a short poem by J. G. Holland pleased me so much by its very suggestiveness, I concluded to copy it for you young brothers:

God give us men/A time like this demands
Strong minds, great hearts, true faith and ready hands. . . .

Scarcity of letters; contraction of currency

109.   March 7, 1889. Ennis. Ann Other.

DEAR MERCURY AND SISTERS: Someone told me some time ago that one of the sisters had asked for Sister Ann Other to come again but not to have one of her bad dreams. Well, I feel as though I had a long dream and not a very pleasant one, either, for different reasons. We failed to subscribe to the *Mercury* last fall when our time expired and when we did subscribe, one lonely paper came closely wrapped in its selfish coat not at all spread out in the social manner it used to come when it came with so many neighbors; and sure enough, it made that one call its last and week after week we have swept and cleaned our mental house and had the table spread for the feast we were sure it would bring with the spices and wine (only jesting W.C.T.U.) and from Marie Labouchere with our sweet fruits, flowers and honey from sister Charitie, and the substantial bread and meat and stabilities of life from Western Reader and the warmth and home comfort of Sister Rebecca, none of which we received in that one selfish wrapper, but were sure all those who so liberally supplied the *Mercury* table in months gone by will still continue to do the same and I am real hungry and want each of the sisters to send me something for my mental table. If you will each send something, the other sisters I am sure will supply such things as they have handy; and I am sure Bro. Tetts and other brothers will bring up their strong streams of thought from their deep flowing and help the spread and perhaps I can get enough in one meal to compensate for this long and forced fast.

Dear Sisters, do you try to write in a house full of noisy merry children, some play, helping others analyze their grammar lessons, and another in her first efforts with fractions? If you do, you will not look for much of interest from such a busy but happy mother.

I see in Gov. Ross' message that he advises caution lest the legislature should crush our railroad monopoly. Alas, for the shortsightedness that would lead a representative to conceive that a pygmy can crush a giant. As the laboring people, they are now so crushed and crowded for money, that votes can be bought for half a dollar or a pair of shoes for the little ones. As long as our currency remains in its present contracted state and a few individual bankers can convulse the whole nation in its finances, as long as we live with our present banking laws, there is no power on earth that can destroy our railroad monopolies and monopolies of all kinds. As to issuing bonds on the counties to build our roads[,] it seems to me no thinking man can contemplate what our national bonded debt has done for us and then authorize the issuing of still more bonds for the present and rising generation to pay. "All things whatsoever ye would that man should do to you, do you even now to them." This is the Golden Rule, Christ's rule, but it must be it is left from the Bible of the monopolist and those who would issue a bonded debt, and it is equally applicable to monopolies of other kinds, and is opposed to a government where man is the integer and woman the cipher and while we are being idle in the great revolution and waiting for time to work it out we should remember time never works; it eats, and rots, and rusts, and destroys. But it never works. It only gives us an opportunity to work. Yours very truly.

Alliance declining; urging on the members

110.   March 7, 1889. Navarro City. Mrs. I. L. Payne.

EDITOR MERCURY: I have been thinking for some time that I would write to let you know that Pinoak Alliance, No. 320 is not quite dead, but some of its members seem to be sleeping quietly; some are punctual to attend and willing to put their shoulders to the wheel at all times to further our grand institution in its noble course. Some of the Sisters as well as the brothers are very careless about attending. Some will say, "I have so much to do, I don't see how I can lose the time to go." Others will say, "It will do no good for me to go, cannot do anything." Let me say to you Sisters, that it is your duty to go, your very presence is encouraging. When we have a full attendance, we all feel encouraged, that we are trying to do something for the advancement of our noble order. Nothing prevents me from attending but some providential hindrance. I have the honor of being treasurer of our Alliance for nearly two years. Some of our members paid off their debts last fall, others who were not lucky enough to have the means to pay them are striving to pay all they owe this year. Our lodge has resolved to not go in debt nor mortgage anything to the merchants this year. Sisters, let us do all in our power to keep our husbands, brothers and children from going into debt this year. I buy all I am bound to have through the summer with butter, chickens, and eggs. That which I cannot buy and pay for, I do without. We need a good lecturer to come and awaken our lodge to their duty. I will quit for fear of taking too much space. Success to our noble paper.

Urging on members

111.   March 7, 1889. Centerville. Mrs. S. E. Watkins.

EDITOR MERCURY: As I have not seen any letters from the sisters in this part of the moral vineyard, I will try to let you all know that we have a little Red Land Alliance down here, but some of our little band have grown careless and do not attend as they should. Now, Sisters, we say we love the Alliance: do we act so? How can we manifest it? I say, by going to the meetings with our husbands and doing all we can for them. We can cultivate our gardens and potato patches and have something at home to help our husbands out of debt. Raise our own chickens and eggs and do without that which we don't really need. Oh, how I long for that time to come when our husbands can come in and sit down by the fire of a cold rainy day and say, "I owe no man anything, and my house is furnished with the necessities of life, and now I can rest from under the burdens and hard labor of the monopolists." Oh, how I would love to see the merchants who have robbed us of our rights go to the plow handles to toil for their daily bread as our husbands had to. Now, Sisters, let's be up and doing as it is springtime and the flowers will soon begin to put forth their blooms, and the bees will soon begin to work, and let us be with them, heart and hand, and lay a store for winter days.

Alliance declining

112.   March 14, 1889. O'Daniel, Guadalupe County. Rena R. Scott.

EDITOR MERCURY: It seems that the suballiances have lost some of their enthusiasm. Why is this? Has the Alliance, where it has had the support of the brotherhood[,] failed in any undertaking? If so I don't know when or where. Why is it that the Alliance is less dear to us than it was two years ago? I say it is our fault. Who will not admit that it is the same grand and noble organization that it ever was? Not one of its principles have been defiled. We can make it one of the best organizations in existence or we can make it nothing. It appears that some have chosen the latter route. They are seldom seen within the walls of our open Alliance and when there, they forget to bring their pocketbooks, so their dues go unpaid. When they are suspended from the roll and are notified they say, "Oh, the Alliance costs too much money. I can't stand it." Alas, deluded brethren, you don't know that you are losing ten times that amount by not attending your Alliance, paying your dues and dealing through the exchange. To prove this, I shall relate an instance of which I was an eye witness. A member this last year saved thirty-nine dollars and a half. He bought a wagon, saving twenty dollars on the price that was given him by the merchants the same day, and saved nineteen and a half dollars on cotton over and above the price offered him on the street the same day. This is no wild dream but a simple fact. If you did not make something, it is simply because you did not do your duty. Many members will go to town, and instead of going to their own house, will do their trading with others because they are told they can do better than with their own firm. Now it seems they put a great deal of confidence in what they are told, at the same time crying class legislation; yet they were told to vote for certain individuals and did so. I like to see confidence, but have a little in yourself. If you have none in yourself, no one else ought to. . . . I visited an Alliance not long since and a resolution was passed, [where members] pledged themselves to not mortgage their cotton crop to anyone. Such a resolution should be passed in every sub-Alliance in the state and strictly adhered to. It will give a chance to hold their cotton or sell through the Exchange, thereby getting the benefit of the Alliance.

Mr. Editor, Guadalupe County is in need of a new lecturer to kindle anew the old flame so the Alliance would go on as of yore.

Support the Exchange

113.   March 14, 1889. Pleasant Run Alliance. Jenny.

Our Alliance is in a prosperous condition, numbers about eighty-five members in good standing, and most of them readers of the *Mercury*.

I wish to ask the brethren a question: Is it our fault or the fault of the gigantic monopolies that are being built up all over our land and country from the products of the unthinking mass of people? I say the fault is around our own fireside: carelessly letting our brains sob and rust out in ignorance, waiting for some other man to cut and dry plans and specifications by which to be governed. Let us crawl out of the old fogy *[sic]*, demoralized ranks and act for ourselves and stand square-toed to the Exchange, patronize it and remember all other Alliance enterprises for the next four years. I think there will be a great change. Respectfully,

The state of one suballiance

114.   March 14, 1889. Union Alliance. S. A. Joiner.

EDITOR MERCURY: As no one has ever written anything from Union Alliance, No. 2104, I will. Our Alliance was organized in 1886, has held out faithful and expects always to. We have about thirty members who seem to be very solid with the exception of a few. It seems as if all can't see and understand alike. I joined the great noble order June 1886. I like it better each time we meet, which is twice a month. My husband is president of this Alliance. We have a lady lecturer, but she don't seem to do much in regard to Alliance duties. Please send us some of those we read of in the *Mercury*. I have been reading the *Mercury* for nearly two years and expect to continue as long as I keep my eyesight and twenty-five cents or one dollar can be had. I feel like we're going to have better times than we've had for several years. We are all trying to live up close and economical. I have been looking for something from Union Alliance for some time. Why is it we are never noticed? I think we are as wide-awake and hardworking a set as ever I saw. Is it for want of sense? No, it is for want of energy. Any of them are more capable of writing than I. Let some sister write some good words for the benefit of our young ladies. We have but one in our lodge. I will close; please do not throw this aside, as it is my first.

Motherhood

115.   March 28, 1889. Ruston, Louisiana. Charitie.

EDITOR MERCURY: Beg pardon, Mr. Editor, I couldn't remain out any longer after seeing the return of Sister Ann Other. So permit me to extend the hand of friendship to one and all, and become a member of the happy family for this once, if no more. It has been quite a while since I put in my oar to help propel the *Mercury*. . . . It seems to progress quite rapidly without my aid.

Well, I have been busy with my home affairs attending to the fruits and flowers that I stored away for winter's use, and also preparing a book for publication. Now, Sister Ann Other, I have no flowers or fruits to bring for this time. All I have to offer is a heart overflowing with admiration for all. I have enjoyed reading all the pleasant witty words and good thoughts of each and every one.

I always overlook the signatures to see if my favorite correspondents are present, and if so I read those first. I have very much missed my Maria Labouchere. Come again and bring more of your spices and wines and tell me about the little Janie and Johnny Goodhope. (My twins['] names are Arthur and Olla.) And you, Western Reader, come with your stabilities of life; and Rebecca with your home comforts, for it takes all to make a happy home. And you, Ann Other, are needed with your W.C.T.U., and Uncle Snort must come too, and bring the music, and won't we all have a jolly time?

Do any of us try to write with a house full of noisy, merry children, asks sister Ann Other. I guess you would think so if you were here around my fireside tonight. The oldest is trying to write a composition on "the pleasure of receiving letters," and to be sure I must assist her; the other two are getting their geography lessons, and my seven year old boy must have a little help with his speech and, of course, mamma must assist.

I live a few steps from a school room. I sit at noon and enjoy seeing the children romp and play so you see I am never without children. My heart is full of pity for the homes without them. . . . What happiness to know that in my children's heart there is true love for me. If death should take me from them now their memory of me would embody all that is pure and good. If they grow to manhood and womanhood and I to old age, how pleasant to feel their strong arms will support me. . . .

I hope that through the medium of the *Mercury,* I am weaving friendly meshes that shall remain unbroken.

Morality and religion

116.   March 28, 1889. Mansfield. Mrs. Lizzie Leonard.

Our obligation as members of the Alliance binds us under one of the most solemn obligations to our order and to each other. Do we fully understand what that obligation means? What does it mean morally . . . ? Must we refrain from obscene language, lying, stealing, keep out of bad company, refrain from intoxicating drinks, adhere to the strictest truth, never defrauding anyone, nor deceiving anyone . . . ? Truth is the foundation on which all great structures are built. Christ, the great law-giver, said, "I am the way, the truth and the light," . . . Do we try to help our members when in trouble? Do we attend the meetings of our lodge when possible? This reminds me of an anecdote of the bear that went into a house. The man jumped into the loft and staid *[sic]* there while his wife took an ax and killed the bear, and then he came down and looked at the dead bear and said, "Ain't we brave, Nancy?" People are afraid not to belong to the Alliance for fear that some great good will come out of it and they will not get their share. But they don't want to spend much time or labor, so they just pay their dues and stay in the loft until the great structure gets to pay, then they will come down and say, haven't we done wonders, but if it should fail they will say, that is just what I thought.

We take the Bible as our waybill through life. In it we find the moral code on which our order is built. Go to Exodus, there you find in the Ten Commandments what it takes to constitute morality. In the history of Samson, the angel's instructions to his mother, when he sent to tell her of his birth, we have the foundation on which we must build all temperance structures, which we must have if we would be strong. Job gives us an example of patience, which we must exercise if we succeed in accomplishing any good. In the Psalms we are taught unity. In Daniel we learn not to fear . . . [indecipherable] . . . Chapter 8, the 12th Verse, we learn our duty and our obligation to our Creator and bountiful benefactor. . . . You may quit the Alliance but that will not lift the solemn obligation you have taken.

Money should not be the only incentive to work for the Alliance. We must make agricultural life more attractive to our sons and daughters so as to keep them from the cities where they will be exposed to so much vice. . . . If we never gain any great financial benefit to ourselves, we will build an order that will be a great legacy to our children and future generations. . . .

Women working in the fields

117.   April 4, 1889. Luna Vista. Frankie Bradford.

EDITOR MERCURY: Although my last letter was not put in print, yet I am not discouraged, so will write again. Spring, the most beautiful season is now here. No doubt the cousins are thankful for such blessings as spring does bring with all its beautiful scenery. The farmers are busy farming. Papa has no boys large enough to help him, and therefore his girls must help. I am not ashamed to confess that I work on the farm, for I am sure it is no discredit to do so; and whoever thinks so, have some lack of knowledge. I believe a girl can work in the field and be so full of grace as one that dwells in a palace; yes, they are more likely to obtain grace and grow therein than those who look down upon them as in disgrace. Let those who say it

Hoeing cotton. Courtesy Photography Collection, Harry Ransom Humanities Research Center, The University of Texas at Austin

is a disgrace to a girl to work in the field take heed to themselves and see if they are in grace. I firmly state that a girl can live a true Christian while working in the field as she can at any other kind of work. She may plow, hoe, plant, pick cotton, etc. Yet, while doing any of those things she can have her heart full of love and grace; speaking to herself in psalms and hymns and spiritual songs, singing and making melody in her heart to the Lord.

Farm life; Alliance declining

118.   April 18, 1889. Oakville. Lucretia M. Dunn.

EDITOR MERCURY: I am a farmer's girl who has just bidden farewell to "sweet sixteen" and belong to that noble order, the Farmers Alliance, the Lebanon Alliance, No. 8612. I don't know of one member who has ever mortgaged his crop before it was planted, though I suppose many of them do buy on a credit. But that is not papa's plan at all; he has always made it a rule never to buy anything unless he could pay cash for it, and although there are twelve of us in the family, not one of us has ever starved to death yet. We raise almost everything we eat at home. We have lived here eleven years and our smokehouse has never been empty, nor have we bought five pounds of bacon or lard.

Now I don't know anything about fine hogs but papa killed two pigs less than eight months ago, one weighing 205 and the other 195 pounds. I don't know whether they would be called fine hogs or not, but they are fine enough for me.

Papa plants cotton only as a surplus crop and never more than we can gather our selves. We have never hired a lock of cotton picked. Our land is very fertile. I don't remember that we have ever gathered less than 1,200 pounds per acre, but one year, and then the best part of the crop was blown out by a storm.

In your letter you alluded to men who go to town and spend all their money for whisky and then growl about monopolies. Now I can say this much for our Alliance, in fact, for the entire neighborhood. I don't know of but one man in this vicinity who ever gets even moderately drunk. I don't remember having seen a drunken man in my life, though I've always lived in a local option county, and if whisky is the horrid thing it is represented to be, I never want to live out of one.

Can you tell me what the best medicine for a sick Alliance is? Am sorry to say that ours is either very sick or so sleepy she can't hold her eyes open long enough to see her almost ruined condition. There are scarcely ever enough members present on the appointed day to hold a meeting, and very often neither president or vice-president is there. Maybe a physician in the shape of a good lecturer who would give our alliance members a rousing speech to wake them up a little and then urge them to take more *Mercury* would be beneficial.

Uncle Snort, you need not go to the piney woods to get out of the mud, for we are out of it here in the Live Oak woods. We have had a lot of rain this winter but the ground is not muddy. Several farmers are planting corn now. The soil is mostly black sandy loam and doesn't get very muddy. The fruit trees are in full bloom.

Mutuality

119.   April 25, 1889. San Saba. Laura Oakly.

EDITOR MERCURY: This is such a rare golden afternoon that I cannot refrain from calling on you all. Our Alliance is in a prospering condition. The sisters think they have missed a grand treat if anything happens to prevent them from attending.

Charitie, I want to tell you how glad I was to read your letter. I like your idea of comradeship among women. This feeling that you and I are linked together by sympathy in a mutual effort (if you will permit such an expression) goes far to strengthen the effort individually made.

Dear family, we never made a greater mistake in our lives than when we judged Rural Widow by her letters. I expected to meet a woman past her youth and extremely cold and haughty. What I did meet was a girl lovely in face and manners—and those blue eyes, they were beautiful enough to make captive every heart. What has become of Rebecca? Come again Rebecca, with your brave, true words. Will Charitie and Anne Other tell me through the family if we are responsible for our thoughts to one? This is a perplexing question.

Duties of Alliance members

120.   May 2, 1889. Stone Point, Van Zandt County. Mattie E. Terry.

EDITOR MERCURY: As the president of our Alliance requested me to write to our noble paper, I will endeavor to give a few thoughts. Although

I am not gifted with the pen as Ann Other, Charitie, and others, my heart is full of Alliance zeal.

Rock Point Alliance, No. 475, numbers about thirty in good standing and I wish to be understood that we will stand. I hear so much cry through the *Mercury* for a lecturer to come and renew them, if not they will surely die. Such nonsense; I say it is very good and nice to have a lecturer to visit us once in awhile, but if we do not have any at all we are not going to quit the Alliance. We have come to stay. Some of us sisters who have little children can't attend very regularly, but we will go as often as we can, and encourage our husbands to go.

Our Alliance has offered a premium for the most corn and cotton raised on one acre of land; there are several striving for the prize.

It was voted on, and I think unanimously carried, that at the roll call all repeat the obligation in answer to their name. I think it would be nice and grand if all the Alliance members would learn the obligation by heart. I don't think there is one-third who belong to the Alliance know anything about it. I am as good a member as anybody, pay my dues and go occasionally. Some others forget the Exchange, the *Mercury,* and anything else they think would take a dime. Poor, stingy member, how can he expect to be benefitted when he is of no benefit to our noble order?

I guess you are tired blotching out errors so I will close by wishing the Alliance and the *Mercury* a never-ending life.

The importance of political education

121. May 9, 1889. Reprinted from an address of welcome, Harbin Literary Society, Dublin. Olia Jones.

LADIES AND GENTLEMEN: I have been chosen by our honorable body, the Harbin Literary Society, to prepare an address of welcome. . . . We first organized our little band in 1884 and have perpetuated it year after year in connection with our school. We are organized into a Literary Society to promote the general welfare and prosperity of our glorious republic through education. It is the key that unlocks the way to civilization. . . . Ours, through education, is not a government of oppression and terror, but one of wisdom, peace, and liberty.

So if we perpetuate our free institution and republican form of government, we must do it by educating the masses in political economy and the science of economical government, with the ballot box closely guarded on one side by common sense and the other by patriotism and honesty.

Out of this little audience, there may be called a statesman to guide the ship of state, a financier to correct our financial errors, a soldier to defend our flag, a sailor to explore the sea, or a politician who will correct political abuses. . . . Hence, the necessity of perpetuating our free schools and literary societies throughout the nation. . . .

Simplify life; mothers' duties

122.   May 9, 1889. Colorado County. Mrs. Maner.

EDITOR MERCURY: Sister Young requests some sister to tell what women can do to help. It seems to me that women are always doing but not always working in the right way. Most women (I mean the middle class) do too much unnecessary work. This everlasting stitch, stitch, cook, cook, wash, wash, iron, iron, is killing our women. It is costing lots of money for doctor's bills and patent medicines; it is making women prematurely old, husbands unhappy and the young folks discontented, driving the boys away from home and making the girls want to go. When will mothers learn that there is something more beautiful in life than tucks and ruffles, lace and embroidery; something more enduring than the pleasures of the palate?

Mothers, dress the little ones in plain comfortable clothes and do away with so much machine and laundry work. Have good wholesome food but not so much variety at each meal, simplify your work; leave off unnecessary things and take time to be agreeable. Don't waste your time, health and life in non-essentials. Cold bread, butter milk, tea or coffee, with a smiling mamma at the table are more enjoyable than hot biscuits and fried chicken with a tired, fretful, unresponsive mother, whose presence chills the warmth and glow of childish joy. . . .

Mothers, it is as much your duty to save yourselves as it is to say your prayers. Take care of your own health and the health of your family, open the doors and windows and let in the fresh air and sunshine; throw back the bedcovers and hang up the children's gowns to air while you get breakfast. Pure air and sunshine are kin to soap and water and all are conducive to health. A bath and clean gown are a sedative for a fretful child and often insure a good night's rest to mother and child. Give your child a happy childhood if you give them nothing else; keep close to the hearts of your children. It is not fine clothes, toys or luxuries that makes a child happy, but the ever-ready, tender sympathy of its parents.

Climate has much to do with a man's physical development, and in the same way the mind of a child grows or decays in the daily atmosphere of home. It is the unconscious habit of thought of parents, the mode of life, the ordinary daily current of conversation, that molds the mind and character of a child.

Death of a mother; mutuality

123.   May 16, 1889. San Saba. Laura Oakly.

EDITOR MERCURY: Since I last wrote, which has been but a short time I have been changed from a lighthearted girl who found nothing but bright, beautiful flowers in her path, to a sad, heartbroken woman. My mother, the one who was my sun by day and guiding star by night, has been taken from me after a short illness and I turn to the family for comfort. I know there are some in this large family who can sympathize with me from experience. I have three little ones left in my care and I feel that I need the prayers of every sister. Oh what a trial it is to try to fill a mother's place. Why this burden has been placed on my shoulders I cannot see, but I know the Heavenly Father doeth all things well. I hope you will forgive me for coming to you so soon and in my happy days I always went to the *Mercury* family for enjoyment, and when sorrow overtook me, I turned to it for sympathy.

Fashion

124.   May 16, 1889. Colorado County. Mrs. Maner.

This is the season for renovating old clothes and happy is the farmer's daughter who was good to her last summer's dresses. She has a reward in having something to make over. By way of suggestion to those who live remote from town and fashion plates, I'll tell what I have seen. A chambry, having plain skirt, basque, and out-of-date drapery was changed by making a wide ruffle (18–20 inches) of the drapery, cutting the basque off at the waistline, and sewing the ruffle to the waist. A nice dark lawn was ripped up, ironed out, and made into a plain full skirt and waist gathered full into yoke, worn with the belt of the lawn. A white bard muslin is to be made into a mother Hubbard and the drapery makes a nice dress for a child. A full skirt, blouse waist, with sailor collars and puffs, the collar and cuffs are briar stitched with red and edged with red braid. . . . Many old dresses can be made over to be nice and stylish; and most girls would rather be out of Heaven than out of fashion. The girls in the in-betweenities are soul-harrowing perplexities to mothers and elder sisters; they have grown so much since last summer, it is difficult to find anything to make over for them and mama must be skillful . . . Calico is cheap and farmer's daughters must learn to wear calico with dignity, for, my dears, you are more respected wearing a calico dress that is paid for than a silk dress that Papa is in debt for.

Fashion, whose fiat is almost as inexorable as fate, has decreed that the bustle must go; it is dying a lingering death, only a hint of bustle is allowable now and puffs and puckers in the back drapery is not much worn. Girls, do the best you can and don't harass papa about buying new things that he isn't able to pay for. Beauty is duty, that is no woman has a right to be ugly. An intelligent, sweet-tempered, kind-hearted, obliging woman is beautiful in any kind of nice fitting dress. . . .

Farm life

125.   May 30, 1889. Oakville. Lucretia M. Dunn.

EDITOR MERCURY: When my letter was printed in the *Mercury*, I hadn't the least idea of assisting the immigration boon to this county, but my pitiful little scrawl has caused me to receive letters of inquiry from different persons which I will answer as well as I can. We raise corn, cotton, hay, sugar cane, both Irish and sweet potatoes, and melons of all kinds in abundance. I don't think small grains will do very well here; as a rule. Vegetables of almost every kind thrive splendidly; plums and grapes do better than other kinds of fruit.

The health of the country is unexceptional. Our timber is mostly mesquite and live oak; there is plenty of it for fuel and fencing. We depend upon tanks and wells for water; the well water generally contains so much mineral that it is used for household purposes, though some of it is good. Fish are not very plentiful. They can sometimes be caught in the Nueces River. Deer and wild turkey are still to be found but not very plentifully. The county is mostly thickly settled and almost every man has his land fenced, so you know there is not much land common.

Fetching water. Courtesy Photography Collection, Harry Ransom Humanities Research Center, The University of Texas at Austin

There are but few negroes here and they congregate in the towns. Mexicans can be found out on the ranches, wherever they can get work.

The country is generally rolling and has a good supply of chaparral and various other kinds of thorny brush. Unimproved land can be bought at two dollars per acre. Crops are in fine condition, corn is tasseling, and I have seen some silks; cotton is ten inches high and forming squares.

Education and morality

126.   May 30, 1889. Post Oak Prairie. Mrs. Minars.

EDITOR MERCURY: I agree with Mrs. Maner that we do not always work in the right way. We spend too much time trying to follow the frivolous fashions of the day which will never enlighten our minds or ennoble our souls or win an hour of happiness or contentment. . . . I think we ought to educate our children in all that is good and true in books and out of them. Teach them that the cut of a coat or the color of a cravat is a second class matter. . . . Let us teach our boys to do any kind of farmwork and our girls to bake and sew and do all kinds of housework in a neat and businesslike style.

Above all, give them employment, for idle hands will find mischief to do, such is the cause of our penitentiaries being full. Parents are too indulgent. Our children spend too much time in loitering.

Love of rural life

127.   May 30, 1889. Gonzales County. P. D. Ellis.

I wish to speak to parents of boys who should be induced by every means to stay on the farm. Ask the farmer's son what he intends to do and he almost invariably answers, "I don't know but certainly not farm." Nothing is done to make the farm attractive. We must educate our sons, send them to college to learn farming as a science, all the best methods and improved implements. He should also read literature; pure, high-toned books and papers are the best educators. Do not let him complain after following the plow all day he is too tired to read or study. Give him a bath and a slice of mother's snow flake bread and golden butter and a goblet of rich buttermilk to refresh him and he will not miss from sleep the hour spent in study. Study every feature of farm life—the most free and happiest on earth in its sweet intercourse with nature. For those who crave the noise and din of the city, the close, dark counting room, there is weariness beyond expression. Those poor oxygen starved creatures would give half their life for your happy privilege of roaming carefree and contented through the cool dark woods, inhaling pure air. Stay at home with mother, whose gentle hands are ready and quickly soothe your slightest pain. How can the stale bread and reeking hash of the boarding house compare to her puffy rolls, nice new eggs and savory tempting ham . . . ? Come back to mother after your college course and with a cultured mind and hands enjoy the happiest life on earth, on the farm.

Importance of education; contentment with rural life

128. June 6, 1889. Reprinted from an address to the District Alliance at Leesville.
        Mrs. Blanch McGarity.

How many of its most zealous members realize the value of our institute? How many think or know what it has done and is doing for the country generally and for the farmer especially? It is noble work and we want more interest. . . . The much abused expression, "the down-trodden farmer," is a misnomer. The farmer is honorable in his noble calling. What has wrought this delightful change? The old fashioned idea that farming does not require an education is hidden away with other false ignorant notions of the Dark Ages, buried never to be resurrected, and in its stead has grown and blossomed and borne wonderous fruit the knowledge that education is not only important but an actual necessity. Each farmer ought to have his own private library and every community its circulating library and reading rooms where the best literature and information about farming can be gotten. Rouse yourself! Be alive, wide-awake, build up and improve constantly, not so restless and always planning to leave the farm. . . .

Why does the overtaxed, nervous city invalid long for the blessed quiet of the farm? Because he remembers too well its carefree happiness. And he knows that nowhere else can he gain such pure air, such ease of mind and body as its calm hours bring. As he leans wearily back in his close dark room . . . there floats in enraptured vision his dear old farm home with its long vine shaded veranda, its rows and rows of bee stands, the deep cool well, and the dairy house nigh it, the babbling brook wherein he waded and fished in his boyhood days, the orchard, the meadow, the deep tangled wild wood and every beloved spot that his infancy knows. All, all comes back to him and his very soul seems to cry out for a draught from the moss covered bucket that hung in the well.

On the farm are modeled some of our most noble characters, instilled with the best principles. Father, see that you make the farm what it should be by honorable example of honest industry, judicious management. Mother, who can estimate your influence? Make it a cheery, joyous home, full of sunshine and pure pleasure. . . .

Women saving egg and butter money to help the Exchange

129.   June 6, 1889. Donalton, Hunt County. Mrs. A. P. Shaw.

EDITOR MERCURY: I am a member of the Donalton Alliance and a constant reader of the *Mercury*. . . . It seems to me that the brethren of suballiances are not doing their duty and are afraid to trust our leaders, or they would pay off the indebtedness of the Exchange. I write to make this proposition to the sisters of the Lone Star state: That we will sell eggs, butter, chickens and garden stuff to the amount of one dollar by the first of

July, to help pay off the debt that hangs over the Exchange. Now let me see in the *Mercury* how many sisters are willing to lend a helping hand to save our head; for the Exchange is our head and if our head be cut off, our body is worthless.

> We will ad to this list as rapidly as the sisters send us their names and addresses—ED.

Urging on the Alliance

130.   June 6, 1889. Kelso Alliance. Hannah Bryant.

EDITOR MERCURY: Our state lecturer was here and lectured for the Kelso Alliance and requested me to write this letter.

New petitions are being sent in at every meeting of our Alliance. The sisters do not attend the Alliance as often as they should. I think it is every sister's duty to attend as often as they possibly can. If we go oftener, it would encourage the men. We must all go to work with all our might. We can't accomplish anything if we wait for some one else to start first. Let us take hold and all "give a long pull, a strong pull and all pull together."

Mutuality and empathy; philosophy of life

131.   June 13, 1889. Harmony Ridge. Rural Widow.

Laura Oakly's sad letter called me out. Laura, you have my heartfelt sympathy in your recent bereavement. I once passed through the trying ordeal of seeing the bonds of love and friendship severed by the cruel hand of death, heard three motherless children asking for "mamma." Yes, verily pity "makes all hearts throb as one." God will surely prepare a way of escape so we must not despair. God knows the keys to the human heart to touch in order to draw out harmonies. They may be the minor keys of sadness and sorrow or the loftiest notes of joy and gladness. "The man who lives without trial dies but half a man." Sorrow is the native soil of manhood and self-reliance. . . . We will all live sufficiently long to see our idols desecrated and the laurels we have woven together in expectant joy for the brow of our idols soiled and trampled by profane feet—it may be the feet of our idols. . . . "Sweet are the uses of adversity, which, like a toad, ugly and venomous, bares yet a precious jewel in its head."

Saving the Exchange

132.   June 20, 1889. Mrs. Bettie Gay, Columbus; and Mrs. A. P. Shaw, Donalton.

THE ROLL OF HONOR

We the undersigned sisters of the Farmers Alliance of Texas, agree to sell eggs, chickens, butter and garden stuff to the amount of ONE DOLLAR, which amount is to be paid by the FIRST of AUGUST, and the total amount so subscribed is to be applied to the payment of the Exchange indebtedness.

The Exchange

133.   June 20, 1889. Columbus. Bettie Gay.

What more can be said? Action is now essential. First of all, let us save the Exchange. Let the lecturers at the July county meetings collect $1 from every member or fifty cents, which would more than pay the indebtedness, and also assist in securing cotton bagging for those who cannot advance money for the present crop. The people need a leader and the majority to follow. There are many who will not do their own thinking, [this] is why the country is in its present condition. . . .

In one of our county meetings the question of taking stock in the New Braunfels mills was discussed nearly all day. Finally, one man arose and said, "I am a poor man and if the county is not able to take two (or five shares, I forget which) I will take from my pocket $1." And in less than twenty minutes the amount was raised. So you see all that is needed is for someone to take the lead and there are thousands who would respond.

It is quite trying on the manager to wait for the people to act; for there has not yet been the proper courses pursued to reach the masses. Many do not read and many do not go to meetings. If it could be arranged for every county to have a barbecue or basket dinner . . . and have a first-class business man speak and take up a collection, I wager we'd have the whole amount needed raised in two months.

I am a woman and with many more like Mrs. Shaw, we can pay out of debt and then stay out.

Mr. Editor, call special notice to Mrs. Shaw's proposition in every number for a month, for some times these things are looked over at one time and at another time they will be read. . . .

The Exchange

134.   June 20, 1889. Donalton. Mrs. A. P. Shaw

Language such as I can command would fail to express my appreciation for the *Mercury* for I think it is the guiding star for the farming class of people . . . Sisters, I beg, I persuade you to come forward with feeling a boldness and love and free our institution from debt. Let me see, Sisters, how many of you in the Lone Star State are willing to lend a helping hand to save our head, for we all fully realize that the Exchange is the head and the Alliance is the body. And if the head is severed from the body, the body will shrivel and decay. Then under this heading place your names: I will sell eggs, chickens, butter, and garden stuff to the amount of one dollar by the 1st of August to help pay the debt of the Exchange. We will not ask the Brothers to place their names under our list, for I believe every true Brother will be in favor of the dues being raised to fifty cents.

Saving the Exchange

135.   June 27, 1889.

ROLL OF HONOR

We the undersigned sisters of the Farmer's Alliance of Texas agree to sell eggs, chickens, and garden stuff to the amount of ONE DOLLAR, which amount is to be paid by the first day of August and applied to the payment of the Exchange indebtedness. Mrs. A. P. Shaw, Donalton; Mrs. Bettie Gay, Columbus; Mrs. L. E. Buckley, Rodgers; Mrs. H. Bittick, and Mrs. S. C. Bowman, Caddo Mills.

Saving the Exchange

136.   June 27, 1889. Rodgers, Bell County. Mrs. L. E. Buckley.

EDITOR MERCURY: . . . I belong to Centennial Alliance no. 3344. I have been a member over three years and have never missed but two meetings. My husband takes the *Mercury* and we both enjoy reading it. I think every member ought to read it and keep posted in their duty.

I say God bless Sister Shaw for her proposition she has made to the sisters to sell chickens eggs and butter to save our exchange. We can everyone do this and it won't hurt anybody. Put my name on the list. I am ever ready to do my duty. I feel that God is with us in this good work.

The Exchange; absence of letters; mutuality

137.   June 27, 1889. Caddo Mills. Mrs. Bittick.

EDITOR MERCURY: Although I feel quite out of place writing to our paper, I cannot help answering Sister Shaw's call. I will send one dollar to the Exchange by the first of July, and I will try not to send mine alone. . . . Our election of officers is over and we had a picnic with quite a number of members present. All seemed to enjoy the day very much. We had a good rain yesterday evening which was very much needed. What has become of all the sisters? I have looked in vain for their nice letters. Ann Other, please write again, and Charitie, come back to your work. If I could only write such letters as you do it would be a pleasure to contribute.

Urging on the members

138.   June 27, 1889. Centerville, Leon County. Mrs. S. E. Watkins.

EDITOR MERCURY: As I see nothing in print from Reedland Alliance I will write again. There are more competent Brothers and Sisters for writing but it seems as if they are careless and do not take the interest in the Alliance that they should. We have a large membership but there are few of us who attend. . . . If you have not got the *Mercury*, send for one. It is one of the best guides in the world to the farmer. We have no crop mortgage this year, neither any stock; so it has stirred us up and caused us to keep out of mortgaging this year. . . . Don't be like the man who climbed the joist and left his wife to kill the bear and when freedom is gained come out shouting "Ain't we brave," when you have done nothing to help gain it. So come to the front, now is the time to work for freedom if you ever intend to.

Saving the Exchange

139.   July 4, 1889.

EDITOR MERCURY: We the undersigned sisters of the Farmer's Alliance of Texas agree to sell eggs, chickens, and garden stuff to the amount of ONE DOLLAR, which amount is to be paid by the FIRST DAY OF AUGUST and applied to the payment of the Exchange indebtedness. Mrs. A. P. Shaw, Donalton; Mrs. Bettie Gay, Columbus; Mrs. L. E. Buckley, Rodgers; Mrs. H. Bittick, Benton; Mrs. S. C. Bowman, Caddo Mills; Mrs. Ella Bush, Benton; Mrs. E. Farris, Benton; Mrs. C. J. McMurrian, Benton; Mrs. S. E. Hutchison, Benton; Mrs. Maner [no location].

140.   July 11, 1889.

EDITOR MERCURY: We the undersigned sisters of the Farmer's Alliance of Texas agree to sell eggs, chickens, and garden stuff to the amount of ONE DOLLAR, which amount is to be paid by the FIRST DAY OF AUGUST and applied to the payment of the Exchange indebtedness: Mrs. A. P. Shaw, Donalton; Mrs. Bettie Gay, Columbus; Mrs. L. E. Buckley, Rodgers; Mrs. H. Bittick, Benton; Mrs. S. C. Bowman, Caddo Mills; Mrs. Ella Bush, Benton; Mrs. E. Faris, Benton; Mrs. C. J. McMurrian, Benton; Mrs. S. E. Hutchison, Benton; Mrs. Maner; Mrs. Maggie Miears, Red Rock; Mrs. L. M. A. Brown, New Caney; Mrs. E. D. Sullivan, New Caney; Mrs. Sarah O. Shelton, Jewett.

141.   July 18, 1889.

Five more add their names.

Tishie Graves, Mrs. L. C. McLain, Mrs. P. A. Neighbors, Mrs. Nannie Newland, Mrs. Mary Graves, all of Donalton, Texas.

About the Exchange

142.   July 18, 1889. Leon County. Mrs. P. F. Copeland.

As I have waited a long time to hear some sister make a start from New Hope Alliance No. 1213, and not hearing from them I will do my best.

I cannot say as some do that our alliance is on a boom. But it is not dead by a jugful. We have lost some but are the better off. When a man or woman do not attend regularly without good cause they have not the correct principle. I have my dollar and one to lend some Sister who has not. No one need to fear for the Exchange, for I have saved enough on one cookstove to pay dues for ten years, besides other things I've saved money on. When you hear a man or woman say the Exchange has done them no good, you can just mark it they haven't tried it. . . .

143.   July 25, 1889.

Three more names are added.

Mrs. Jennie Du Bois, Jewett; Mrs. Caroline Schernick, Center Lane; Mrs. C. J. Munroe, Center Lane.

Holding the fort

144.   July 25, 1889. Manor, Travis County. Mrs. M. E. Turner.

We are still trying to hold the fort; there are a few amongst us who have not been cowed but many may be staying home to see how things work. There are many in the world who soon grow weary and imagine that everything can be accomplished in a day and because reformation cannot be affected in a day or a year, they become discouraged and stay at home and grumble at those who are laboring for their good and the suppression of that giant, monopoly, which is everywhere to be found in our land.

145.   August 1, 1889.

Two more names.

Mrs. Calley J. Bell, Blanket; Mrs. Anna J. Jordan, Drane.

Saving the Exchange

146.   August 1, 1889. McKinney Alliance, Guadalupe County. Mrs. P. H. Hall.

I see in your valuable paper that some of the sisters have solved a plan to save our Exchange. I will tell you of the plan that my Alliance sisters have made. We gave a picnic dinner in the schoolhouse and all the men and the boys from fifteen years up paid us for their dinner so we received fifteen dollars which we sent to the Exchange. The husbands barbequed most all of our meats. All the ladies gave a willing hand. Only a few gave excuses that they were sick or had sickness in their family. . . . After dinner, we held our alliance meeting and received four new petitions for membership. These were the first who have joined in nearly a year, so I think our picnic has done some good. . . .

On not overworking; mutuality

147.   August 1, 1889. Ruston, Louisiana. Charitie.

EDITOR MERCURY: Sunday morning! A dear bright day after an abundance of rain and it will be the industrious farmer who will "make hay while the sun shines," as there has been but little sunshine of long duration. But nature is not idly dreaming time away. Her work is important; much depends upon it too. She reads an eloquent lesson in the most winning tones and language to her listeners. She warns us from wastefulness, needlessness and slothfulness. Recreation is reading found in her presence; stores of thoughts she has treasured for weary folks no less than the tireless ones.

As I sit this morning listening to the church bells, not feeling well enough to attend church, deliberating on which, among the varied subjects that occurred to my imagination, I should bestow to the paper of today. Reading one of the back numbers of the *Mercury,* some of my lady friends inquire, "Where is Charitie?" So it is for answering them I take my pencil and paper today. . . .

I am still in the land of the living and ready once more to occupy my easy chair in the circular. I regret seeing so few old familiar faces. Perhaps like myself they are worked to death. "Oh, foolish and perverse generation." The condemnation of centuries past is deserved today. When will women learn the lesson of working wisely and realize that overwork is a sin? "Softly, softly!" says a wise voice, "do not hasten; there is time enough." We drown these words saying, "Life is short; we must work, work!" And we work till our strength fails. . . .

I was reading the other day that in England it is considered ill-bred to overwork and the women there make the care of health their first duty. Daily walks in the open air are a matter of course. How delightful it would be to have ourselves and children with bright eyes, rosy cheeks, good spirits and radiant health.

I am pleased to see the women coming to the front and lending a helping hand on behalf of the Exchange. All honor to Mrs. Shaw and other ladies who have come forward and shown "what women can do. . . ."

What a sad thing it is that some men think that their wives seem to be accounted for nothing but drudges or fit for little else but to prepare food for them and their lots of friends. Ah, well, thanks to the most High, the world progresses and each year brings with it [a] more enlightened view in regard to the old exploded idea that it is not necessary for a woman to know anything. . . .

Where is Ann Other, Marie Labouchere, Western Reader, Rebecca and Saucy Birdie, and other of our friends, and some of our brothers? Give an account for yourselves, for you all are not forgotten but remembered. . . . Yours,

148.   August 15, 1889.

Eight more names are added.

Mrs. Ellen Jones, Travis County; Mrs. M. J. Moore, Telephone; Mrs. M. A. Gates; Benton; Mrs. S. C. Bauman, Caddo Mills; Mrs. L. E. Madeley, Rodgers; Mrs. A. McFarland, Atoka; Mrs. P. F. Copeland, Marquez; Mrs. M. W. White, Belton.

Women pitch in to save the Exchange

149.   August 15, 1889. Benton. Mrs. M. W. White.

You will find enclosed $1 to be applied under Mrs. Shaw's proposition. I have no eggs, butter, chickens, or "garden truck" to spare but I am taking care of a little orphan boy at $6 per month. I cheerfully send $1 of this hard earned money to help lift the cloud that is now hovering over us.

Saving the Exchange

150.   August 15, 1889. Leon County. Mrs. P. F. Copeland.

EDITOR MERCURY: Here I come with my $1 as I promised, and you please add my name with the good sisters. Now I offered to lend my other dollar, but no one has said they wanted it or would put in with me. May God bless the good sisters who are trying to get the Exchange out of debt. I am in favor of trying men until we get one that will not go in debt and will just hold the fort. Why the Exchange don't do better is because people don't trade through it. It is a strange idea that men will work against their interests—have as good a thing as the Exchange and not use it.

Now, sisters, I know it is right to help all we can; not one stand back and wait for the other, but push together. The cripple the Exchange has had did it great harm. I hope our leaders will go slow and be sure they are on good ground before they move again.

Our suballiance is about clear of the weak-kneed ones.

We are suffering for rain, corn is good, army worm is here and the boll worm has done much damage. People are burning lights in their cotton of nights. May God bless the order, our paper, and leaders. . . .

Morale boosting

151.   August 22, 1889. Delta County. Essay by Mrs. Garrett.

Mr. President, Brothers and Sisters: . . . Great are the wonders performed by the Alliance for the farmers, educating them morally, socially, if not financially! The time will come when they will be able to cope with all the combined power of capital if they will only remain true to each other and never forsake the sacred obligations which bind them to the Alliance cause.

I ask where is the proud American eagle? You left liberty's golden bowl unguarded at the political cistern and your proud bird swooped down to drink; designing politicians came and by wiles and art have stolen him and made him a prisoner in the congressional halls of these United States, and he will remain there until the farmers and laborers rise up in their might and demand its release. I will tell you where the gold is that should be in circulation among the working people. Railroad kings own about ten millions. . . .

Paying Alliance dues

152.   August 22, 1889. Anderson, Grimes County. Mrs. H. A. Whitfield.

EDITOR MERCURY: Grimes County Alliance can once more hold up her head and say she has made arrangement to pay her warehouse debt which has hung like a dark cloud over her nearly two year. She also . . . sanctioned raising the dues to fifty cents per quarter. I think that it would be the best for the whole amount for the year to be due in the first quarter of the Alliance year. The members not being expelled; but suspended until the end of said year.

I see from reports in the *Mercury* quite a number of Alliance have voted down the increase of dues, and I cannot feel otherwise than disgusted at such economy (?). If I had the power I would raise them and let those who were not willing to pay get out of the order; and really it could do better if not hampered by such folks. In one sense of the term it would be like a law passed by the legislature or congress. They would not be prosecuted if they withdrew and refused to comply. Please print a copy of the synopsis of the railroad commission bill that was defeated last winter. Have been told it calls for three men to act in all cases as jurors in all railroad trials instead of twelve as is customary. I do not believe it; for instead of working against it, the railroad would have worked for it and would have been much easier to have bought those three men for all time than it would to have been always buying twelve at every trial. I desire this information . . . for every voter in the county.

Grimes County is going to wrap her cotton with cotton bagging if she can get it. With much zeal for the cause of the Alliance, I am respectfully,

153.   September 5, 1889.

The women agreeing to sell eggs, chickens, butter, and garden stuff
to the amount of one dollar now numbered fifty-five. It included:

Mrs. R. B. Lott, Mrs. M. A. Davis, Mrs. A. J. McMillan, Mrs. M. A. Henry, Mrs. V. R. Howard, Mrs. Shell Parker, Mrs. Jessie Smalley, Mrs. E. C. Rogers, Mrs. M. C. Rutledge, Mrs. N. J. Mitcher, Mrs. Ellen Swindler, Mrs. J. M. Jones, all of Bryan; Mrs. L. E. Buckley, Centennial; Mrs. M. E. Otis, Mrs. A. L. Otis, Burke; Mrs. Sarah Smith, Senior; Mrs. Mamie Johnston, Mrs. Florence Taylor, Mrs. Ellen O'Quinn, Mrs. Mollie Garnet, Mrs. Jennie Boulter, Mrs. Mamie Wintams, all of Goldthwaite; Mrs. N. A. Butler, Wortham.

Woman's sphere

154.   September 5, 1889. Harmony Ridge. Rural Widow.

EDITOR MERCURY: I was much pleased at finding so many of the sisters letters in last weeks paper. As the editor is so kind as to give us part of his valuable paper, it is our duty to make it as interesting as possible. I was delighted with Charitie's letter; she is right, woman's work is unhappily, to some extent, depreciated—that is, if a man and a woman of equal capacity apply for the same place or try to do the same work, the man will have two chances of success to the woman's one. I know whereof I speak, having had some experience. But strict justice forces the admission that for this, women are largely to blame. Until women recognize and abide by the stern logic and the sternest requirements of the laboring world, this depreciation must inevitably be their portion. The sooner they learn to screen themselves or their efforts behind their protective wall of sex, the better it will be for the immense rank and file of workers. I found out early in the fray that in the whole battle field of work, there must be neither men nor woman, but simply so much force, be it brain or muscle.

Woman's work today is depreciated because in time past, women unknowingly, I believe, did imperfect work. Her will was good but she had not gone into the fight rightly equipped; therefore she put before her employers a deficient result, expecting the deficiency to be supplied by consideration for her delicacy of temperament or constitution or some other such ill defined and suitable feminine quality. Now the pendulum begins to swing to the other side.

Women realize that if they are to receive equal compensation they must give in all respects an equal service and this "equal service" from the very nature of the case, must always press harder upon the women, consume more of the precious life-blood, makes larger demands upon the brain and nerve force[,] for speculate as we might, the God-favored and indestructible fact remains the same. Women are weaker than the men and less fitted for the stern and pressing work of the world.

If we could return to the God-appointed order of things, all this talk about the depreciation of women's work, whether it be to save the Exchange or be president, would cease. It is the work of the plodder that is most effective in the practical world; and a large majority of men are plodders. By contrast with the quick nervous unequal effort of women, man gains much in power and effectiveness. A woman will go to her work today and meet its most exacting requirements; tomorrow she will lag a little, the third day, urged on by some magical impetus, she approaches perfection; the fourth day she has sick-headache and fails utterly. On the other hand, the man plods on in an ox-like fashion; he makes no extraordinary success, neither does he chronicle any failures. . . . Work is simply his means to a required end, money. But with women, it becomes an ever-present, ever-following shadow. She lets it consume her vital energies, sap her strength, undermine her health and steal her life, yet intuitively know[s] she is sinning before high heaven and while it is unlady-like to be overworked, she still persists.

Cotton bagging

155.   October 24, 1889. Keith. Mittie Keith.

[Front of letter obliterated] . . . We have a very good Alliance here, although we are few in number. . . .

My father was a delegate to the State Alliance and he said he never had a better time. He bought a photograph of the Exchange and I think it is a beautiful building. How can the people of Texas lose such a building? They cannot.

I want to say a word about cotton bagging. The farmers here using it think it so much prettier than the old jute. I think when the jute men carry their cotton to town, they ought to keep it covered up to keep it from making Alliance men sick, for it is enough to make them sick to see farmers working against their own interest. I will hail the day with joy when the farmers will all work in unity; for in unity there is strength and victory. . . . Perhaps someone would like to know how old I am. I will say that I am something less than fifty years old and they say I am awful mean but don't believe a word of that for I am the best single girl in the family. Long life to the *Mercury*.

Suballiance report

156.   October 31, 1889. Houston County. Mary P. Hodges.

Health generally good. We have had so much rain that farmers are backward gathering crops. All seem to be in fine spirits. We've had some glorious meetings in and near the settlement. We regret the death of Mrs. Trudy Patton, the wife of William Patton. Our alliance is not dead, the ladies are raising chickens to ship to the Exchange. Can anyone give any information concerning a young man by the name of Bennie Morgan? Left Cherokee County four years ago with a man by the name of Bob Williams: Went to west Texas. Any information will be gladly received and appreciated.

Self-esteem

157.   December 12, 1889. Angelina County. Margenie.

As I am sitting by the bedside of my sick husband I cannot think of any-thing to do but to try to write a few lines to the dear old *Mercury*. I do not write thinking anyone will be made any the wiser, but to draw some one out to correct what I have written, or to show the readers of the *Mercury* that Angelina county is not filled up with such thick-skulled people as I am. . . .

I think that Mary J. Smart's letter is a good one. "What is the use of poor farmers' wives and daughters buying fine clothing, trying to look or dress as fine as those who hold the farmers' money purse?" If they want to turn the cold shoulder to us and turn their noses up, or give us the back seat at church because we wear calico, five-cent lawn, or perhaps twenty-cent worsted, it should not hurt us. Let them stick their heads in a flour-barrel and put on their silk and satin and sit in church pretending to swallow every word the preacher says. When they go home, ask them what the text was and they will most likely tell you they don't know for Miss or Mrs. Somebody was dressed in her old five-cent lawn, which has been washed a half-dozen times. I do not think such people ought to come to church. They think because we dress that way we should not hear a sermon. But dear Sisters, do not let that bother you, for there never was a bird that flew so high but it had to come to the ground for water.

I have just become a member of the Alliance and hope to learn about it and do some good.

They say of some of us women that we never know when to stop talk-ing, but I think I do. It is when we can think of nothing else. Wishing God's blessings on the dear old *Mercury*.

Love of rural life

158.   December 12, 1889. Tarrant County. Lettie Reynolds.

I have waited and watched so long for something in the *Mercury* from some of the Alliance men of this community that patience is fairly exhausted. There is some good material here but it seems dormant. I have been read-ing Blue-Eyed Lena's letter. I, too, live on a farm and like it.

I am glad there are so many sensible girls and women that are not blindfolded by folly and fashion; but I long for a reformation in the ways of some of our country boys, who work hard all week, probably for fifty cents per day, just for the satisfaction of sporting a cane and wearing a Prince Albert on Sundays. If they would only save their hard-earned money and buy homes and educate themselves upon their own interests, we could look forward to the time when all shall enjoy equal rights with special privileges to none. O! Young men of thought be up and stirring, night and day. There is a midnight darkness changing into grey; men of thought and men of action clear the way.

O! for another Cincinnatus, that can leave the plow and rule a nation, and return again to the humble farm without any feelings of mortification. Sisters, let's be up and doing, keeping our eyes wide open to the duties and responsibilities reposed in us. Let us not despise farm work; let us make home as pleasant and attractive as possible.

Most of the people have gathered their crops. Old Jack Frost made his appearance the other night.

Love in marriage

159.   February 6, 1890. Harmony Ridge. Rural Widow.

Here I am again, dear family. I came only in answer to Star's [a *Mercury* columnist] request that I try and straighten that kink that has gotten in Laura O.'s brain. I would that I could answer your first question, sweet Laura, but it is beyond human ken to say whether one will be happy after marriage. Love in marriage is desirable, but I don't think positively necessary to happiness. Some of the happiest marriages that I know of, the persons were unacquainted save by a letter, until a very short time before marriage. I am persuaded that if all the women who have married men who professed to love them could but lift the veil from the hearts of their husbands, three-fourths of them would find there a face not their own, on which was written "my idol," in burning letters of love. Love need not necessarily be "woman's whole existence" in this day when the wife may have her work as well as the man. Women are odd creatures. Because of medieval ideas, they are content to fold white hands idly in their laps and dream of how much they love their lords and masters, but marriage, Laura, is not a failure; some people are, I grant you, and degrade everything they deal with, but marriage cannot be, or if it is, heaven and all things holy are.

For shame, Laura, if you knew me, which I don't believe you do, you knew that I only took the old crepe off that my Xmas dress might look a little fresher. Please tell me when and where you saw me. . . .

> *From April 24, 1890, until July 3, 1890, no significant letters from women were printed in the* Mercury. *"The Home Circle," which included a "Boys and Girls' Department" and a "Woman's Column," replaced "The Family" in the July 3 issue; Mrs. Jennie Dixon, wife of Sam Dixon and a temperance advocate, was its main editor. The "Boys and Girls' Department" focused instruction on the youth of the Alliance, "the cousins." Its announced "special aim" was "to develop literary talent and to nurture a taste for the pure and good in reading and learning." The "Woman's Column" was "devoted to a discussion of and interchange of ideas, as to the needs, duties and rights of the farmer's wife." In it, Jennie Dixon offered much advice. Letters from Alliance women appeared occasionally.*

160.   August 7, 1890. Duplex. Hattie Hickman.

I ask through your paper, is there any reason why ladies should not join the Alliance? Some object to it, but I think it is our duty to do all we can to assist in the cause. . . .

Grace Danforth, a doctor and ardent feminist, on fashion

161.   August 21, 1890. Terreus. Grace Danforth, M.D.

Our beloved state president has requested a contribution on dress reform for your columns. To please her, and not with the hope of making one convert, the task is attempted. Hercules never approached the twelve labors with half [as] much trepidation as I felt over influencing woman to better ways of arraying herself. The idea that what little influence woman wields is through her "beauty" is so deeply rooted in her nature she is loath to risk it [changing her dress]—her ideal of beauty being a misshapen production of the [corset]. . . . If woman realized how much her powers physically and mentally are crippled by her costume, there would be some hope, but the vast majority are perfectly satisfied and would not make an effort to change even if they knew the blessings of health that are in store for them. It will [take] a generation that knows something about the circulation and how it is affected by dressing one part of the body thick and another thin and any part cramped at the expense of motion and circulation[before fashion will change]. So long as women insist upon suspending the weight of heavy skirts from their waists, corsets are a necessity. The popular idea that the weight is borne by the hips is all a mistake. The soft walls of the abdomen are constricted and pressed downward with what fatal effects only the anatomist realizes. Suppose our beasts of burden had their loads attached to a band tight around their stomachs. Do you suppose we would have horses to do our work? The corset prevents bands from cutting, distributes the weight more evenly and makes the victim fail to realize the damage that is being done. When health fails it is charged to overwork, nervous exhaustion, climate, anything but dress. . . .

162. September 25, 1890. Mrs. Jennie Dixon [editor of the *Mercury's* "The Home Circle" section]

Dear Sisters—This has been repeatedly and truthfully called the woman's century, and truly she has been, and is, making wonderful strides toward enlightenment in all the walks of life. Many of us can remember when our mothers and older sisters thought their condition very low in the social scale, if they had to work in any way to assist in the support of the family, and then there were only two avenues open for the aspiring woman, teaching and sewing. Now there is practically no employment that is not open for woman, and so faithful and efficient has their labor been found that they are fast coming to the front, and almost universally receive the same salary as men. Now I hope none of you will misunderstand me when I say that I candidly think there is no "sphere" that is more unwomanly for a woman than hard work in the field. If our farmers, who are as a class very conservative as to woman's position, would give their daughters the advantage of college education, and fit them for some business, they will prove to them a help in time of need, when that mortgage on the farm is about to be foreclosed, or when a drought or worms cut short the crop, or when much needed but expensive piece of machinery is to be bought. Keep the boys on the farm, the honest work will develop their strength and manhood, and suits them; but your delicate daughter needs an easier place to earn her share of the family fund. Moreover, if your son is in a position to make money, he will, if he chances not to be a spendthrift, and very apt to think that he must lay up his own home which he expects soon to found. Not so with the daughter; for if she is looking forward to a home of her

The first reaper in Potter County, Texas, 1890.
Courtesy Texas Department of Public Safety

own, she also thinks of the strong arm that has promised to provide it, and how delighted she is to help father who was the means of her success, and how glad she is to put a help in the kitchen for mother, in the place of one she lost when daughter went to college. . . .

A young girl's thoughts

163.   September 25, 1890. Willow Creek, Texas. Maudalene.

A sample letter from the Mercury's *"Boys and Girls" section.*

DEAR COUSINS: Our Jennie says the aim of this department is to develop a taste for good sound literature. Let us try to make it a real home circle, where we can come together to get and give strengthening, ennobling thoughts and sentiments, not a place in which to tell how much cotton one has picked and that "papa belongs to the Alliance." Like you, Stella, I think Cousin Mary K. is altogether wrong on the business of corresponding with an unknown person. We treat them just as we do one to whom we are introduced in person; if we find them unworthy, social rules allow us to cut their acquaintance—and just so with correspondents. I fail to find where a girl can compromise herself by writing to an unknown person. We feel no timidity in stating our views on any subject. We can give our imagination unbounded sway; we can discuss books, music, and any and all sentiments of the human heart and feel no fear in treading on any personality. I have books, music, flowers, shell[s,] and rare specimens of writing which have been sent by persons whose faces I have never seen; Still, they are dear to me. . . . This one tells the bitter struggle of a youth who is trying to rise above circumstances and this one is from a grey-haired gentleman in whose letters are many bright gems of thought. Another one comes from a bright-eyed laughing boy of eighteen who tells many stories and describes his future wife, but his ideas are all chaste. Though we have never met in person yet I feel we are kindred spirits. Say cousins, all, what you think of waltzing . . . ?

The correct behavior for young girls

164.   September 25, 1890. Jennie Dixon.

DEAR BOYS AND GIRLS: There has never been occasion for me to comment very seriously on many of your letters but I feel bound by sisterly interest to advise with Maudalene about promiscuous correspondence. There is evidently no impropriety in very little boys and girls exchanging a letter or two with each other but when they come to Maudalene's age, a girl cannot be too particular in their intercourse with boys whether in their company or through letters. My dear girls, you do not know whose eye your letter might fall under, and to have it criticized, even the spelling, and picked to pieces by a thoughtless and may hap, vicious crowd of boys, would cause a painful blush of wounded pride to mantle your cheek.

And oh, Maudalene, we should never give our "imagination unbounded sway" in writing, for sure the world is so that it will all come back to us, a mass of silly gushing nonsense, which, like a ghost, will rise to distress us in later life. For most young girls I should say when asked about corresponding with young men, even those we claim as friends, "Don't do it."

On fathers

165.   October 2, 1890. Fannie Armstrong.

Dear Sisters—Seeing a copy of the *Mercury* and reading The Home Circle, a cold wave of loneliness passed over me and I seemed for a moment to be drowning. Reaching out my hand of faith I felt solid rock, for heaven is my home and no changes ever come to it. . . . Our editor says we may talk about anything that interests us . . . what a large theme. . . . Dear Mothers, do you know that I think you do not make companions out of your children as you should? This night, on the very verge of my 49th birthday, I thank God that I was the friend and companion of my parents. Many a time have I sat on our old horse behind my father, holding on to his coat and hearing the thunder crash and the lightning flash along the skies. And sometimes great pines would fall near us while we quietly talked about God's voice in the rolling thunder. I never knew what fear meant. My mother's daily conversation was the best school I ever attended. My father told me who varnished the beetle's wing and painted and folded the rosebud so beautifully within its emerald calix. He used to read the old standard authors to me and sing the songs of old Scotia and his own beloved Erin's green isle. So I think if fathers would put on the brakes in regard to this reckless money-making for their children, and if mothers would spend a little less time on ruffles, feathers, and biscuits, and watch the sunset and talk about God, Heaven, holiness, humanity and the power for good in their children, I know by my own happy experience that many precious seeds would be sown to bear fruit when you are living under the quiet stars. . . .

The power of women

166.   October 9, 1890. Mrs. Jennie Dixon.

DEAR SISTERS: I have heard it said that one reason why women do not take their places more rapidly by the sides of men as bread winners is because while men will catch at the first thing that offers, hoping by faithfulness and industry to win his way higher, when the same place is offered a woman, she will hesitate and consider; and it is said that the woman who hesitates fails. This is very true. We must have confidence in ourselves, else how can we hope to impress others. Women must merit every preference given her, hence the question is not so much a matter of propriety as of fitness, for there are absolutely no closed doors for the efficient hand. The secret of success is to learn one thing thoroughly. The wide awake, energetic girl of today has forsaken the old beaten paths and is striking out for herself. They are studying architecture, designing, and many other profitable and interesting things. They are even laying out gardens and paths.

They are numbered among our foremost lawyers, doctors, dentists, reporters, merchants, jewelers, clerks, and in one town in Kansas, the whole city government was for two years carried on by women—and they were the wives of the bankers, lawyers and merchants, the first families in the town. They are members of many of our school boards, and many states elect women as county superintendents, and one state has a woman candidate for state superintendent of education, with great assurance of being elected. Now, what will be interesting news to many of us; these women have lost none of their womanliness or "motherliness." They are wives and homemakers just the same and just as dedicated to the care of their loved ones. . . .

Marriage

167.   October 23, 1890. McKinney, Collin County. [Name obscured.]

Is the farmer's wife a miserable woman? Not all. There are thousands of happy country homes where husband and wife work for each other's happiness. I, for one, believe that most of those who are miserable are to blame because they do not exercise their own common sense. . . .

So many are seemingly in a great hurry to get married. Girls will marry men who are drunkards and know all along they are not going to quit. Girls will marry men who have been at work for themselves, or should have been, for years and have nothing but a few clothes. Now if they can't support themselves, how under the sun can they support a family? I think that the girls who marry this sort of man are they that plod about in coarse shoes, go to church under sunbonnets and ride in the farm wagon with the rusty plow gear. Farmers' wives have a great deal of work to do in the house, and it is not a woman's place to work in the field. They are to blame if they do for they will gain very little and if they commence it, it may be expected of them. Commence to be a lady and be one; if you don't you are to blame. . . .

Absence of letters; pride in the writers; concern about alcohol

168.   October 23, 1890. [No location.] Ellen D.

Sisters: I have long been a constant reader of the *Mercury*. I have watched the woman's department with much pride and interest, until, alas! it completely failed to make its appearance at all. Our talented writers have deserted us, however, "our Jennie" cannot fail if we know what we are at, for we must, and will lend her a helping hand. Dear Charitie, what are you doing these beautiful autumnal days; are your motherly cares so oppressive that you cannot find time for one of your comforting, helpful chats with the sisters? Since I have written to the *Mercury,* I have felt all the anguish that a soul can bear. My only sister died some two years ago. While time is a great healer to a sorrowing heart, no one can ever fill the places of my dear sister, and my dear parents, too.

I most heartily approve of the total abstinence society. Let our motto be "Touch not, taste not, handle not" that which has cursed so many homes. I took the pledge when a child and in spite of the many temptations, have swallowed but very little in all the years. I do not feel afraid of whisky ever harming me but I have six brothers aged 19 to 9 years, who will be men soon, and I do not want them to fill a drunkard's grave or live the degrading life which are the fruits of frequenting saloons. I have been a member of the Alliance for nearly five years; joined when our Alliance was first organized. There! I came near telling my age. I am afraid you will consign my letter to the bad place; I am not small enough for the children's corner and not wise enough for the Ladies' Department.

Our Alliance is struggling along, trying to live. One of our neighboring Alliances has its lady members pay up their dues in eatables and they have a supper and a fine time generally which keeps up an interest. I think we ought to adopt the same plan. Of course our ladies are splendid cooks, especially the widows, who are noted for their fine picnic dinners.

I have been reading one of Dickens' books—*Old Curiosity Shop.* Like you, I was delighted with Little Nell.

Women working in the fields

169.   October 30, 1890. Wortham. Alice E. Miller.

DEAR SISTERS: I have been reading your good letters now for several years and have often been constrained to write but would put it off from time to time on account of not having any education. As I was a farmer's daughter and had three brothers and seven sisters, you may know my education is quite limited. I agree with Mrs. Dixon in regard to women working in the field, although every woman I see has been picking cotton. It seems that they are just bound to work in the field to help make a support.

I do not think it is a disgrace although I do not think we were made to do hard field work or we would have been as stout as men. If it gets much worse, I think women will have to take the lead in the field. This is one thing that is ruining the women's health of today as well as tight lacing. Let us work, watch and pray and perhaps we will see the day when we have more time for reading and brightening ourselves up. Let us be as cheerful as possible and always have a smile and good word for our tired husband when he comes from the field.

Field work

170.   October 30, 1890. Jennie Dixon.

DEAR SISTERS: . . . Alice Miller, you must not think that I for a moment believe that there is any disgrace attached to any kind of honorable work. I simply think that the work on the farm is too heavy for delicate women and I, for one, wish to see other employments open to them where they will receive equal pay for the same kind of work that men perform. A reform of some kind is needed to improve the affairs on the farm but wiser heads than mine have failed to discover it. I feel sure though that it is not more work or better management or more scrupulous economy on the part of the farmers' wives. It would help if a great many of our farmers would institute a thorough and rigid boycott of the saloon on their weekly visit to the towns. The farmers of all others should determine that not one of his hard-earned honest dollars should enter the coffers of this non-producing, leprous element in our midst. . . .

Absence of women

171.   January 22, 1891. Columbus. Mrs. Bettie Gay.

Letter in the Mercury's *regular "Correspondence" section.*

TO THE MERCURY: The women have been cut off from your columns for nearly two years, and the interest of the order, too, has been slumbering, not dead, but the heart bleeding, has been pent up till now. Thank Heaven the columns are open once more to those who suffer most. With your permission I will invite the Western Reader, Mrs. Shaw, and others to the rescue of our order and let us reinstate our order where it was two and three years ago. And let us show the men of Texas, as of old, that it is not well for man to be alone. He may feel very large in his own estimation, until he gets into deep water and then he cries for help. Now in this hour of need, and a great need too, come out from behind the barn and let us go to victory in '92. We have the *Mercury,* the *Texas Labor Journal* and the *Educator.* What more can we ask? Let us ask for a genuine revival next spring or summer. Invite L. I. Polk of North Carolina, Ralph Beaumont, Mrs. Lease, Mrs. Emery [all Alliance leaders and lecturers] and others of equal distinction. Why let Texas lag when other states are doing so much? Let some one decide where the best location is and get the railroads to let us have reduced rates, and commence now to work up the encampment and I warrant it will put new life in the land, and every one will do more than ever, and we can command instead of being commanded, and if we should elect any one and are mistaken in him, get him to resign. Do not let them create contention, which is easily done by continued mistakes, but for the good of all concerned put the right man in the right place and we can have an army that can move the world. Our Exchange would have been paid for, and our factory too, would have been a success. It makes me tired to see men want to become popular without patriotism, only for greed, reminds me of painting the U.S. flag on pitchers, jugs and other things to show how much it is appreciated that it means liberty when there is not such thing in America. Give the people liberty and they will appreciate it without ever seeing a flag. I am in for education, organization, and agitation. Give us free schools, free teachers, and free books. The money that is wasted or given to pet officers, go to have books free for the children of Texas. Let the trustees who do all the work without pay, sign the teachers' vouchers and let the treasurer pay the money to the teacher; save more than enough money to have free books and then more poor children can have a chance to go to school and learn to be a free American citizen and enjoy some of the luxuries that our kid-gloved gentry do and get it by robbing the children out of their education and that million dollars. How much suffering would that relieve. And how many books would that amount pay for? And how many taxpayers of Texas care if Chicago is advertised or not? And how many will be able to go to the World's Fair?

Look at Texas! Look at her fine jails (and ours are full—thirty criminals—twelve murderers) and courthouses, and see how our law-makers are advertising her! Is Chicago any better? They make laws to create crime and then make laws to punish crime. How can this state of things be changed? By sending men to make laws that think more of their fellowmen than they do of mammon. We, the toilers, run a man on that ticket and at nearly all the precincts [he] was far ahead, but the other man was counted in and the *Galveston Weekly News* has a list of lawmakers elected and among them our man's name, sixty-seventh district, B. H. Neal. Now will some one rise and explain? The old adage is, "Silence gives consent." How are we to get justice when there is so much fraud in the land and in high places, so to speak? Educate, keep a standing list of reform books in your columns.

Look what Kansas has done; why not Texas? Are there more brains in Kansas than in Texas? No, not that; but her people have been educated and her labor papers have done it. God bless the people of Kansas. They are doing noble work.

Let us hear from all who are concerned in the encampment; make suggestions and come to some understanding. Have it in the most convenient place, so that those from a distance can go on the railroad. Invite everyone who is willing to affiliate with us and let brotherly love be the ruling sentiment of the occasion.

On December 6, 1894, the Mercury *ran the following editorial:*

Some of our equal rights people have taken exception to the article appearing in the *Mercury* of November 22 relative to the woman suffrage results in Colorado . . . which complains . . . of woman suffrage because the [Colorado] women did not vote the Populist ticket. . . . Woman suffrage became a reality in Colorado by the amendment to the state constitution through . . . mainly . . . the Populist party . . . [which] championed the suffrage question. . . .

Despite these facts the women not only voted against reform and in favor of the party or parties that had brought ruin upon the country but also against the party that had championed their cause. . . . This, the *Mercury* states now, is incontrovertible evidence that women are not sufficiently educated in the duties of citizenship to exercise the functions conferred on them, by the ballot, safely and considerately. . . .

The following letters no longer appeared in the section called "The Family" but were spread around, some in a news announcement section near the front of the Mercury *and others in a "From the People" column near the back.*

172.	December 27, 1894. Columbus. Bettie Gay.

I listen to men talk sometimes till I think they ought to be disfranchised til they learn self-protection, to vote for self-protection and the protection of oppressed humanity. Talk about woman suffrage! Many of the women are better posted on political economy than many of the men. We have a nation of cowards, because our women have been slaves.

173.	December 27, 1994. Granger. Grace Danforth, M.D.

What an unjust and an unfair thing it is to expect women in one election to right all the wrongs masculine rule has fostered upon society! The women of Colorado had no angels to vote for when they deposited their ballots. They had only men and they are largely whisky-loving animals, no matter what political party they chance to belong. The enclosed clipping is from the *Women's Tribune* of Washington, D.C., whose editor, Clara B. Colby, is a Populist. What a contrast it is to the unkind item in regard to the same thing in the last *Mercury!* Because some of the officials elected by the women favored the measure, they (the women) must bear the blame. It is the same old cowardly tale in one of its most Protean forms: "The women tempted me, and I did eat." Seems to me sometime men would get ashamed of following example of that pusillanimous ancestor of theirs.

The Mercury *answered in the same issue:*

No, doctor, the "whisky-loving animals" did not expect the women to convert earth into a paradise at one election. Nothing of the sort, but they did expect for the women of Colorado to exercise the right of suffrage in the interests of morality and temperance, which it appears from the record they did not do.

Now, doctor, the *Mercury* objects to going back to the morning of creation in this controversy, and dragging Adam into the muss. From what little we know of Adam, he was a very nice man; in fact, the best citizen— male citizen—of Eden, but he was hen-pecked. He lacked the courage of his convictions, and instead of obeying his God he listened to the wiles of Mrs. Adam, which got him into trouble[,] and it has been so since the foundation of the world.

Eve was an advocate of equal suffrage. She was made equal, but like her Colorado descendants, at the very first election after her enfranchisement, she got the whole neighborhood into trouble, Adam included, and when God got after Adam, she, no doubt, hid behind her sex.

Now the *Mercury* wouldn't have said a word about Adam, or Eve either, if Dr. Danforth hadn't begun it. The time has come, in the opinion of the *Mercury,* for the women to stop abusing Adam. He was the first man infatuated by woman, and induced thereby to do very foolish things, but he was not the last one by a large majority. . . . We right here and now protest against Dr. Danforth calling our greatest grandfather a "pusillanimous ancestor." Don't do it, Grace! He is your ancestor as well as ours. . . . Adam did eat, didn't Eve shake the apples off for him? There now! Be just, and don't lay all the blame on Adam . . .

174.   January 3, 1895. Groesbeck. Mary Raborn.

The Populists elected a majority of the peace and constables, the county judge and representatives of this (Limestone) county, I am glad the *Mercury* lets the woman suffrage question take a back seat. We don't want any more ignorant voters than we have now. It is time to stop howling for woman's suffrage when not one woman in five hundred has ever read the Declaration of Independence and would not know the Constitution of the United States from a patent office report. We feel sure of sweeping the county in '96, for we will see that the elections are conducted fairly then.

On January 3, 1895, the Mercury *carried the following editorial:*

The women who are crying like John the Baptist in the wilderness of their desolation for equal rights should define the measures they propose to champion when they secure equal rights. The enfranchisement of several hundred thousand voters in Texas is an important proceeding. This vote would have the balance of power, and might be wielded for good or evil. In Colorado it was wielded for evil. The populists at least desire to know whether the women of Texas are going to vote for reform or not before that party helps lift the yoke of bondage from the necks of down-trodden female humanity.

A January 10, 1895, Mercury *editorial proposed the following:*

As Dr. Grace Danforth is so fond of writing, the *Mercury* will make her this proposition: if she will sketch out the position occupied by the seekers for equal political rights, as enunciated in the resolutions of the equal rights conventions heretofore held, so as to have it authoritative on the leading reform questions of monopoly, money, land and transportation, and boil it down to a column space, the *Mercury* will be pleased to publish it. We want to [print] authoritative expressions of the equal righters' minds on these questions.

Prosuffrage; education

175.   January 17, 1895. Columbus. Mrs. Bettie Gay.

The *Mercury* of Jan. 3 asked that the women of Texas define the measure[s] they propose to champion should they secure the right to vote. John the Baptist lived in the wilderness till he came forth to herald the time of the coming of the Savior. The women have been in the wilderness for one hundred years. According to the prophecy of John, it is time for them to come out of the wilderness[,] for John says: "And all flesh shall see the salvation of God." There may be those in the People's Party who, like Herod, would be willing to behead them, but the wise women of Texas will yet lead the men out of darkness, as they (the men) have been a failure in the management of governmental affairs. We propose to have a say in the laws that govern us, as intelligent beings, and not as idiots and criminals. We propose to elect representatives, not debauchees. We are the natural guardians of our children, and we want laws that the most innocent can understand. No party will give women her rights till she demands them. The time is not distant when she will demand, and not ask, any party to recognize her. All that is needed is the proper education, and that is going on faster than any party is aware of.

I am surprised at any intelligent editor laying the cause of defeat of the Populists in Colorado to women voters, when the democrats and republicans fused there to beat the Populists, and spent piles of money to buy up the floating population. All the fraud that is perpetrated hereafter in Colorado will be laid upon the women. I suppose they can stand it for they have been the burden-bearers time out of mind: but they propose to share the burdens hereafter with the would-be lords of creation. Light is dawning and humanity will soon assert its rights.

To fully define our position would take too long an article for a newspaper. If all the women were like myself they would not ask man for any rights. What more rights have they than we? Ignorance on the part of woman has kept her in slavery.

176.   January 24, 1895. [No location.] Margaret L. Watson.

. . . Mary Raborn of Groesbeck, Texas, goes on and abuses the women for wanting to vote; says they cannot tell the Constitution of the United States from a patent office report, then says: "We feel sure of sweeping the country in '96, for we will see that the elections are conducted fairly then." Oh, "Mary, Mary—so contrary!" What on earth have you to do with elections? Go and read your patent office report.

177.   January 31, 1895. [No location.] Susan B. Anthony.

The 27th annual convention of the National American Woman's Suffrage Association will be held in Atlanta, January 31 to February 5. The object is to educate women into a knowledge of their rights and duties as citizens and through them, to arouse the nation to a sense of the national wrong perpetuated by the disenfranchisement of half the people of the United States, in opposition to the principles of government declared by our laws and constitutions. While Colorado's full enfranchisement of women in 1893 is encouraging, the defeat of the suffrage amendments in New York and Kansas in 1895, shows how largely men still fail when called upon to put in practice the principle they enunciate.

Though twenty-six states have granted some slight concessions to women citizens, in no states of the union, save Wyoming and Colorado[,] are women yet admitted to the dignity of equal rights in citizenship. In only six states of the union are mothers conceded to be the legal owners of their own children.

Such being the sad and shameful state of affairs, it behooves all lovers of justice to rally at the call to speed the next step in human progress—the full development of the mother of the race, the greatest factor in the coming civilization. . . .

178.   February 21, 1895. Groesbeck. Mary A. Raborn.

I am sorry the equal suffragists can see nothing better to fight for than female suffrage. I know there are many women who can be intelligent voters, but to offset all these, there are thousands and thousands of not only ignorant, but degraded women, both black and white, who would be as easily purchased as the ignorant voter of the male sex. What help would these be to reform? For my part I see something better, grander, and greater to be desired than the right to vote. . . . It does seem to me that the three great and principal questions now confronting us are fully set forth in the people's party platform: namely money, land and transportation. Let us all work (if we don't and can't vote) for a wise solution of those questions first. Then it will be time to take up minor issues. I never like to be criticized, but suppose I can bear it, however, I would like to say to Margaret L. Watson that I did not "abuse the women for wanting to vote." I only accused the mass, i.e., the majority, of ignorance. Yes, Margaret, I'll have a hand in helping hold the next election. I have a husband, three sons and two sons-in-law, all Pops, who will be there. Later on two more sons will be added. Don't you think I'll quote just a "leetle bit"? As for reading my patent office reports, you forget I am a subscriber to the *Mercury*, consequently am not forced to such dry stuff for literature. To be serious with you my dear Margaret, what is the platform or principles of the equal suffragists? I have never read it. Perhaps if I understood what they are doing, I would be an equal suffragist too. You ought to try to convert me if you think I am wrong.

A Mercury *announcement reported the following on March 7, 1895:*

The *Mercury*, in common with all her knew her, regrets most sincerely the death of Grace Danforth, one of the intelligent women of the state.

Grace Danforth was an active worker in the equal rights cause . . . advocated equal suffrage with her pen and from the platform with marked ability . . . was a friend of humanity and a good shepherd to the lowly and oppressed of both sexes. . . . Surely there is a rest and reward for all such God-fearing and humanity-loving women as Grace Danforth.

Against prize-fighting

179.   July 25, 1895. Bazette. Lizzie Cornwell.

I highly endorse the *Mercury*'s sentiments in opposing Corbett and Fitzsimmons fighting* at our fair southern city. Every citizen advocating reform and Christianity should at once take an active part in suppressing this savageness. The Woman's Equal Rights association and every other organization seeking justice should demand of the civil authorities that the fight, this brutal demonstration, this exhibition of brutality, be prohibited on Texas soil. . . .

    * *Robert Fitzsimmons became the world boxing champion in three divisions, includ-*

ing heavyweight, when, in 1897, he defeated Jim Corbett in fourteen rounds in Carson City, Nevada.

Prize-fighting

180.   August 1, 1895. Columbus. Mrs. Bettie Gray *[sic]*.

Let me appeal to the Texas women to condemn the Corbett and Fitzsimmons prize fight, and each and every one obligate themselves not to attend the Dallas fair if such is to be carried on there. Is there a mother in this great state that is willing for her son to witness such brutality? I for one am not. If we are such Christians let us condemn it. Shall we go back to barbarism or go on and upward in the paths of progress? Women! are you a power in the land? I say you are. You have the power, if you will properly exercise it, to stop this brutal combat that is to disgrace our fair land. Where are the churches and the Alliance people? They should condemn it on every occasion. I look to the women of Texas to stay the hand and let us be rescued from such a fate.

Bibliography

Archives, Eugene C. Barker Texas History Center, University of Texas at Austin.

Arendt, Hannah. *The Human Condition*. Chicago: University of Chicago Press, 1958.

Abbott, Shirley. *Womenfolks: Growing Up Down South*. New York: Ticknor and Fields, 1983.

Barnes, Donna Ann. *Farmers in Rebellion: The Rise and Fall of the Southern Farmers Alliance and the People's Party in Texas*. Austin: University of Texas Press, 1984.

Barr, Alwyn. *Reconstruction to Reform: Texas Politics, 1876–1906*. Austin: University of Texas Press, 1971.

Bernhard, Virginia; Betty Brandon; Elizabeth Fox-Genovese; and Theda Perdue, eds. *Southern Women: Histories and Identities*. Columbia: University of Missouri Press, 1992.

Blocker, Jack S. "The Politics of Reform: Populism, Prohibition, and Woman Suffrage, 1891–1892." *Historian* 34 (1972): 614–32.

Brady, Marilyn Dell. "Populism and Feminism in a Newspaper by and for Women of the Kansas Farmers' Alliance, 1891–1894." *Kansas History* 7 (Winter 1984–85): 280–90.

Buck, Solon. *The Granger Movement, 1870–1880*. Cambridge, Mass.: Harvard University Press, 1933.

Cannon, Charles A. "The Ideology of Texas Populism, 1886–1894." M.A. thesis, Rice University, 1968.

Cotner, Robert C. *James Stephen Hogg: A Biography*. Austin: University of Texas Press, 1959.

Cott, Nancy F. *The Bonds of Womanhood*. New Haven, Conn.: Yale University Press, 1977.

Degler, Carl. *At Odds: Women and the Family in America from the Revolution to the Present*. New York: Oxford University Press, 1980.

Diggs, Annie L. "The Women in the Alliance Movement." *Arena* (Boston) 6 (July 1892): 161–79.

DuBois, Ellen Carol. *Feminism and Suffrage: The Emergence of an Independent Women's Movement in America, 1848–1869*. Ithaca, N.Y.: Cornell University Press, 1978.

Dunning, Nelson A., ed. *The Farmer's Alliance History and Agricultural Digest*. Washington, D.C.: Alliance Publishing Company, 1891.

Epstein, Barbara. *The Politics of Domesticity: Women, Evangelism, and Temperance in Nineteenth-Century America*. Middletown, Conn.: Wesleyan University Press, 1981.

Gay, Bettie. "The Influence of Women in the Alliance." In *The Farmers' Alliance History and Agricultural Digest*. Edited by Nelson A. Dunning. Washington, D.C.: Alliance Publishing Company, 1891.

Goodwyn, Lawrence. *Democratic Promise: The Populist Moment in America*. New York: Oxford University Press, 1976.

———. *The Populist Moment: A Short History of the Agrarian Revolt in America*. New York: Oxford University Press, 1978.

Hawks, Joanne V., and Sheila L. Skemp, eds. *Sex, Race and the Role of Women in the South*. Jackson: University Press of Mississippi, 1983.

Hays, Samuel P. *The Response to Industrialism, 1885–1914*. Chicago: University of Chicago Press, 1957.

Hewitt, Nancy A., and Suzanne Lebsock, eds. *Visible Women: New Essays on American Activism*. Urbana: University of Illinois Press, 1993.

Hicks, John D. *The Populist Revolt*. Minneapolis: University of Minnesota Press, 1931.

Hofstadter, Richard. *The Age of Reform: From Bryan to FDR*. New York: Vintage Books, 1955.

Humphrey, Janet G., ed. *A Texas Suffragist: Diaries and Writings of Jane Y. McCallum*. Austin, Tex.: Ellen C. Temple, 1988.

Jeffrey, Julie Roy. *Frontier Women: The Trans-Mississippi West, 1840–1880*. New York: Hill and Wang, 1979.

———. "Women in the Southern Farmers' Alliance: Reconsideration of the Role and Status of Women in the Late Nineteenth-Century South." *Feminist Studies* 3 (Fall 1975): 72–91.

Jensen, Joan M. *With These Hands*. Old Westbury, N.Y.: Feminist Press, 1981.

King, Keith Lynn. "Religious Dimensions of the Agrarian Protest in Texas, 1870–1908." Ph.D. diss., University of Illinois at Champaign-Urbana, 1985.

Kraditor, Aileen S. *The Ideas of the Women's Suffrage Movement, 1892–1920*. New York: Columbia University Press, 1965.

McMath, Robert C. *Populist Vanguard: A History of the Southern Farmers' Alliance*. New York: W. W. Norton, 1977.

Macune, Charles W. "The Farmers Alliance." Typescript, 1920. On file at Eugene C. Barker Texas History Center, Univ. of Texas.

Marti, Donald B. *Women of the Grange: Mutuality and Sisterhood in Rural America, 1866–1920*. New York: Greenwood Press, 1991.

Martin, Roscoe C. *The People's Party in Texas: A Study in Third Party Politics*. Austin: University of Texas Bulletin, 1933.

Miller, Worth Robert. "Building a Progressive Coalition in Texas: The Populist-Reform Democrat Rapprochement, 1900–1907." *Journal of Southern History* 52, no. 2 (May 1986): 163–82.

Moreland, Sinclair. *The Texas Women's Hall of Fame*. Austin, Tex.: Biographical Press, 1917.

Myres, Sandra L. *Westering Women and the Frontier Experience, 1800–1915.* Albuquerque: University of New Mexico Press, 1982.

Nieuwenhuizen, Patricia B. "Minnie Fisher Cunningham and Jane Y. McCallum: Leaders of Texas Women for Suffrage and Beyond." Senior thesis, University of Texas at Austin, 1982.

Nugent, Walter T. K. "How the Populists Lost in 1894." *Kansas Historical Quarterly* 31 (Fall 1965): 245–55.

———. *The Tolerant Populists.* Chicago: University of Chicago Press, 1963.

Pollack, Norman. *The Populist Mind.* Indianapolis, Ind.: Bobbs-Merrill, 1967.

Ryan, Mary P. *Women in Public: Between Banners and Ballots, 1825–1880.* Baltimore, Md.: Johns Hopkins University Press, 1990.

Sachs, Carolyn. *The Invisible Farmers: Women in Agricultural Production.* Totowa, N.J.: Rowman and Allanheld, 1983.

Schwartz, Michael. *Radical Protest and Social Structure: The Southern Farmers Alliance and Cotton Tenancy, 1880–1890.* New York: Academic Press, 1976.

Scott, Anne Firor. *Making the Invisible Woman Visible.* Urbana: University of Illinois Press, 1984.

———. *The Southern Lady: From Pedestal to Politics, 1830–1930.* Chicago: University of Chicago Press, 1970.

———, ed. *Unheard Voices: The First Historians of Southern Women.* Charlottesville: University Press of Virginia, 1993.

Scott, Stanley Howard. "Angry Agrarian: The Texas Farmer, 1875–1896." Ph.D. diss., Texas Christian University, 1973.

Sims, Anastatia. "The Woman Suffrage Movement in Texas." Senior thesis, University of Texas at Austin, 1974.

Smith, Ralph. "'Macuneism' or the Farmers of Texas in Business." *Journal of Southern History* 13 (May 1947): 220–42.

Southern Mercury (Dallas, Texas), 1886–1907.

Stiller, Richard. *Queen of Populists: The Story of Mary Elizabeth Lease.* New York: Dell, 1970.

Swierenga, Robert P. "Towards the New Rural History." *Historical Methods Newsletter* 6 (1973): 111–21.

Taylor, A. Elizabeth. *Citizens at Last: The Woman Suffrage Movement in Texas.* Austin, Tex.: Ellen C. Temple, 1987.

Wagner, MaryJo. "Farms, Families, and Reform: Women in the Farmers' Alliance and Populist Party." Ph.D. diss., University of Oregon, 1986.

Weddel, Connie. "Annie Diggs." M.A. thesis, Wichita State University, 1980.

Wiedenfeld, Melissa Gilbert. "Women in the Texas Farmers' Alliance." M.A. thesis, Texas Tech University, 1983.

Willard, Frances, and Mary Livermore. *A Woman of the Century.* Chicago: Charles Wells Moulton, 1893.

Winkler, Ernest William. *Platforms of Political Parties in Texas.* Austin: University of Texas Bulletin, 1916.

Woloch, Nancy. *Women and the American Experience.* New York: Knopf, 1984.

Woodward, C. Vann. *Origins of the New South, 1877–1913.* Baton Rouge: Louisiana State University Press, 1971.

———. *Tom Watson: Agrarian Rebel.* New York: Macmillan, 1938.

Index